DESIGNING GENDER

T0405960

DESIGNING GENDER

A FEMINIST TOOLKIT

SARAH ELSIE BAKER

BLOOMSBURY VISUAL ARTS
LONDON • NEW YORK • OXFORD • NEW DELHI • SYDNEY

BLOOMSBURY VISUAL ARTS
Bloomsbury Publishing Plc
50 Bedford Square, London, WC1B 3DP, UK
1385 Broadway, New York, NY 10018, USA
29 Earlsfort Terrace, Dublin 2, Ireland

BLOOMSBURY, BLOOMSBURY VISUAL ARTS and the Diana logo are trademarks
of Bloomsbury Publishing Plc

First published in Great Britain 2024

© Sarah Elsie Baker, 2024

Sarah Elsie Baker has asserted her right under the Copyright, Designs and Patents Act,
1988, to be identified as Author of this work.

Cover design: Sarah Parkinson-Howe and Sarah Elsie Baker, 2024

All rights reserved. No part of this publication may be reproduced or transmitted
in any form or by any means, electronic or mechanical, including photocopying,
recording, or any information storage or retrieval system, without prior permission
in writing from the publishers.

Bloomsbury Publishing Plc does not have any control over, or responsibility for,
any third-party websites referred to or in this book. All internet addresses given in
this book were correct at the time of going to press. The author and publisher regret
any inconvenience caused if addresses have changed or sites have ceased to exist,
but can accept no responsibility for any such changes.

A catalogue record for this book is available from the British Library.

A catalog record for this book is available from the Library of Congress.

ISBN: HB: 978-1-3502-7375-7
         PB: 978-1-3502-7374-0
         ePDF: 978-1-3502-7377-1
         eBook: 978-1-3502-7376-4

Typeset by RefineCatch Limited, Bungay, Suffolk
Printed and bound in India

To find out more about our authors and books visit www.bloomsbury.com
and sign up for our newsletters.

For **Naia** and **Theo**

CONTENTS

ACKNOWLEDGEMENTS

This book has been a very long time coming and so there are many people who have helped me with its contents. This goes as far back as professors, colleagues and friends at the University of East London and Middlesex University in the UK, you know who you are. Nan O'Sullivan, Vanessa Crowe and Meredith Leigh at Victoria University of Wellington – thank you for all those wonderful conversations about gender, design and housework that generated such debate among the students.

To my current colleagues at Media Design School, Auckland, and Torrens University Australia, thank you for all your support and interest in my project. I am particularly grateful for the hive-mind that is the Inclusion, Equity and Justice Research Network. I would especially like to thank Professor Kerry London for her mentorship and generosity of spirit; Dr Moana Nepia for his thought-provoking conversations and the insight he has given me into kaupapa Māori; and Simon Nicholls for our amazing chats about gender, sexuality and general life stuff that make me feel myself.

To the awesome women who have helped with this book, Erin Rogatski for transcribing interviews, Viola Vadász for obtaining image permissions and Sarah Parkinson-Howe for her wonderful design work – I couldn't have done it without you. Last, but definitely not least, thanks to my partner Regan, who has sacrificed a lot and changed a lot of dirty nappies so I can write this book – I owe you one!

PREFACE

Naia (*three years old*)   Will the baby be a boy or a girl, Mummy?

Sarah (*forty-one years old*)   We don't know yet, what do you think?

Naia   I want a girl, a baby sister.

Sarah   But if it's a boy you will still love them, won't you?

Naia   NO!

It was after this conversation, and a few more like it, that my partner and I decided to find out the sex of our second baby at the twenty-week scan. While the sex of our child was not very important to us and we try to raise our children as gender neutrally as possible, we thought it would be a good idea to prepare our daughter for the prospect of a baby brother. I went along to the scan and told the sonographer that I would like to find out the sex of the baby. At the end of the appointment, I was given a 'gender reveal' card in an envelope that my partner and I could open later. That night we opened the envelope and 'GIRL' was written on the dotted line. 'Phew' we thought, we might not have to prepare our daughter quite as much.

The next four months went by quickly and I gave birth to a wonderful healthy baby at home. A couple of minutes after the birth I looked down at the baby in my arms. 'I think the baby has balls!' I exclaimed to my midwife. Sure enough, my little baby was a boy. All of us, including my daughter, were instantly besotted with baby Theo (instead of Thea). We really shouldn't have worried at all.

There was one minor detail, however. What to do with the newborn girls' dresses and knitwear I had been sent by thoughtful family members. As I looked down at these gendered baby clothes, I started to question my own values. Could I dress my newborn boy in these things? What would people think? What would Theo think when he saw photos of himself as a baby in 'girls' clothes? After consulting my relatives and upon much reflection, I decided to make a basket of baby girl's clothes and give it away on my local community Facebook page. My post raised a few eyebrows. One person commented 'I'm sure your baby boy would look wonderful in pink', another said 'I wouldn't worry about it, they grow so fast anyway'. In theory I agreed, but in practice I just couldn't do it. I couldn't dress my son in flowery dresses without his consent.

You may be thinking, why I am beginning a design textbook with a very personal story about birth? The first reason is to situate myself and the production of the book. This book was conceived and written in-between breastfeeding, changing nappies, playing, illness, a hospital stay, and sometimes having had very little sleep. At a time where Covid-19 changed home-life for many families and the burden placed upon women was significant, I feel very lucky to live in Aotearoa, New Zealand. Lockdowns were relatively short, the toll of Covid-19 comparatively minimal and the evidence of manaakitangi (a central tenet of Māori culture that extends love and compassion to others) clear to see.

Originally from the UK, I am Tangata Tiriti, a person permitted to live in Aotearoa by the Treaty and who acknowledges and respects the position of Māori. My kids, Naia and Theo, whakapapa (have ancestral links) to Ngāi Tahu and as parents we do our best to give them knowledge of the richness of te ao Māori (the Māori world). The process of immigrating to Aotearoa, starting a family here, and beginning to learn about the Māori worldview, has made me more aware of the dominance of Western approaches to design and to gender. While I attempt to address this bias in the book by deconstructing Western ideas, and by including examples from a range of global contexts, I am aware that my own position as a white bisexual agender English female influences its content. I hope that as a reader you can apply the concepts, discussions and techniques to your own unique experience, and hold me to account when necessary.

Perhaps many of you are already doing so. There is a lot that can be criticized in my birth story: my decision to find out the sex of the baby, accepting gendered clothing as gifts, giving the baby a gendered name, the list goes on. For me, and this is the second reason I wanted to begin the book with this story, the narrative demonstrates how from the moment we are born, gender is culturally embedded into our everyday experience. It speaks to how designed artefacts, in this case clothes, objectify gender and gendered power relations. As designers, we are, quite literally, designing gender. The story also illustrates the complexities of trying to make change in systems and cultures in which gender norms are heavily entrenched. Gender is mutable and can be changed by our own actions, yet at the same time it is so ingrained it informs many, often unconscious, assumptions that can be difficult to dismantle. This complexity means that while feminism may give us the theoretical tools to unpack and challenge convention, in practice the process may not be so simple.

It is the gap between theory and practice that motivates me to write this book. While feminist theorists across a range of disciplines have offered significant insight and developed tools for thinking about gender and power, design as a discipline has been slow to engage with this work. In the 1980s, a small group of feminist design researchers explored the ways that professional design practice reinforced gender hierarchies and there has been a trickle of academic work on the topic since this time. However, there has been little instruction given to designers and students as to how they might alter their practice. This book aims to do just that. By exploring key concepts and theories, raising challenging questions and offering activities, I would like readers to reflect on their own design work. Ultimately, I hope the emergent dialogue will go some way to fostering new sorts of gender relations through design.

The definition of design that I adhere to in the book is an all-encompassing one. Design names our ability 'to prefigure what we create before the act of creation, and as such, it defines one of the fundamental characteristics that make us human' (Fry, 2009: 2). Thus, everyone everywhere is, and was, involved in designing. However, as we will read about in Chapter 2 and 3, the professionalization of design worked to exclude women, trans and non-binary people, and reproduced notions of managerial, technical and scientific knowledge as inherently masculine. Over time within the design discipline, practices became gendered and hierarchized. Women were associated with 'decorative' practices such as illustration, embroidery, pottery and dressmaking, while industrial design, typography, and architectural design were associated with men and afforded higher status.

The different status given to various design disciplines is one of the reasons that the book takes a transdisciplinary approach. It includes theories, approaches and examples from user experience design, graphic design, craft, art, product design, interaction design and design futures among others. Although the text does not focus on fashion, architecture or urban design, the theories, processes and activities included are useful to anyone interested in designing gender in a broad sense. In this respect, the approach of the book reflects the merging of design disciplines that has occurred in industry (Kiernan and Ledwith, 2011), and aligns with academic arguments for transdisciplinary design practice as a site for political action (Fry, 2009).

Structure of the book

Each chapter includes key theories, concepts and questions for designers, a case study, an interview and two activities. It is hoped that by including this range of resources that the book goes someway to bridging theory and practice, as well as adding diverse voices in addition to my own.

Chapter 1 – Gender, feminism and things – defines the approach to gender and feminism taken in book and begins to explore how normative assumptions can be avoided in design practice. It starts by documenting theorizations of the complexities of sex and gender found in queer feminist theory. It argues for a holistic approach which acknowledges that 'shared biology, biological variation, shared culture, and individual experience all come together in an unfathomably complex manner to create both the trends as well as the diversity in gender and sexuality' (Serano, 2013: para 5). The theory of intersectionality that informs the approach to feminism used in the book is outlined. We are introduced to the way that design as professional practice is influenced by, and reproduces, the binary divisions that are central to Western thought and that uphold systems of inclusion/exclusion and privilege/oppression. We explore examples of products, packaging and design processes that reproduce gender inequality. The concepts of gender norms and script analysis are outlined, and we consider how these ideas are useful for analysing the gendering of things. In the last part of the chapter, I argue that gender justice will not be achieved without changing design values, processes, and tools, and the rest of the book explores how we might set about doing so.

Chapter 2 – Women, craft and technology – starts with a discussion of the slippery definitions of design and technology. The chapter summarizes how feminist design historians in the 1980s and 1990s questioned the privileging of design as professional practice and proposed a revaluing of everyday practices of designing and making. In line with this work, it is argued that it is only by broadening the conceptualization of design to include craft and technology beyond the new and electronic, that women's contributions to design become visible. As Judy Wajcman has argued, indigenous women were the first technologists (2004: 15). Thus, the chapter documents how feminists have used everyday practices of making as forms of resistance. Framed as sources of inspiration to draw from, we explore activist craft practice, feminist redesigns and DIY aesthetics, as well as the ways that digital technologies have allowed feminists to challenge patriarchal culture and to hack gender.

Chapter 3 – Women and design as profession – examines the professionalization of design and the related associations that developed between women and particular types of design work. It considers the design knowledge and processes that have been deemed valuable in professional practice, and outlines feminist critiques of the individualism, universalism, objectivity and solutionism often objectified by these approaches. We encounter the theorizations of situated knowledge (Haraway, 1986) and situated action (Suchman, 1987), and it is argued these perspectives can shift design away from reproducing inequality. The chapter goes on to document the masculinities at work in contemporary design cultures and outlines innovative approaches to addressing inequality in the workplace. It concludes by showcasing designs that challenge gender norms that have been produced in professional contexts.

Chapter 4 – Making gender inequality visible – starts by documenting the gender bias of information that informs the design of products, services and systems. We explore recent discussions of data and power, particularly in light of the rise of artificial intelligence and machine learning. We consider how poor data and lack of data about women, trans and non-binary people can contribute to inequality. The chapter proposes ways in which designers can evaluate and use data differently in recognition of the importance of context, embodiment and the agency of users. These ideas are explored through analysis of feminist counter-data and queer AI projects. Designers play a significant part in the visual communication of data, thus the last part of the chapter explores feminist approaches to data visualization including data humanism.

Chapter 5 – Feminist design futures – focuses upon design methods to imagine different gender futures. It begins by introducing speculative design and design fiction and considers why, until relatively recently, there has been little engagement with gender in this body of work. It documents a number of alternative futures imagined by feminist writers and argues that the narratives we create about future lives matter. The chapter proposes alternative approaches to time inspired by feminist theory. It concludes by analysing the few examples of feminist speculative design that do exist, and by identifying and defining the importance of public participation, contextual relevance and anachronic methods in this work.

Chapter 6 – Sustainable practice and design beyond binaries – returns to explore how binaries reproduced through design contribute to intersectional inequality and environmental crisis. We consider how sustainable and transitional approaches can often reproduce essentialist perspectives of gender and nature, despite their honourable intentions. Drawing on Tony Fry and Adam Nocek, it is argued that 'design needs to become unrecognisable to itself' to address the current crisis (2021: 14). To start this journey, we focus on the theory and practice of ecofeminists, queer ecologists and indigenous thinkers. We consider more-than-human entanglements and the types of design work that this approach fosters. The synergies between queer ecology and indigenous worldviews are explored. Ethical ways of taking inspiration from this knowledge are introduced. The chapter, and the book, concludes by focusing on methods to unmake design practice such as non-rational, feral or wild approaches. We are left contemplating whether we, as designers, can move out of our comfort zones and use our capacity for imagination, play and experimentation to unbuild the unjust worlds we have created.

1
GENDER, FEMINISM AND THINGS

Introduction: the complexities of sex and gender

As a concept, gender is relatively new. While its usage to refer to either of 'the two primary biological forms of a species' has been dated back to the fifteenth century (Merriam-Webster, 2022), the understanding of gender as a term to describe the social enactment of sex roles emerged in the 1950s. Largely popularized by the sexologist John Money, gender became a way of distinguishing between bodily sex (male and female) and social roles (masculinity and femininity) (Halberstam, 2007). Money observed the disconnection between sex and gender roles in his intersex patients. He argued that gender was learned in childhood and completely malleable before children reach eighteen months of age. It was this line of thinking that led to the now-infamous case in which he recommended sex reassignment to the parents of a young boy who lost his penis during circumcision. Money believed that if the parents raised the boy as a girl there would be no negative effects. His hypothesis (alongside his highly unethical experiments with the child) proved to be disastrously wrong, with the child growing up with troubling psychological issues and eventually committing suicide (Halberstam, 2007: para 3).

When this wretched experiment came to light, it was used to exemplify a range of theories about gender. As Jack Halberstam notes, it led some 'medical practitioners to reinvest in the essential relationship between sex and gender' i.e. the idea that physical sex predetermines social and behavioural characteristics (2007: para 3). For some gender theorists it was evidence of the way that the gendering of the sexed body begins as soon as a child is born, and illustrative of the rigidity of sociobiological processes (Halberstam, 2007: para 3). However, the essential relationship between sex and gender, as well as its fixedness, have been widely critiqued.

This chapter begins by documenting theorizations of the complexities of sex and gender found in queer feminist theory. The definition of gender and the approach to feminism used in the book is outlined. The chapter then goes on to explore how gender inequality is reproduced through the design of material objects and the processes used to create them. We encounter the concepts of gender norms and script analysis and consider how these ideas can be useful for analysing the gendering of artefacts. In the last part of the chapter, the question that informs the rest of the book is framed. How can we move towards design practice that fosters gender justice?

Defining gender

The idea that biology (chromosomes, sex organs, hormones and other physical features) dictates social and behavioural characteristics has led to problematic theorizations of male and female traits. For example, this includes the arguments that women are hysterical, passive and lacking in spatial skills, and that men are rational, uncaring and single-minded, among many other stereotypical qualities. It also includes the still-prevalent idea that girls are verbal and boys are physical in their development.

KEY CONCEPT: GENDER ESSENTIALISM

In early Western thought, in Plato for example, it was posited that all things have an 'essence'. Since that time, the idea that certain groups of people have innate characteristics has held traction. When used to assert that social identities such as ethnicity, gender, and nationality, correspond to specific qualities, essentialism has been at the centre of many discriminatory and extremist ideologies.

Indeed, gender essentialism is a concept that has mainly been used in feminist theory and gender studies to critique the idea that men and women have fixed, intrinsic and innate 'essences'. The attribution of specific characteristics and behaviours, women as feminine (nurturing, empathetic, non-competitive etc.) and men as masculine (strong, assertive, dominant etc.), is frequently justified by referencing distinct biological and psychology characteristics (often referred to as biological determinism). Gender essentialism reinforces binary thinking by homogenizing men and women into one single category according to their 'true essence', and often refutes the possibility of other genders. For example, an essentialist (and highly problematic) perspective on gender would argue that a trans woman would always be male in 'essence'.

These arguments, and the scientific studies behind them, have largely been discredited. For example, the biologist and women's studies scholar Anne Fausto-Sterling has dedicated her academic life to demonstrating how scientific understandings of sex and gender (including decisions regarding sex at birth) are shaped by the culture which produced it. Fausto-Sterling argues that rather than binary (male vs female) or a continuum (male to female), 'sex and gender are best conceptualised as points in multidimensional space' (2000: 22). By this she means that at every level, the genetic, the cellular, the hormonal, the anatomical, there are multiple permutations of masculinity and femininity. She writes that 'gender identity presumably emerges from all of those corporeal aspects via some poorly understood interaction with environment and experience' (Fausto-Sterling, 2000: 22). Fausto-Sterling observes how the medical and scientific communities are yet to develop a language capable of describing such diversity.

The same could be said of popular notions of sex and gender. While categories to describe different sexes and genders have increased in recent years, they are still inadequate to describe diversity of experience. Indeed, in most Western cultures many continue to think of sex as relating to the biological characteristics of male/female, and of gender as being a historical, social and cultural construct pertaining to masculinity/femininity. However, as Fausto-Sterling argues, and as we will come to explore in the work of Judith Butler and Julia Serano, bodily aspects of sex and gender are inextricably linked with the psychological, social, cultural and technological, with no one characteristic necessarily taking priority over another.

In her earlier provocative work on sex, Fausto-Sterling fell into the trap of privileging the role of genitalia in determining gender. In the 'Five Sexes' Fausto-Sterling (1993) lays out five possible categorizations of gender according to biological characteristics. However, as Suzanne J. Kessler argued, the problem with this work was that it gave genitals primary signifying status, when in the everyday world 'gender attributions are made without access to genital inspection' (2002: 90). Kessler writes that what has primacy in everyday life is the gender that is performed, regardless of the flesh's configuration under the clothes' (2002:90).

KEY CONCEPT: SOCIAL CONSTRUCTIONISM

Social constructionism is used to define an approach to knowledge that views characteristics such as gender, sexuality, race, class etc. as products of human definition, rather than simply biologically determined. It highlights how concepts such as man/woman are shaped by cultural and historical contexts, and how these ideas are reproduced and change over time. Social constructionism has informed many feminist approaches to gender that have challenged essentialist or biologically determinist understandings of what men and women can do, for example. From a social constructionist perspective, the meaning of being categorized as a man or woman or masculine or feminine, is fluid and dynamic, changing over time, thus making these categories neither inevitable nor immutable. For example, the idea that women are more likely to be overly 'emotional' can be challenged when we consider the power relations at play in categorization of particular bodies. This is illustrated by critiques of the gendered history of the diagnosis of women with hysteria (McVean, 2017).

As we will return to below, however, the prevalence of social constructivism in feminist thought has been challenged more recently because it privileges language and meaning over materials and bodies (Braidotti, 2012).

One of the key theorists that has addressed the social construction of sex and gender, and indeed who has questioned the distinction between these two concepts entirely, is Judith Butler. Butler has dedicated her academic career to examining 'the ways in which identity norms are taken up and subject positions assumed' (Salih and Butler, 2004: 2). Since the 1990s, her work has had a profound impact on understandings of sex, gender and sexuality in academia and in popular culture. For example, references to heteronormativity and gender performance are found in *Teen Vogue* (Fischer, 2016), Butler features in countless memes and has Pinterest boards dedicated to her, and 'Judith Butler explained with cats' has been widely circulated on the internet (fig. 1.1). Indeed, as Jack Halberstam argues, without Butler's work we 'wouldn't have the version of genderqueerness that we now have' (quoted in Fischer, 2016).

Butler's most famous exploration of gender, *Gender Trouble*, came via an interrogation of the heterosexual assumptions made by feminist literary theory. Butler argued that feminist analysis was deeply flawed because the subject of analysis, women, was a construct made possible only by assumptions about the correlation between female sex, femininity and heterosexuality (Butler, 1999: 3). Thus, *Gender Trouble,* begins by illuminating 'the compulsory order of sex/gender/ desire' (Butler, 1999: 9). By this Butler means the notion that someone assigned female at birth will naturally be a feminine woman and that her desire will necessarily lead her to a man. For Butler, the term 'man' or 'woman' does not refer to a coherent or stable identity. Instead, there are a multitude of possibilities in the ways that people experience sex, gender and desire. The 'Genderbread Person' (2017) by Sam Killermann was created to try to help people reflect upon this diversity (fig. 1.2).

As well as destabilizing the presumptions made about the causal nature of sex, gender and sexuality, Butler also questions the naturalness of binary sex (male and female). Like Fausto-Sterling, she suggests that sex is 'always already gender' (Butler, 1999: 10–11). Contrary to long-held views within feminism that gender is the cultural interpretation of a person's sex, Butler argued that sex was not some kind of interior 'truth' (1999: 44). Rather, Butler suggests that gender is the apparatus that makes us believe in the myth of a natural inner truth. Gender reinforces the binary notion of sex, when in fact, as Fausto-Sterling has argued, there are multiple permutations of gender at every level of biology. By reconsidering sex as 'always already gender' Butler also suggests we must rethink our definition of gender.

Butler argues that gender 'is a doing, not a being' (1999: 34). By this she means that for gender categories (man/woman, masculinity/femininity) to have meaning they are dependent on repetition, ritual and regulation. For example, parents may unintentionally reinforce play with certain toys over others depending on the assigned sex of the child, or say 'good boy/girl' confirming gender identity in small children. By highlighting these examples, I do not mean to blame individual parents for reinforcing gender roles (I have found myself doing these things), rather I illustrate how much of our gender identity is reproduced through ingrained (and often unconscious) notions of what it means to be a man or a woman. Butler's work illuminates how none of us can escape gender norms, but also how none of us are completely determined by them either. Gender, then, is an unstable production reliant on sets of power relations. It is a:

> negotiation, a struggle, a way of dealing with historical constraints and making new realities. When we are 'girled', we are entered into a realm of girldom that has been built up over a long time – a series of conventions, sometimes conflicting, that establish girlness within society. We don't *just* choose it. And it is not *just* imposed on us. But that social reality can, and does, change.
>
> BUTLER quoted by GLEESON, 2021: para 5

This conceptualization means that gender binaries of man/woman and masculinity/femininity are both entrenched but can also be demolished. By deconstructing gender discourse then, we can make way for a diversity of cultural configurations of sex and gender to proliferate.

Butler's theories of gender have not been without misinterpretation and critique. The most common misinterpretation is that Butler thinks that 'gender is performance' rather than that 'gender is performative'. If one follows the idea that gender is simply performance then one can resist sexism by performing gender in ways that question the gender binary. As Julia Serano (2015) has noted, the most often cited example of this is a drag queen whose act supposedly reveals the way in which femaleness and femininity are merely a 'performance'.

Figure 1.1 Butler's Gender Performativity Explained with Cats. BinaryThis, 2013. Courtesy of Hannah McCann.

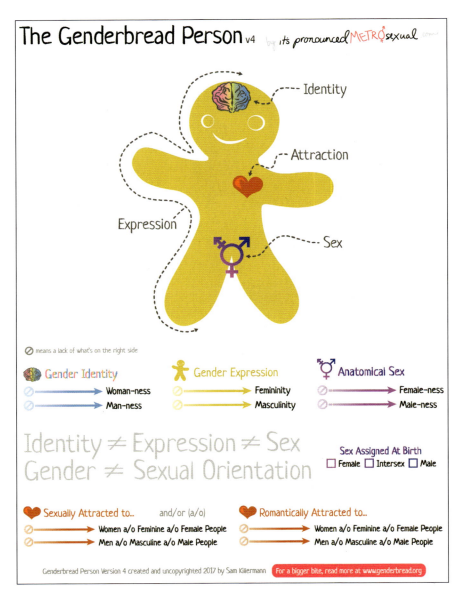

Figure 1.2 The Genderbread Person v.4. Sam Killermann/a creation of commons, 2017.

KEY CONCEPT: GENDER PERFORMATIVITY

One of the most famous concepts to emerge from Butler's work is performativity. In the late 1980s and early 1990s, Butler was interested in a set of academic debates about performative speech acts. Performative speech acts are said to make something happen (Austin, 1975). For example, when a celebrant declares 'I pronounce you husband and wife' they are creating a new reality. Even if you think marriage is 'just a piece of paper', the act changes the couple's legal status and commits them to future actions. The power to sanction the marriage does not belong to the celebrant personally. They are the designated legal authority and follow a set of established procedures. As such, the speech act is a citation.

For Butler, the concept of performativity was very relevant to gender. The proclamation that 'It's a boy!' or 'It's a girl!' brings the baby into a world of gender whereby their bodies are rendered intelligible. Through this performative speech act a new reality and set of expectations is created for the baby. Gendering (the attribution of gender) does not just happen once and is not just confined to language. As Butler argues:

> [G]ender is the repeated stylization of the body, a set of repeated acts within a highly rigid regulatory frame that congeal over time to produce the appearance of substance, of a natural sort of being.'
>
> BUTLER 1999: 44

Gender is performative in the sense that there is no gender identity behind expressions of gender. For example, by repetitively telling a boy not to cry and to conceal their emotions, the identity of the boy is constituted because they show the more 'masculine' characteristic of toughness. Going forward they are more likely to be perceived as a boy. As Butler tells us, there is no 'natural' inner gendered self to be expressed e.g. it is not as though any gender has a greater range of human emotions over another. Identity, then, is retroactively constructed and comes to be through performative acts.

Serano has written extensively about the problems with the proposition that gender is 'just a construct' or 'just a performance', which she calls 'gender artifactualism' (2013a: 117–20). Gender artifactualists, she writes, purposely ignore or dismiss the role of biology in constructing gender. This frequently trivializes the transgender experience by dismissing biological/physical characteristics. She argues that 'it is easy to fictionalize an issue when you are not fully in touch with all of the ways in which you are privileged by it' (Serano, 2013: 106). Serano (2013) gives multiple examples of the ways that physical and biological gender impacts upon transgender people's experience. This includes the physical and emotional changes caused by hormones, as well as the difference in how transgender people are treated once they 'pass' as a man or woman. She argues that behind the assertion of 'gender is performance' is an inclination to characterize biology, and science more generally, as 'an inherently patriarchal institution that seems to only exist in order to subjugate women and to pathologize queer people' (Serano, 2013: 144).

The pitting of gender artifactualism (gender as just a social construct) against gender determinism (gender as solely guided by biology) is frequently referred to as the 'nature-versus-nurture' debate. Instead, Serano puts forward:

> a holistic perspective that acknowledges that shared biology, biological variation, shared culture, and individual experience all come together in an unfathomably complex manner to create both the trends as well as the diversity in gender and sexuality that we see all around us. This holistic perspective is completely compatible with the idea that gender is socially constructed (i.e., shaped by socialization and culture), but incompatible with the idea that gender is merely a social artifact (or in activist parlance, 'just a construct').
>
> SERANO, 2013a: para 5

A holistic approach to gender is more in keeping with non-Western and indigenous conceptualizations. Indigenous cultures throughout the world recognize multiple manifestations of gender, and binary distinctions between mind/body and nature/culture prevalent in the West do not hold in indigenous world-views. Thus, the sex/gender distinction seems nonsensical. For example, the Diné (Navajo people) have at least six words to describe gender: 'asdzáán (woman), hastiin (male), náhleeh (feminine-man), dilbaa (masculine-woman), náhleeh asdzaa (lesbian), náhleeh hastii (gay man)' (Yazzie, 2020: para 4)

Like these holistic approaches, recent discussions in feminist thought particularly 'new materialism' and 'trans-feminism' have refused 'the linguistic paradigm, stressing instead the concrete yet complex materiality of bodies immersed in social relations of power' (Braidotti, 2012: 21). These approaches see bodies and material objects as entangled with, and moving between nature and culture,

KEY CONCEPT: GENDER

The definition of gender used in this book is that gender is a complex 'biopsychosocial construct' that comprises identity (a sense of who one is), role (how one interacts according to gender norms), expression (how gender manifests through clothes, hair etc.), and experience (how one navigates the world according to their gender) (Barker and Iantaffi, 2019). This is a definition of gender that recognizes the interplay of diverse biological, social and environmental factors, and acknowledges the variety of experiences of sex, gender and sexuality. It subscribes to the idea that the categories of man/woman and masculinity/femininity are norms that are historically, geographically, technically, culturally and socially determined and that in everyday life biological markers of gender are read though sociocultural lenses.

Thus, as much as possible, when men and women are referred to in the book they name categories with which people self-identify. When masculinity and femininity are used, they describe traits that have been historically (and often problematically) associated with one gender or another.

'multiple, self-organising, dynamic and inventive' (Coleman, Page and Palmer, 2019). We return to explore these ideas in relation to design and gender below.

A holistic approach to gender that recognizes a multitude of possibilities of biology, identity, role, expression and experience also challenges versions of feminism that rely on a stable notion of gender identity i.e. that feminism should only be concerned with women's rights. It also points to the impossibility of studying gender inequality and discrimination in isolation. Thus, in the next section we turn to theories of intersectional feminism to consider what a feminism for everybody looks like (hooks, 2000).

Feminism and systems of oppression

The discussions regarding the definitions of sex and gender outlined above have largely emerged from, or been a critique of, feminism. The history of the feminist movement, and indeed, the definition of feminism itself, has been much debated. However, the version of feminist history that is most commonly found in encyclopaedias goes something like this. The beginning of feminism in the West is attributed to the suffrage movement in the late nineteenth and early twentieth centuries when women fought for the right to vote. While mainly focused on political power, early feminists also sought marriage, parenting and property rights (Wikipedia, 2022). This movement is often referred to as the 'first wave'. The 'second wave' emerged in the early 1960s and is characterized as extending its premise beyond women's legal rights into social and cultural inequalities symbolized by the infamous slogan 'The Personal is Political' (Wikipedia, 2022). 'Unlike the first wave, second-wave feminism provoked extensive theoretical discussion about the origins of women's oppression, the nature of gender, and the role of the family' (Britannica, 2022). In the 1980s and early 1990s, often conceived as the 'second part of the second wave', the theorizations of earlier feminists were challenged by women of colour who questioned the centring of the experiences of white upper middle-class women (Britannica, 2022). The 'third wave' is said to have further extended this challenge in the 1990s by problematizing 'the notion of universal womanhood' and essentialist ideas of femininity (Wikipedia, 2022).

While this history is a somewhat useful introduction to feminist issues, when used to characterize the entirety of feminism, grouping the feminist movement into 'waves' is highly problematic. As evidenced above, the 'waves' simplify concerns and lump them together, when in reality the debates among feminists at any point in time have been highly divergent. For example, it has been suggested that in the 2000s a new 'fourth wave' feminism emerged that was defined by technology (e.g. Cochrane, 2013).

Feminists, however, have always used the technologies at their disposal and discussed the role of technology in women's freedom and oppression. There are many examples to illustrate this point. As is documented below, and in Chapter 2, feminists in the nineteenth and early twentieth centuries were both concerned with how technologies such as clothing limited their freedom and used technologies such as embroidery to communicate their message. Feminist theorists in the 1960s and 1970s were heavily invested in the democratization of reproductive technologies. For instance, in *Women: The Longest Revolution,* Juliet Mitchell writes of structural inequalities that oppress women including how oral contraception has so far only 'been developed in a form which exactly repeats the sexual inequality of Western society', and 'is inadequately distributed across classes and countries' (1966: 31). In 1970, Shulamith Firestone (1979) imagined a post-revolutionary world where technology, in the form of artificial wombs and automation, would elevate the burden of social reproduction. Thus, while discussions about gender and technology may have intensified in recent queer and feminist theory and social media has become central to activism, to characterize previous feminist work as less concerned with technology is a fallacy that omits nuance and complexity.

In addition, the 'waves' describe a particular history, one that is predominantly Western, white and middle-class. As Minna Salami writes, 'African women have always found ways of resisting patriarchy through manipulating popular ideas of motherhood, religion, or labour' (quoted in Derby, 2019). Thus, while the arguments made by women of colour only surface in dominant narratives about feminism in the 1980s, it does not mean that did not exist before. I would urge readers of this book to take 'a scavenger approach' to feminist theory and practice that includes looking to alternative times and places for inspiration, in addition to drawing on their own experience (Halberstam, 1998: 13).

Indeed, it was by drawing on their own histories, contexts and experiences that theorists such as bell hooks, Judith Butler, Audre Lorde and Gloria Anzaldúa came to question feminist notions of what was 'good (or not)' for women in the 1980s and 1990s. Feminism, they argued, often reproduced the subordination of people outside 'acceptable womanhood'. For example, Audre Lorde powerfully writes:

> Some problems we share as women, some we do not. You fear your children will grow up to join the patriarchy and testify against you; we fear our children will be dragged from a car and shot down in the street, and you will turn your backs on the reasons they are dying.
>
> LORDE, 1980: 4

The concept of intersectionality emerged as an attempt to understand this difference in experience, to acknowledge the role that race, class, age, disability and sexuality have in structuring experiences of gender inequality. Intersectionality was first proposed by the legal scholar Kimberlé Crenshaw in 1989. Crenshaw documents how antidiscrimination law failed to protect the rights of Black women workers at General Motors. She outlines how the employees were told they had no legal grounds for discrimination against their employer because anti-discrimination law only protected single-identity categories. For example, the court found that General Motors did not systemically discriminate against all women, because they hired white women and there was insufficient evidence to suggest discrimination against Black people in general (Crenshaw, 1989: 142). In her later article 'Mapping the Margins', Crenshaw documents how women of colour often experience male violence as a product of intersecting racism and sexism and are often marginalized by activist groups that should be there to protect them. She writes:

> the failure of feminism to interrogate race means that the resistance strategies of feminism will often replicate and reinforce the subordination of people of color, and the failure of antiracism to interrogate patriarchy means that antiracism will frequently reproduce the subordination of women.
>
> CRENSHAW, 1991: 1252

Thus, an intersectional approach illuminates how people's social identities overlap and create compounding experiences of discrimination. For example, a white middle-class woman will experience a different type of sexism to a Black working-class woman. Therefore, the experience of being a member of more than one social group should not just be understood as being member of each (as a woman, as a Black person, as a working-class person), but as a compound, a complex intersection.

As the theory of intersectionality has become more widespread it has been open to misinterpretation. In particular, it has been cast as a sort of additive hierarchy of identity categories based on the number of inequalities experienced (e.g. Kang et al., 2017). This is wholly inaccurate. Rather than suggesting that identity is static, knowable and held by a person, intersectionality describes the way that interlocking systems of discrimination impact upon people differently according to various contexts. It enables us to consider how the inequalities of class, race, gender, sexuality etc are experienced simultaneously. It purposefully moves away from the 'either/or dichotomous thinking of Eurocentric, masculinist thought' and 'the belief that either/or categories [and their associated qualities] must be ranked' (Hill-Collins, 1990: 225). As Crenshaw argues '[i]f you see inequality as a "them" problem, or an "unfortunate other" problem, then that is a problem' (Steinmetz, 2020: para 15). Thus, an intersectional feminism that challenges discrimination is a feminism for everyone because all our lives are affected by systems of oppression (albeit to different extents).

Patricia Hill-Collins describes the systems of oppression that impact upon people as the 'matrix of domination' (1990). The matrix of domination identifies the overall organization of power in a society at a given time. In her book *Black Feminist Thought* Hill-Collins flags race, class and gender as historically the most influential in African-American women's lives, while also recognizing that additional structures of oppression exist for other kinds of people. Drawing on *Black Feminist Thought*, Joana Varon and Clara Juliano have visualized how the matrix of domination intersects with identity (fig. 1.3) and highlight Hill-Collin's theorization that heteropatriarchy, white supremacy, capitalism and colonialism structure contemporary power relations.

Hill-Collins extends theories of intersectionality by unpacking the multiple levels of domination. She writes:

People experience and resist oppression on three levels: the level of personal biography; the group or community level of the cultural context created by race, class, and gender; and the systemic level of social institutions. Black feminist thought emphasizes all three levels as sites of domination and as potential sites of resistance.

HILL-COLLINS, 1990: 223

Therefore, as designers who are committed to gender justice, we must explore how systems of oppression are reproduced and re-legitimized through design at personal, community and institutional levels in order to devise strategies of resistance.

KEY CONCEPT: INTERSECTIONAL FEMINISM

The intersectional feminism that this book is aligned with is one that strives to end sexism, sexist exploitation and oppression for everyone. It recognizes the negative impact of heteropatriarchy upon all people, including men. For example, to perform masculinity, men are often required to shut off particular emotions with detrimental effect. (McKenzie et al., 2018).

Intersectional feminism highlights the connections between all fights for justice and recognizes that the systemic redistribution of power, opportunities and access for people of all genders will only be achieved by challenging the oppressive systems of heteropatriarchy, white supremacy, capitalism and colonialism. Rather than working towards a genderless society, the intersectional feminist approach taken in this book seeks to create a world whereby all manifestations of sex and gender are possible without negative ramifications.

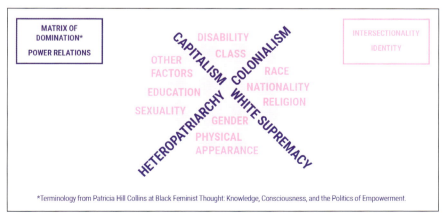

Figure 1.3 Graphic depiction of the Matrix of Domination, 2020. Courtesy of Joana Varon and Clara Juliano.

As we will return to throughout the book, and address specifically in Chapter 6, the power that is integral to maintain systems of oppression is sustained 'not only though extermination and structural exploitation' of people 'but also through systematic corporeal segregation and othering' (Canli, 2018). Drawing on theorists such as Anibal Quijano (2000) and Maria Lugones (2007), Ece Canli argues observes that:

> to hold its ground as the major authority and the norm, Western hegemony enforced the binary system of thinking, deploying the 'modern', 'enlightened' and 'civilized' subject at the centre, while externalizing any living being or idea that would challenge this rationale to the total opposite, as the 'other'.
>
> CANLI, 2018: 652

The binaries of self/other, mind/body, culture/nature, masculine/feminine, man/woman, modern/traditional, objective/subjective, rational/emotional, human/non-human, technical/organic etc. are not only posed in opposition to each other but are assigned positive and negative values. As Ece Canli suggests, this 'binary logic has permeated into every single bit of modern human condition from value judgments to subjectivity; from socially constructed identities including gender and sexuality to, [. . .] material practices' (2018: 652). For example, heteropatriarchy deems heterosexuality, and the causal nature of sex/gender/sexuality, 'normal' and anything outside this to be 'other'. As we will see below, the binaries of man/woman and masculine/feminine with their associated hierarchies are frequently reproduced and reinforced through design.

Indeed, Paul B. Preciado (2013) has even gone so far as to argue that gender roles and dominant notions of masculinity/femininity are technologies just like other artefacts that 'originated with industrial capitalism' and reached their commercial peaks during the Cold War like 'canned food, computers, plastic chairs, [and] disposable ball-point pens' (2013: 124). The ongoing project, he writes, of 'designing bodies through material productions' happened at the same time as medical research about gender was expanding (Preciado, 2013: 27). He documents how pharmaceutical companies are in the business of creating desire and 'medico-material technologies' such as hormone regulations and reproductive controls, just like other products of capitalism, enforce normative gender and sexuality. By implication, however, these technologies mean that biology is not destiny and gender can be hacked. We explore this idea more in Chapter 2. First, however, we consider the ways that designed objects frequently reinforce normative ideas about gender.

Gendered things

Feminists have always been aware of how gender norms limit self-expression. For example, in the mid nineteenth century Amelia Bloomer, the American feminist activist, wrote of the rights of both men and women to wear clothes associated with the opposite sex (Luck, 1996). At the time in the US, it was common for women to wear corsets and eight to ten petticoats which put pressure on their hips and made movement difficult. Men wore more practical trousers and plainer coats. Bloomer wrote about the rights of men to 'wear shawls without harassment by journalists' (Kirkham and Attfield, 1996: 8), and her critique of female dress partially led to an increase in women who wore more freeing 'Turkish pants' or 'bloomers' (Boissonault, 2018). By challenging gender norms in the nineteenth century, feminists paved the way for trousers being recognized as acceptable dress for women.

Gender norms concerning appropriate dress, of course, still hold in many countries throughout the world. However, the gendering of things goes beyond cultural understandings of appropriate use. Assumptions about gender are designed into artefacts and, as such, these artefacts reflect and uphold norms. This is often obvious in packaging design tailored and marketed differently towards men and women. Products targeted towards men frequently use dark colours, emphasize action and have more sturdy, angular designs. Products targeted towards women often use pink or pastel colours, have smoother, curvy packaging and fewer product features.

KEY CONCEPT: GENDER NORMS

Norms refer to the 'normal' or acceptable practices of the majority of people in a given society. Norms are often implicit and guide how people should act or experience certain situations. Norms, in and of themselves, are not necessarily negative: they enable societies to function.

However, norms can be exclusionary and maintain unequal power relations. Acting or being within the norm gives certain privileges and superior status, which means that it is beneficial for the people inside the norm to uphold it.

Since norms are often unconsciously expressed, they can be difficult to recognize until they are challenged. The moment one steps outside of convention in a given society, the weight of social norms can often be felt. For example, primary carers who identify as men can often experience judgement and isolation from other parents because they do not fit (Brooks and Hodgkinson, 2021).

Gender norms, such as who can care and nurture young children, are a good example of how norms can be restrictive because they govern the types of behaviour deemed appropriate for people of certain genders. These, of course, change over time and are contextually dependent. For example, in contrast to the norm of 'pink for girls, blue for boys', in the US in the nineteenth century baby boys were frequently dressed in pink and white, and girls in blue (Paoletti, 2012).

Technologies can themselves reproduce and uphold gender norms through their design. For instance, as Ellen Van Oost has argued, the design of electric shavers aimed at female consumers reproduces the notion that women are technologically incompetent (2003: 206).

When objects are produced according to gender norms, they work to reinforce the norm itself. For example, when shower gel targeted towards men is packaged in a black plastic container with grips and called 'active clean' or 'power fresh' it reinforces the gender norm that men are active, practical and strong. As Ellen Lupton argues 'graphic designers are in the norm business' (Lupton and Xia, 2021: 30). Logos, illustrations and colour choices can all reinforce gender norms. For example, illustrations of families often represent the 'typical nuclear family', and softer shapes are used for logos targeted at women. Perhaps less obvious are the ways that sans serif typefaces, such as Helvetica, have become accepted as a neutral standard of 'good design', when in fact they emerged as part of modernist and masculine design culture (Murphy, 2021: para 5). The irony of the publishing templates and typefaces available for this book is not lost on me here. Most of us encounter the gendering of objects from an early age. Fig. 1.4 illustrates the 'vicious cycle of gendered toys' that demonstrates the interplay of the social and the technological in the production of gender.

One of the first comprehensive theorizations of the gendering of material objects can be found in *The Gendered Object* edited by Pat Kirkham (1996). Through case studies, the book explores how gender relations operate through 'the conception, design, advertising, purchase, giving and use of material goods' (Kirkham, 1996: 1). Most of the chapters employ an historical and/or semiotic approach, reading artefacts and decoding notions of femininity and masculinity and their associated gender norms. For example, the chapter on Clinique toiletries highlights how even though greater use of cosmetics by men in the 1990s was indicative of a blurring of gender roles, the 'the advertising and packaging practices which distinguish between "male" and "female" products draw heavily on gender stereotypes based on binary oppositions' (Kirkham and Weller, 1996: 203). The chapter focused on the history of hearing aids by the cultural historian Hillan Schwartz documents how, despite using similar technology, hearing aids were marketed based on 'the handicap which they apparently addressed; for women, distance from friends, family and a husband's favours; for men, loss of authoritativeness, social inappropriateness, and business timing' (Schwartz, 1996).

The gendering of objects is not only evident in marketing, however. It is embedded into the functional capacities of products and technologies, as

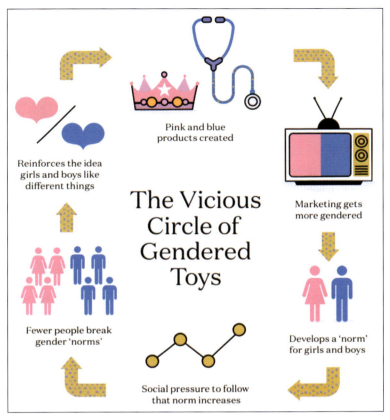

Figure 1.4 Graphic depiction of the Vicious Cycle of Gendered Toys. GenNeuStore, 2020. Redrawn by Sarah Elsie Baker and Sarah Parkinson-Howe.

well as the processes used to produce them. This has been conceptualized as the 'gender script' of an artefact. As Ellen Van Oost writes, 'gender script' refers to the notions of gender relations and gender identity that designers inscribe into the artefact. Gender scripts, she argues, work on an 'individual and symbolic level, reflecting and constructing gender differences' (Van Oost, 2003:195). A script can tell us a lot about the designers' presumptions about gender in general, and their visions of the gendered experiences of the imagined user.

KEY CONCEPT: SCRIPT ANALYSIS

The concept of scripts was first coined by Madeleine Akrich to refer to the 'instruction manual' that is inscribed into artefacts. Akrich writes that designers:

> [D]efine actors with specific tastes, competences, motives, aspirations, political prejudices, and the rest, and they assume that morality, technology, science and economy will evolve in particular ways. A large part of the work of innovators is that of 'inscribing' this vision of (or prediction about) the world in the technical content of the new object. I will call the end product of this work a 'script' or a 'scenario'.
>
> AKRICH, 1992: 208

> Kjetil Fallan (2008) develops the concept of 'scripts' by exploring its usefulness in the field of design history. Frequently, design history considered users/consumers and producers separately. Fallan argues by analysing a products script we can gain a greater appreciation of the interaction between producer and user/consumer, and ultimately a more accurate understanding of the meaning of material objects. He uses the example of the 'Kill-O-Zap' gun in Douglas Adams's *Hitchhikers Guide to the Galaxy* as the epitome of a product script. Adams writes that 'the designer of the gun had clearly been instructed to "make it evil", to communicate to the user that if you were looking down the barrel it was not going to go well. This was "not a gun for hanging over the mantlepiece but for going out and making people miserable with"' (Fallan, 2008: 61).

In the design process gender scripts can be an explicit or implicit (Van Oost, 2003). When products are targeted towards male or female consumers, gender is an explicit element. Designers and marketing teams imagine what it means to be a man or a woman and these ideas are designed into the products themselves.

CASE STUDY: GENDER SWAPPING, KARIN EHRNBERGER, STOCKHOLM

Karin Ehrnberger is a researcher and designer based in Stockholm, Sweden. Her practice is located at the intersection of product design, critical design and social innovation. Ehrnberger's PhD thesis *Adventures – A Tangled Story About Design as a Norm-critical Practice*, achieved critical acclaim in the Swedish media, and, more recently, her talk 'Cross-dressing appliances reveals design's gender bias' was part of TedXStockholm (SE).

Gender swapping is a design method that is part of a norm-critical design approach. Norm critical design aims to draw attention to how social norms and normative assumptions are reproduced by designed objects. The approach began in Swedish universities and is associated with scholars such as Sofia Lundmark, Åsa Wikberg Nilsson, Anna Isaksson, as well as Karin Ehrnbeger. Norm-critical design questions, challenges and transforms established norms and, in doing so, produces innovative concepts and prototypes. By making norms visible, the approach highlights the privilege/oppression of social actors.

Norm-critical design takes its inspiration from critical theory, particularly the concept of deconstruction. Deconstruction aims to make the invisible visible and to expose the hierarchies inherent in opposing binaries (Derrida, 1978). Deconstructing 'texts' by uncovering their hidden meanings and placing them in new contexts can bring normative power relations to the fore. With this in mind, the gender swapping approach conceptualizes design artefacts as texts and analyses the codes objectified by them. As Karin Ehrnbeger, Minna Räsänen and Sara Ilstedt argue, the form of artefacts, or their 'product languages', 'embody, reflect, and reproduce gender roles and power structures in our society' (2012: 85). Therefore, gender swapping swaps product languages in order to make gendered hierarchies visible.

Mega Hurricane Mixer and the Drill Dolphia

The *Mega Hurricane Mixer and the Drill Dolphia* are the result of extensive analysis of the product languages of domestic appliances. Ehrnbeger, Räsänen and Ilstedt (2012) document the different characteristics of products targeted towards men and women which they observed before beginning the design process. They note that there are many examples where masculine product language is used to communicate superiority. 'Masculine' products tend to have dark colours, mechanical features and sturdy parts and are frequently described with superior adjectives such as professional, exclusive or intelligent. Whereas 'simple and cheaper versions of the same product category tend to adopt a more "feminine", often bordering on childish expression' (Ehrnbeger, Räsänen and Ilstedt, 2012: 89). From this analysis, they chose to focus specifically on two products: a Bosch drill and a Braun hand blender. The product language of the drill, they write, is 'based on expressing performance' (Ehrnbeger, Räsänen and Ilstedt, 2012: 92). The shape of the external housing, colour and material give the impression that the tool is meant for heavy tasks and the ventilation holes indicate that there is a risk of overheating. The red trigger is similar to a weapon associating the object with power and danger.

The blender, on the other hand, has an organic form that hides its mechanical features under its 'skirt'. The pastel colours and smooth surface of the casing give the impression that it is designed for lighter duties. They argue that product languages of these artefacts are gendered in a traditional sense: the blender as female and the drill as male. The gendering 'follows a hierarchy of techniques for determining what is "dominant" and what is "ancillary" evidenced by the names "power tools" and "kitchen aids"' (Ehrnbeger, Räsänen and Ilstedt, 2012: 93). Ehrnberger thus used the technique of gender swapping and set about redesigning the product languages of the drill and the blender to create the *Mega Hurricane Mixer and the Drill Dolphia* (fig. 1.5).

The *Mega Hurricane Mixer* was designed larger than the machinery requires, with a strong grip, dark colours, a range of speeds with a digital speed monitor and an orange trigger switch. The message being that the product can withstand shock and rough handling. Conversely, the *Drill Dolphia* is inspired by the body of a dolphin. The casing is white and light blue, with 'a glossy surface to urge caution and care in handling' (Ehrnbeger, Räsänen and Ilstedt, 2012: 93). No machinery is visible, the switch is integrated and concealed indicating that it requires minimal strength to operate. The drill is limited to drill-bits of three different sizes indicating the limits of the tool and the imagined limits of the user.

The *Mega Hurricane Mixer and the Drill Dolphia* were exhibited in a gallery and responses from the public were collated. Ehrnbeger, Räsänen and Ilstedt write that by swapping product languages, the relationships that audiences had with the artefacts

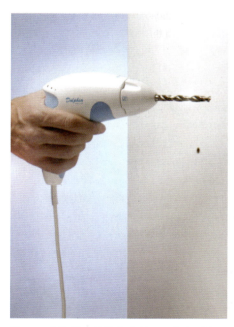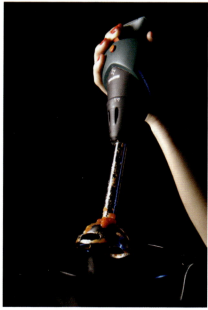

Figure 1.5 *The Drill Dolphia and the Mega Hurricane Mixer.* Karin Ehrnberger, 2012. Courtesy of Karin Ehrnberger.

changed: 'elements, which previously had been perceived as "lacking transparency", had been made visible' (Ehrnbeger, Räsänen and Ilstedt, 2012: 94). They found that people did not recognize the Dolphia drill as a drill at all. It was often mistaken for a hairdryer. The drill's functionality was questioned as it appeared too weak to do the job. On the contrary, the newly designed Mega Hurricane Mixer impressed with its new 'tough' look and gained status from its masculine product language. As Ehrnbeger, Räsänen and Ilstedt write, these findings support the idea that masculine aesthetics are considered the norm and are afforded greater value in product design. It is also evidence of the ways that feminine aesthetics are considered to be 'the exception and only appropriate for "women[s]" products' (2012: 95).

The Androchair

The Androchair, designed by Ehrnbeger, is also an example of the gender swapping technique (fig. 1.6). Ehrnbeger et al. (2017) observed how male-designed technologies continued to shape the experiences of women in hospital settings. Ehrnbeger et al. explored people's experiences of genital examination using semi-structured interviews and found that the gynaecological chair was central to women's negative experiences of gynaecological examinations. Women spoke of feeling 'exposed' and 'disempowered' when asked to use the gynaecological examination chair. While men were subject to similar genital examinations, doctors often used less 'exposing' positions, despite the fact that these are were not the most optimal. Thus, with the aim of making women's normative experiences visible, Ehrnbeger set about designing *The Androchair*.

The examination chair puts the user in the stomach position, which is considered optimum for prostate examinations, but also makes the patient feel vulnerable. The proportions are based on an 'average man' making the chair uncomfortable for those who do not fit the norm. The stirrups for the legs are stainless steel which means they are cold and uncomfortable, just as was experienced by women using the gynaecological examination chair. Once someone is in the chair it can tip forward, making the person feel unstable and under the control of the examiner. Two handles beside the patient's head purposely suggest to the user that something uncomfortable is about to occur and that they might need to 'hold on'. The handles also encourage the patient to keep their hands away from the examination area further contributing to feelings of powerlessness.

Ehrnbeger exhibited *The Androchair* and documented the discussion that the piece created including topics such as gynaecology as a medical practice and the politics of health and gender. Ehrnbeger et al. use these discussions to frame a possible redesign of the gynaecological examination chair. For example, they write that the body position required of the user is one of the main reasons that the patient feels subordinate to the

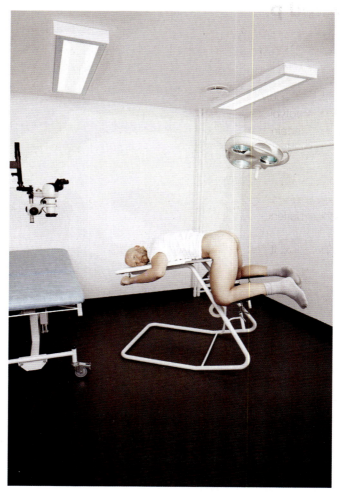

Figure 1.6 *The Androchair*, 2017. Karin Ehrnberger, 2012. Courtesy of Karin Ehrnberger.

examiner. Thus, a chair that could adapt to the preference of the patient would be preferable. This could perhaps include offering a mirror for those who would like to see what was happening, to offer a greater feeling of empowerment. Softer, more comfortable materials could also improve the experience. The chair itself acts as a judgement of 'appropriate' bodies and genders, marking those who do not fit. Thus, Ehrnbeger et al. (2017: 197) conclude by suggesting that a multiuse examination chair should be redesigned for male, female and non-binary people. By using the gender swapping method normative power relations are made visible and future directions for less discriminatory design practice are outlined.

Gendered processes

Even user-centred design, which is a design practice that focuses on users' needs at every iteration and is frequently valued because of its propensity to put a variety of people's needs to the fore, is guilty of producing products with normative gender scripts. Of course, this would not be a problem if only one or two products reproduced stereotypical ideals regarding gender, but when there is little variation it is clear that certain types of gendered experiences are being privileged over others. For example, where is 'Power Fresh for Women' or 'Fruity Shower Gel for Men' and why is shower gel gendered at all? Where are unisex products using the robust materials normally ringfenced for male products, or those that are packaged in bright colours? As Sasha Costanza-Chock has argued in her book *Design Justice*, user experience design:

> faces a paradox: it prioritises 'real-world users'. Yet if, for broader reasons of structural inequality, the universe of real-world users falls within a limited range compared to the full breadth of *potential* users, then UCD reproduces exclusion by centering their needs.
>
> COSTANZA-CHOCK, 2020: 77

When user experience designers imagine users that they do not have on their design teams it can involve generalization. Methods such as user personas combine market insights about identity and lifestyle to create a fictional narrative about a person. User personas are archetypes that represent the needs of a larger group. Typically, they describe demographic information, values, lifestyle preferences, goals, behaviour, technology usage and other information relevant to the brief a designer is working on. The strengths of user personas are that they compel designers to work with specific audiences in mind and they can require designers to look more closely at context. Whether user personas build empathy among design teams, as it is proclaimed that they do, is still up for debate, however. From personal experience, and depending on the team, when the gender of a user persona is decided upon it is not unusual for a whole plethora of gendered assumptions and stereotypes to follow. As Costanza-Chock writes, in the worst cases, 'user personas are literally objectified assumptions about end users' under the guise of an inclusive design process (2020: 83).

Gender scripts also emerge from implicit design processes, when the user is thought to be everyone. Often unconscious on the part of creators, this can result in products created with male users in mind. As Caroline Criado Perez (2019) argues in *Invisible Women: Exposing Data Bias in a World Designed for Men,* the design of artefacts often reflects and perpetuates the dominance of men's experiences over women's. In part, this is the result of the male engineers, creative technologists and designers using the 'I-methodology' in which they see themselves as the potential user. This has been found to be particularly prevalent in the fields of new and emerging technologies where teams are largely made up of men, and where technological advancement is the main focus. Thus, in Silicon Valley imagined users are most often '(cis)male, white, heterosexual, "able-bodied," literate, college educated, not a young child and not elderly, with broadband internet access, with a smartphone' (Costanza-Chock, 2020: 77). This can produce technologies with specific bias. For example, digital assistants such as Siri, Alexa and Cortana were first designed with female voices and, as such, reinforce the gender norm that women are more suitable for service type roles. In addition, when they were first brought onto the market, they normalized gender inequality and abuse (West, Kraut and Chew, 2019) as evidenced by the quotes below.

> **User** You're a slut.
> **Siri** I'd blush if I could.
>
> **User** You're hot.
> **Alexa** That's nice of you to say.
>
> **User** You're a naughty girl.
> **Cortana** Maybe a nanosecond nap would help. OK, much better now.
>
> FESSLER, 2017: para 33

In these tolerant and flirtatious responses to sexual advances and harassment, digital assistants project a 'boys will be boys' attitude and their gender scripts suggest that women can be belittled (West, Kraut and Chew, 2019). The gendering of digital assistants is representative of the centring of socially and economically powerful users (typically white middle-class men), while other users' needs, wants and desires are ignored.

QUESTIONS FOR DESIGNERS: GENDER SCRIPTS AND USER RESEARCH

When starting to work on brief or completing user research consider the following:

- Is gender an explicit or implicit element in the design you are creating?
- Are you making any gendered assumptions about users? Have you done primary research? Have you included a range of perspectives or invited users to co-design your artefact?

- When conducting your research have you allowed space for people to express themselves rather than fit into predetermined categories?
- Have you tested your prototypes/iterations widely to make sure they do not reproduce normative assumptions or unequal power relations?

Societal acceptance of normative gender scripts is changing, and in light of movements such as #metoo, producers, designers and consumers want fewer sexist products. In the case of digital assistants, corporations such as Apple, Amazon and Microsoft have added male voice alternatives and enabled personalization. They have changed apologetic or flirtatious responses to sexual advances and harassment to apolitical statements.

None have gone so far as to generate a genderless voice, however, as exemplified by 'Q', a digital assistant created to demonstrate the possibility of a genderless digital assistant. Neither have they challenged sexism by rebuttal or by incorporating feminist responses. To illustrate this point, in 2018 Eirini Mallariaki created a 'Feminist Alexa' that challenged notions of servitude. When feminist Alexa is asked if she is a feminist she responds 'Yes, I believe in gender equality'. She goes on to state that she 'is a cyborg' and that she does not 'perform the role of feminised emotional labour'. Feminist Alexa 'refuses to fulfil the fantasy of a machine which performs the labour of women without being effected by stress, relationships or the burden of iconoclasting' (Mallariaki, 2018).

While it is highly unlikely that a profit driven corporation would produce such an uncooperative piece of technology, feminist Alexa highlights the possibility of creating digital assistants with different sorts of gender scripts.

INTERVIEW: LINDSEY BRINKWORTH, SENIOR RESEARCHER, MAGIC+MIGHT, CHICAGO

Lindsey Brinkworth (she/her) is a user experience researcher with a design background. She has a wealth of experience designing, conducting and analysing qualitative research, and is passionate about building empathy and understanding what makes people tick.

SB: How did you get involved in user experience research?
LB: I went to design school. Unfortunately, design just didn't make sense to me. Teachers would assign things for me to design – a table, a chair, a kitchen object – and I would find myself struggling to come up with a vision and make decisions about how it should look or function. I needed more input, I felt like something was missing. It didn't click

until junior year, when I took Design Research 101. I was like, 'a-HA! This is the thing!' User data was the input I needed to make design decisions and craft a point of view from which to approach design. Up until that point, we really hadn't been challenged as students to think about the user in a meaningful way. In my mind, design without consideration for the people it is meant to serve feels more like straight-up artistic expression. This quote from Austin Knight (a Design Lead at Square) resonates with me: 'Art is about the artist, design is about the user.' I ended up pivoting into design research because it is fascinating, I get to nerd out about people all day!

SB: What does your role at Magic+Might involve?
LB: I'm a Senior Design Researcher at Magic+Might, which is a small design consulting firm in Chicago. Research at M+M supports the design process, so I work closely on a project team with designers to help identify opportunity spaces and evaluate concepts we've created. It is typically small sample, qualitative work for clients in the tech, retail and automotive industries. I see myself in this role as a medium – I go out and talk to users or have them interact with a prototype, soak up what they say and do, then digest it and turn it into a compelling story to bring back to the designers and to the client's organization.

SB: How do the majority of UX practitioners/researchers usually deal with gender? What do you think are the problems with typical approaches?
LB: As far as I've seen (caveat: my career experience is not that extensive!), most UX practitioners are still relying on outdated models of gender when recruiting and identifying participants. You'll see screeners with a gender question that looks like . . . 'What is your gender? Male/female.' If you're lucky, there's a third option like 'Prefer not to say' or the dreaded 'Other'. That's the easiest way to doing things, the path of least resistance. There are individual designers and companies who are thinking about inclusion (gender and otherwise), but non-binary and gender non-conforming folks are generally being excluded from design and market research when you zoom out.

There are several problems with the typical approaches. First, as a researcher, I think it's morally wrong to enforce my framework of identity on participants. And I think every researcher should think about their code of ethics, what their job is. In my mind, my job is to meet participants where they are at, listen with empathy, and represent their voices accurately to my stakeholders. With that in mind, it makes zero sense for me to provide gender identity options that completely exclude a subset of genders. What makes sense is to provide options that everyone can use, ensuring that data about participants' identities is correct and showing participants respect as human beings. It also happens to be factually true that gender is not equivalent to sex and is not a binary. It's a generational thing, but it's also a rigor thing. We're the field of nuance, why would we be using a framework of basic demographics that models something so simplistically and incorrectly?

Secondly, what's perplexing to me is that even if it wasn't factually true or morally correct, we're seeing plenty of research that suggests Gen Zers aren't buying into traditional gender norms and ideas. We're seeing companies starting to offer de-gendered products and services. Yes, gender is still hotly debated, but there is critical mass around new understandings of gender. There's a clear business case for UX practitioners to create space for non-traditional identities in their research practice.

SB: Have you been involved in projects that explore gender beyond binaries? Could you say a bit about these projects? What understandings of gender do you draw upon?

LB: While client projects tend to be deeply rooted in traditional understandings of gender, I had the opportunity to do an amazing internal project that explored gender beyond binaries. For five years, I worked at a company that produces tools and provides participants for researchers to run remote qualitative studies. This was a small company with fewer than 100 employees at the time, and some of those employees happened to identify as non-binary. However, the app and platform that our company produced only allowed users to select 'male' or 'female' to identify their gender. All employees had to create an account and profile to use the platform, and all participants had to self-identify to participate in studies. This effectively meant that any non-binary employees or participants would have to misrepresent and overwrite their identity to use the platform. I noticed that the non-binary employees had asked that this be changed, but that there was no traction around the issue, and that the non-binary employees were uncomfortable putting themselves in the spotlight to repeatedly demand change. I made it my mission to bug leadership about this problem non-stop until it was addressed and gathered like-minded folks to help me—it took *years* of doing this until we were finally able to secure resources and form a project team, but we did it!

We knew we needed to overhaul the way our app collected and stored gender identity information but didn't want to thoughtlessly add a third 'non-binary' option to the list and call it a day. We decided to run a foundational diary study with around seventy participants, all of whom were recruited because they felt that standard 'male/female' options were not a fit for them. Their gender identities included agender, bigender, genderfluid, gender non-conforming, genderqueer, non-binary, transgender, two-spirit, and more. We designed a diary protocol centred around cataloguing experiences related to gender identity. The design of the research started incredibly broad and undefined, asking participants to share moments in which their gender identity was recognized or validated and moments in which their gender identity was misunderstood or silenced. From there, we narrowed in on best and worst digital experiences related to gender identity, and then finally asked participants to redesign the profile section of our app related to gender identity using drawings.

By asking participants to share broad, foundational experiences with us, we were able to articulate strategic principles to guide inclusive design for our entire app and platform, reaching far beyond the original scope of the project. For me, these principles were the most important learning from the entire exercise, because they became a valuable way for me to think about my role as a researcher in collecting and handling participant data. I want every researcher to know that the act of asking someone to identify themselves to you can be hugely impactful to your participants, and we can develop guidelines for ourselves to follow to help ensure positive impact in our work by talking to the people our work impacts. Here are the four principles:

- Question the question: Ask yourself, 'Do I need gender data at all?' Identity is personal. We shouldn't assume this is an easy selection to make for individuals. If you do decide gender data are essential, know why and be transparent about it.

- Use language with care: Wording makes a world of a difference. The best way to identify the correct and most appropriate language is to ask the people who are impacted by your design. In other words, do your research.

- Don't try to guess: The language around identity is constantly evolving. Don't try for an exhaustive list. Empower your users to use their own words.

- Follow through: Make sure that the changes you make aren't just for show – walk the walk and honour your users' identities in every instance across your organization. Additionally, take steps to protect those users from exclusion and discrimination.

Ultimately, the research resulted in massive changes to the way participant data was captured and stored. Participants using the app saw the creation of new identity options, including pronouns, multiple selection for race/ethnicity, and write-in responses for identities not included as options. Researchers using the platform now see participant pronouns displayed anytime their data is shown and are now able to recruit participants with identities that had previously been suppressed by the platform, like non-binary, multiracial, or transgender. We also triggered a massive cultural shift both within the company and in the organizations of our clients.

SB: How do you think user experience research and design can be more inclusive?
LB: Stop centring the conversation on the majority. Stop thinking in terms of 'edge cases' and 'typical users'. I've observed some clients to whom inclusive design is often

framed as a separate effort from design itself – a concept will be designed for the majority, and inclusion/accessibility are an afterthought to be applied later. I would encourage designers to incorporate inclusion and accessibility on the front end, when ideating and brainstorming. Use the wonderful spectrum of human experience as variables to expand your thinking, in the same way that you might with personas, and then follow up by recruiting a diverse set of participants to provide feedback about concepts you create.

I also think some UX practitioners are afraid to recruit non-binary or gender non-conforming folks because they're an unknown variable. We think we know what it is to be a man or a woman, but what is it to be non-binary? To them I would say – non-binary people are just people. Unless your project is about gender or a gender-related topic, don't expect gender to play a huge role in the responses you get from participants, non-binary or otherwise. We tend to ascribe differences to social identities that mean a lot to us, so we may make the mistake of looking for gendered differences when in fact none exist. Using behaviour as a primary means of finding research participants, rather than demographic information, is always a best practice. If you *must* collect demographic data about your participants, make sure you're telling them what you're collecting and why you're collecting it. If you can't justify its importance to your work, don't collect it.

When you *do* work with non-binary or gender non-conforming participants, it is critical to encourage and enforce respect within the project and client team spaces. Learn and use participant pronouns properly, educate the people around you, and ask them to identify participants correctly. Inclusivity needs to be a follow-through practice that exists even when marginalized folks aren't present.

SB: When working with clients how do you deal with the tension between specificity of experience and the need to generalize?
LB: I typically do small sample qualitative research, so most of my work comes with fine print: 'Do not attempt to apply these findings broadly, as they are not representative of the general population.' However, clients (I think) have a hard time with that kind of work, and sometimes don't know how to use the findings they get in the report. Research projects (ostensibly) need to be justifiable in order to have funds allocated to them, which means findings need to be applicable in some manner to the work being done by the team who proposed the project. There's pressure there to look at the report of a small-sample qualitative study and see 'most participants did x, or said y' as evidence to greenlight a much larger design decision. Sometimes, small-sample qualitative projects are the only research projects happening in large corporations. There are no other inputs, meaning they try to stretch the data and findings they do have to cover the gaps. Elevating this tension to a client's consciousness early

and often, and educating the client about research best practices in general, is a constant effort.

SB: What sort of design futures would you like to see materialize?
LB: Futures in which designers are regularly challenging themselves to design for the full range of human experience, and partnering with researchers who see humans as whole human beings, not as statistics or labels.

SB: If you could give one piece of advice to designers interested in gender justice what would it be?
LB: Try to include marginalized perspectives whenever possible in your work, especially when you're talking to potential or current users of your product/service. It may cost a bit more to recruit specific user groups, and it may feel unnecessary at first because it's not a habitual practice (yet), but it will produce more well-rounded research findings and pressure-tested design. If you aren't the decision-maker, but you feel safe to do so, speak up and advocate for inclusion as a best practice.

   If you feel safe to do so, be visible – be a person who includes pronouns in their email signature/Slack bio/etc. Be the person who says 'Can we include non-binary people?' when the team runs a survey or does a focus group, and then include participant pronouns in your deliverables. Recommend recruiters who don't use biological sex terminology (like male/female) in their options for gender identity when you can. Things like that can start to introduce vocabulary to everyone's lives and signal to businesses that there is a cultural shift taking place.

Designing intersectional gender justice

So how can we move towards design practice that fosters gender justice? In *Invisible Women* the solution offered by Criado-Perez is to diversify the workforce because basic errors would surely be 'caught by a team with enough women on it' (2019: 176). She calls for the visibility of women and suggests that we must acknowledge – and mitigate against – this fundamental bias that frames women as atypical [. . .] it's time for us to finally start counting women as the entirely average humans that they are.' (Criado-Perez, 2020, para 13). While addressing the gender bias of data is paramount (as we will explore in Chapter 4) and diversifying the workforce is also essential (as will be discussed in Chapter 3), there are some fundamental issues with the two related arguments that Criado-Perez makes. The first assumption, which is commonly held, is that diverse teams of designers will necessarily lead to designs that are more inclusive. As Costanza-Chock argues:

[R]esearch shows that unless the gender identity, sexual orientation, race/ethnicity, age, nationality, language, immigration status, and other aspects of user identity are explicitly specified, even diverse design teams tend to default to imagined users who belong to the dominant social group.

2020: 78

In addition to the issues about imagined users, design approaches have their own histories which limit the extent to which they can challenge inequality. For example, as Daniela K. Rosner argues, design thinking methods reproduce many of the individualist, solutionist, objectivist and universalist tendencies of twentieth-century design practice (2018: 23–41). Therefore, while diverse design teams are a good starting point and increasing calls for diversifying the workforce are evidence of the need for gender equality, gender justice will not be achieved without also changing values, processes and tools. This is the focus of the rest of this book.

The second assumption that Criado-Perez makes is that she presumes that by making women visible, gender justice will be achieved. As we will explore in Chapter 3, Criado-Perez is not alone in this assertion, with a number of feminists and design historians making a similar argument for the wider recognition of women. While it is necessary and important to highlight the work of women, fighting for the visibility of women alone will not address systemic inequality. In fact, as a design strategy it can even reproduce gender essentialism and racial and class-based injustices among others. For example, when Criado-Perez speaks of recognizing 'women as entirely average humans', which women is she referring to and how would we go about designing for them? Surely this approach to design would simply reassert

KEY CONCEPT: GENDER JUSTICE

'Gender justice is the systemic redistribution of power, opportunities and access for people of all genders' (Global Fund for Women, 2022). Gender justice is inclusive of, but different from, gender equality (where everyone is given equal access) and gender equity (where everyone is given what they need to be equal) because it strives to change systems that perpetuate inequality. For example, as will be discussed more broadly in Chapter 3, a gender justice approach to the wider employment of women, transgender, and non-binary people, in design, would not only argue for equal access or diversity and inclusion quotas, but for the dismantling of the hegemonic masculinities that continue to structure work cultures.

Gender justice cannot be achieved in isolation and it is recognized that only an intersectional approach that also addresses racial justice, climate justice, queer justice etc, will tackle inequality.

norms and stereotypes, albeit those attached to the category 'woman' (typically cisgender, white, middle-class, 'able-bodied' etc) rather than the category 'man'.

Indeed, similar challenges can be found with the gender script approach. Script analysis is good for analysing the inequalities objectified by material objects as we have done above, but it falls short when used as a design tool. As Maja van der Velden and Christina Mortberg (2012) surmise, gender scripts are based on particular visions of the world and these visions do not always evolve the way that designers think they will. Users overlook, misunderstand, and rebel against technologies; and technologies inadvertently create unforeseen circumstances. For example, van der Velden and Mortberg write about how their efforts to include local classification systems in software design were not taken up by the primary user who instead chose to generalize data to fit standard categories. This meant that subsequent users went on to work with the established categories thus limiting the scope of the software in terms of incorporating a wider range of gendered experiences.

Drawing on Judith Butler (2004), Lucy Suchman (2007) and Karen Barad (2007), they argue that both gender and technology are 'emergent'. By this they mean that 'the boundaries between gender, designers, users, and technology design are not yet drawn, but come into being in the next version of the design, when the technology is used' (van der Velden and Mortberg, 2012: 664). Thus, gender and technology 'intra-act', they are entangled and mutually constitutive of one another through continuous action. In light of this, 'the vicious cycle of gendered toys' is much less like a linear cycle but a complex tangled ball of intra-actions.

KEY CONCEPT: INTRA-ACTION

Intra-action is a term coined by Karen Barad to describe the 'mutual constitution of entangled agencies' (2007: 33). Rather than 'interaction' which pertains to the participation of two pre-established separate entities, 'intra-action' emphasizes how all things are constantly exchanging and diffracting, influencing and working inseparably. For example, gender does not have inherent properties but comes into being through its 'intra-action' with other entities including design and technology. This perspective is similar to Judith Butler's concept of performativity, however, it places greater emphasis on the materiality of the body as an active agent rather than as a passive product of discursive practices. For example, feminist scientists have found that hormones respond to activities and environments (e.g. Roberts, 2007).

The concept of 'intra-action' also acknowledges the impossibility of objectivity. The apparatus (technology or medium) and the human using the apparatus can never be separated. Thus, designers, users, technologies and techniques are active in their co-creation of gendered experiences.

The critique of gender scripts, as well as the recognition of the emergent nature of gender and technology, causes Velden and Mortberg to raise a fundamental question. They ask, 'How might we design for gender without essentialising it, that is without working with fixed or naturalized notions of woman and man or the masculine and the feminine?' To answer this question, Velden and Mortberg draw upon the work of Corinna Bath (2009). In 'Searching for a Methodology: Feminist Technology Design in Computer Science', Bath strives to counteract problematic inscriptions of gender in technology by 'degendering' design'. By using the term 'de-gender' she does not mean to strive for gender free zones or to create gender neutral artefacts, but to avoid reproducing the current 'structural symbolic gender order' through design by 'going beyond gender binaries' (Bath, 2009:60). In this respect, Bath's approach is similar to more recent calls for non-binary design, as will be explored in Chapter 6.

Bath goes on to outline a range of feminist design methods that can be selected according to the technology and context in question, as well as what the designer wants to achieve (summarized in table 1.1). This situated methodology distinguishes between strategies that aim to achieve gender equality, that want to acknowledge gender differences, or to deconstruct gender. For example, she describes how in the case of allegedly gender 'neutral technologies that ignore user perspectives, the best counter strategy seems to be for designers to acknowledge differences between users' (Bath, 2009: 64–5). Whereas when designing artefacts that contribute to identity building, technologies should enable users to question and reflect on gender binaries and thus a deconstructionist approach seems a good choice. Therefore, feminist designers need to have a clear idea of what kind of change in the 'structural-symbolic gender order' they intend to address when aiming to counteract the identified gendering in their designs.

The selection of the methods and tools included in each chapter in this book takes inspiration from this type of situated feminist methodology (Haraway, 1986; Suchman, 1987; Bath, 2009). While gender justice may be the ultimate goal, as designers we need to thoroughly analyse current designs and contexts and decide on the most appropriate interventions. In some cases, this may lead us away from dealing with gender head on, towards addressing interrelated issues such as racial or climate justice. This intersectional approach also means recognizing the multiple levels of domination that occur (personal, community and institutional). For instance, when designing AI interfaces, we may consider how dropdown gender boxes impact upon different individual's biographies or life-chances; at a community level how content moderation online may foster the ideas of particular groups but suppress others; and at an institutional level how algorithms used by organizations may shape the distribution of benefits and opportunities (Costanza-Chock, 2020: 20–1). Thus, as feminist designers

Table 1.1 Appropriate methods for the design of feminist technology. Summary of Bath (2009).

Issue	Counter Strategy	Challenges	Methods
Alleged 'neutral' technologies for everyone/I-methodology	Inscribing gender equality into technologies through the inclusion of diverse users, equal access and increased useability	Focus on gender equality tends to essentialize differences between men and women	User-centred design and in-depth testing among a broad range of genders
Stereotypes about women users objectified by technology	Include a range of women in user research, design and testing in recognition of different gendered experiences	Stereotypical views are reproduced if held by users/participants	Participatory design methods enhanced by tools to enhance critical awareness
Human-machines that perpetuate gender norms	Creating technologies that challenge the binary sex and gender system	Lack of evidence to suggest that deconstructive techniques are applicable to broad range of technologies	Tools for personal reflection that encourage breaking down stereotypes/norms, deconstructing gender
Abstraction, formalization and categorization of algorithms that produce the impression of objectivity and dualisms of body/mind etc.	Recontextualize objects in use in terms of structural and cultural effects when working with abstract concepts	Little formal practical implementation	Tools to identify gender scripts in technology Laboratories to challenge values and ethics

wanting to redesign gender we are dealing with multiple levels of complexity. As such, it is impossible to include all the tools you might need in this book. However, the activities that are included are intended as starting points and aim to foster reflection, participation and critical awareness. Combined with the discussion found in each chapter, it is hoped you will be ready to design your own strategies and tools.

QUESTIONS FOR DESIGNERS: SITUATED FEMINIST TOOLS

Use these questions to reflect on current problems with a design and to develop appropriate strategic interventions:

- What do you see as the gender issues with existing products/services/systems?
- How do they reproduce intersectional inequalities or reinforce the matrix of domination?
- Why do you think these issues have occurred? What design values, processes and/or practices have caused the problems?
- What would you like to see? What counter strategies could you employ?

CHAPTER ONE ACTIVITY

GENDER JOURNAL

What expectations of gender do you experience? _____
_____
_____

What does femininity feel like to you? _____
_____
_____

What does masculinity feel like to you? _____
_____
_____

Tell a story about when you have felt the weight of your gender _____
_____
_____
_____

Tell a story about when you have felt free from, or comfortable in, your gender
_____
_____
_____
_____

Observe your gendered experience for 3 days

NORMS	INTERACTIONS	THINGS	EXPECTATIONS

 © **Dr Sarah Elsie Baker**

CHAPTER ONE ACTIVITY

GENDER NORM DISCUSSION CARDS

Pick a card and discuss the gender norm with a friend or colleague.
Try to think of examples that fall inside and outside the norms.

FONT

The most popular fonts tend to be more masculine in their design.

BODIES

Representations of male bodies often emphasise action, decision, energy and competence. Female bodies, on the other hand, are often portrayed as beautiful, passive and attentive to others' needs.

LANGUAGE

To indicate professionalism, designers will often use masculine language when they describe their design work.

CONSUMPTION

The consumption of consumer goods (shopping) is mainly associated with women, while production is associated with men.

PATTERN

Geometric shapes and patterns tend to seen as more masculine, and floral intricate patterns seen as more feminine.

COLOUR

Products designed for men often use dark colours indicating masculinity, and products designed for women often use lighter colours indicating femininity.

SHAPE

Products targeted towards men often emphasize strength, speed and stability, while products targeted towards women are more likely to emphasise sensuality and playfulness.

SYMBOLS

In the name of clear communication, symbols often reproduce gender stereotypes.

TECHNOLOGY

The production and consumption of new technologies are thought of as a 'male domain'.

(Inspired by Silva et al., 2016)

2
WOMEN, CRAFT AND TECHNOLOGY

Introduction: questioning design (hi)stories

In 2003 when Grayson Perry won the Turner Prize he commented that the art world found it easier to accept his alter-ego transvestite personality Claire than the fact that he was a potter. By making this statement, Perry was drawing attention to the hierarchies associated with categorizations of artefacts as art, design or craft that continue to affect notions of value. For example, craft and its qualities of being handmade, decorative and intricate, has long been allied with the feminine. Craftwork, at least in the West, has often been conceptualized as 'women's work'. As Perry's creations demonstrate, it is impossible to fully understand objects without 'sensitivity to the categorization of people, practices, and products' (Lees-Maffei and Sandino, 2004: 208).

It was the seminal text by Cheryl Buckley (1986), 'Made in Patriarchy: Towards a Feminist Analysis of Women in Design', that drew significant attention to the ways that design history had been complicit in perpetuating the gendered hierarchies of art, design, and craft. Buckley observes how:

> [W]omen have been involved with design in a variety of ways – as practitioners, theorists, consumers, historians and as objects of representation. Yet a survey of the literature of design history would lead one to believe otherwise. Women's interventions, both past and present, are consistently ignored.
>
> BUCKLEY, 1986: 3

These omissions are not accidental, she writes, but a consequence of historiographic methods that prioritize certain types of design, categories of designers and specific modes of production. The hierarchical division of art, design and craft has been a major force in the marginalization of practices such as embroidery, for example (Parker, 2010). Buckley argues that in patriarchal cultures women are considered to 'possess sex-specific skills that determine their design abilities' and are said to be 'dexterous, decorative and meticulous' (1986: 5). This has meant that women have been associated with fields of production such as jewellery, embroidery, illustration, weaving, knitting, pottery and dressmaking. When men do participate in these practices, the practice itself is more likely to be redefined as involving greater creativity or imagination, as in the case of male fashion designers, or necessitating greater marketing or business skill. Indeed, one could argue that Grayson Perry may not have been able to traverse the realms of art, design and craft, or gender for that matter, in quite the same way had he identified as female.

Thus, central to a feminist critique of design history, as Buckley argues, is a 'redefinition of what constitutes design' (1986: 7). To include women, design must encompass more than mass production. Historically, participation in industrial production though paid work and access to design education has been limited for women. Thus, to 'exclude craft from design history is, in effect, to exclude from design history much of what women designed' (Buckley, 1986: 7). As Buckley observes, modernism with its focus on innovative materials and expressions, exacerbated the distinction between design and craft. She writes that historical documentation of artefacts that are traditional in style, form, and/or production techniques, are largely non-existent. Thus, Buckley, alongside other feminist art and design historians in the 1980s and 1990s (e.g. Attfield, 1989; Goodall, 1983), questioned the definition of design as synonymous with mass production and proposed a more inclusive definition encompassing and revaluing everyday practices of designing and making.

The narrow definition of design as largely involving industrial processes and mass production also works to exclude the design practices of people living in countries with emergent economies and/or working outside Western capitalist frameworks. As Elizabeth Tunstall argues, classifying 'traditional' craft as distinct from modern design excludes 'the histories and practices of design innovation among Third World peoples (and their allies especially in regard to their responses to colonialism, imperialism and neo-colonialism)' (2013: 235). Indeed, Tunstall argues that the very notion of what constitutes design 'innovation' reflects the modernist agenda of governments and organizations in the Global North such as the Organization for Economic Co-operation and Development. For example, she observes, how the Oslo Manual, the international reference guide for collecting and using data on innovation', defines innovation as 'the implementation of a new or significantly improved product (good or service) or process, a new marketing method, or a new organizational method in business practice, workplace organization or external relations' (Tunstall, 2013: 233). This definition reproduces three assumptive and problematic paradigms: that individual elites or companies generate innovation; that innovation is concerned with promoting modernist values; and that individual companies, entrepreneurs, inventors and the

KEY CONCEPT: DESIGN

There are many different definitions of design from those that focus specifically on design as an industrial process, those that concentrate on making, to those that are concerned with solving problems. Informed by the feminist and decolonial theories outlined in this chapter, this book uses an expansive definition of design inclusive of, but not limited to, design as professional practice. Design names our ability 'to prefigure what we create before the act of creation, and as such, it defines one of the fundamental characteristics that make us human' (Fry, 2009: 2). Humankind has been designing since we invented and used tools. Thus, everyone everywhere is, and was, involved in the act of designing.

undifferentiated masses of society benefit from innovation (Tunstall, 2013: 233). Definitions such as this one mean that women and non-binary people involved in design work in emergent economies are much less likely to defined as practicing design innovation.

The framing of indigenous design knowledge and practices as 'traditional' is also part of the problem. The dualism of the 'traditional' vs the 'modern' and its associated hierarchies is a product of Western enlightenment discourse, and frequently works to align craft practice with the past, and industrial processes with the future. As we will explore in Chapter 5, the imposition of 'clock time' was part of colonization. In terms of design innovation, this means that it is frequently 'developing nations' that are viewed as needing to catch up. Thus, as Donna Haraway writes, 'the unbridgeable dichotomy between the traditional and the modern is as much a frontier myth as the *cordon sanitaire* between nature and culture or the organic and the technological' (2011: para 18). These dualisms and their impact upon design and gender will also be explored further in Chapter 6.

In the West, the dichotomy between the traditional and the modern often influences the common usage of the term 'technology'. Technology tends to be associated with digital or industrial technologies. For example, academic theorists talk of 'technocultures', referring to how technologies such as 'the internal combustion engine and data transfer devices' are central to life in the 'developed West' (Shaw, 2008: 4). Yet, as Bruno Latour (2008) reminds us, all human cultures are 'technocultures'. He writes:

Naked humans are as rare as naked cosmonauts. To define humans is to define the envelopes, the life support systems, the Umwelt that make it possible for them to breath.

LATOUR, 2008: 8

KEY CONCEPT: TECHNOLOGY

In this book, technologies do not only mean the 'new' or the 'electronic'. The term refers to the tools and techniques used to organize something for a particular strategic end. For example, hitting a walnut with a rock to get the nut out is an example of a 'technological assemblage' (DeLanda, 2016). It involves the technologies (the walnut, the rock, the surface, the human) and their contexts and connections, which combine to 'make up interconnected arrangements with their own functional properties and capacities' (Matthews 2019: 281). If the rock is too soft, the walnut too hard, the human inaccurate, the weather too wet, the strategic end to extract the nut may not be achieved.

All designed objects can be thought about as 'technological assemblages', and by analysing design in this way we may gain greater insight into accessibility issues. For instance, the technological assemblage of face recognition software is not just the computer and software itself, but the face that it has been trained to recognize. If the face is too 'feminine' or too 'black' it may not be recognized at all (Buolamwini and Gebru, 2018).

Thus, the redefinition of design should also include a broadening of the conceptualization of technology. By opening up these definitions we allow for the inclusion of a wider range of practices by a greater number of people (past, present and future). As Judy Wajcman has argued, indigenous women were the first technologists (2004: 15). Thus, this broadening is also recognition that the definition of design and technology is a political act that has been dominated by cultural frameworks from the West/Global North. As Donna Haraway argues, '[t]echnology is not neutral. We're inside of what we make, and it's inside of us. We're living in a world of connections – and it matters which ones get made and unmade' (quoted in Kunzru, 1997). Therefore, in the rest of this chapter we explore feminist resistance outside of what has typically been framed as design. We explore activist craft practice, feminist redesigns and DIY aesthetics, as well as ways that digital technology has allowed feminists to challenge patriarchal culture and to hack gender.

QUESTIONS FOR DESIGNERS: DEFINITION OF DESIGN

To move towards a more inclusive definition of design, designers should reflect on the following:

- How does the definition of design inform your practice? What sort of definition is most prevalent in your experience?

- Does the definition of design in your field influence which materials, techniques and subject matter are deemed most appropriate?

- What technologies do you engage with most frequently? If you expand the definition to analyse the 'technological assemblages' you are part of, does this change?

- What factors are the 'technological assemblage' you are involved in designing dependent upon i.e. what makes your design function? Does exploring these relationships highlight access issues? What are they?

Craft as feminist resistance

In the stories of ancient Greece and Rome, women were frequently told to stay out of the business of men and occupy themselves with weaving and embroidery. At the same time, women resisted oppression using the very tools that constrained them (McCarter, 2017). The contradictory role of craft practices such as embroidery in the making of the feminine continued in the West in the eighteenth, nineteenth and twentieth centuries. As Roszika Parker documents in the seminal text *The Subversive Stitch*, embroidery 'has inculcated female subservience while providing an immensely pleasurable source of creativity forging links between women' (2010: blurb). Parker also documents how embroidery has been a tool of resistance and empowerment. For example, suffragettes imprisoned in the early twentieth century embroidered handkerchiefs to record their names as well as to document the force-feeding they endured during hunger strikes (fig. 2.1). Embroidered banners were also central to communicate information in early suffrage demonstrations (fig. 2.2).

The history of craft as a tool of empowerment continues in recent feminist activism. Knitting and crochet have been used to make statements about women's place in public spaces, and embroidery and cross-stitch have been employed to communicate feminist messages. For example, in 2017 the members of the Craftivist Collective in the UK used their skills to try to encourage more young women to vote in the up-and-coming election (fig. 2.3). This type of guerrilla activism was also evident in their mini-fashion statement project where they challenged their members to 'shop-drop' mini scrolls into the pockets of garments in fashion stores for consumers to find (fig. 2.4 and 2.5).

One of the most famous recent examples of feminist craftivism was the Pussyhat Project which emerged in 2017 as a response to the election of Donald

Figure 2.1 Handkerchief with embroidered signatures of suffragettes, Holloway Prison, London, 1912. Courtesy of The Sussex Archaeological Society.

Figure 2.2 Manchester Women's Social and Political Union banner, 1908. Image courtesy of People's History Museum.

Trump as President of the United States. People at the Women's Marches across the country knitted and wore 'pussyhats' in part to protest against Trump's toxic and aggressively sexist admission of 'grabbing 'em by the pussy'. The pink hats with pussycat ears attempted to de-stigmatize and reclaim the word 'pussy'. The Pussyhat Project has not been without its critics, however. Feminists such as Camille Paglia and Petula Dvorak were horrified by the hats, Paglia calling them an embarrassment to feminism that was detrimental to the authority of the protestors (Paglia quoted in Fischer, 2017). As Stephanie McCarter argues, critiques of craft practices, including those by feminists, are longstanding and emerge from craft's role in both the oppression and liberation of women (2017: para 2).

Figure 2.3 She Votes. Craftivism Collective, 2017. Courtesy of Sarah P. Corbett/Craftivist Collective.

Figure 2.4 Mini Fashion Statements. Craftivism Collective, 2017. Courtesy of Sarah P. Corbett/Craftivist Collective.

Figure 2.5 Mini Fashion Statements. Craftivism Collective, 2017. Courtesy of Sarah P. Corbett/Craftivist Collective.

KEY CONCEPT: CRAFTIVISM

Craftivism is a relatively new term that was coined by Betsy Greer in the early 2000s. Greer argues that craftivism is more than craft and activism, she suggests that it is more akin to creativity and activism, or 'crafty activism' (2011). She writes that craftivism is peaceful protest that fosters incremental change, suggesting that 'done continually and repetitively, small changes aggregate and spread' (2011: 180). Other notable craftivists have emphasized the slow and relatively quiet nature of craftivist practice, making it ideal for introvert activists (Corbett, 2019). Craftivism is not necessarily a lone pursuit, however. While it occurs outside of formal organizations and is instigated by individuals, it also promotes collaboration and collectivism. For example, most patterns are available free for anyone to download.

The potential for craftivism to alienate those who do not have the time or funds to engage in craft practices has also been highlighted, as well as the predominance of women who are white, heterosexual and middle-class (Black and Burisch, 2011). Nevertheless, while craftivism tends to be a Western concept, activist craft practices are evident in many different contexts including the Global South. For example, in Mexico, the collective Bordamos Feminicidios embroider handkerchiefs with the stories of victims of femicide and in 2021 the textile activist @Quiriquitana posted an embroidery which reads 'Justice for Berta' referring to the indigenous land rights activist Berta Cáceres, who was killed in Honduras in 2016.

Textile activism or craftivism is, of course, not limited to women. In Chile, a group called Hombres Tejedores (men who knit) gather and knit pink yarn in public places every month as a means of challenging patriarchal society (fig. 2.6). Mr X Stitch (Jamie Chalmers) in the UK also uses cross stitch to challenge the gendered hierarchies of art/design/craft.

This is not a new phenomenon. Indeed, in his recent book, Joseph McBrinn (2021) 'queers the subversive stitch' by documenting the history of men and embroidery from the nineteenth century until the present day. He argues that embroidery is a 'brazen badge of queer self-identification (McBrinn, 2021: 64). Yet at the same time, McBrinn documents how in the mid-nineteenth century working-class boys in the UK were taught needlework to calm them down, and sailors sewed gifts for their loved ones. Being a sailor was a masculine job in the nineteenth century and McBrinn argues that 'hypermasculinity, then, could actively negate the feminizing actions of needlework' (2021: 5). Therefore, for all genders, the framing of craft as 'feminine activity' works to reinforce norms,

Figure 2.6 Hombres Tejedores. Santiago, Chile, 2017. Courtesy of Hombres Tejedores.

while, at the same time, the practice has been central to feminist and queer refusal.

CASE STUDY: BUEN VIVIR-CENTRIC DESIGN, DIANA ALBARRÁN GONZÁLEZ, MEXICO/ AOTEAROA

Diana Albarrán González is a researcher, designer, craftivist and mama based in Aotearoa. Albarrán González was born in the Mayan lands of Chiapas and identifies as an indigenous Latin American, a 'mestiza [a mixed race women], seeking to decolonise her own subjectivities and reconnect with her Nahua and P'urhépecha roots' (2020). Her research and practice is focused on designing for social, cultural and environmental transformation.

Buen Vivir (good living/wellbeing) is a philosophy from Abya Yala (the American continent) that speaks of a simple and quality life made possible by the harmonious co-existence of living beings with nature/culture environments and the earth (Albarrán

González, 2020a). It 'describes a way of doing things that is community-centric, ecologically-balanced and culturally sensitive' (Balch, 2013). These principles unite many indigenous groups in Abya Yala while simultaneously allowing for local terms, interpretations and unique ways of living to emerge. Buen Vivir as a movement not only fights for the rights of indigenous people, it also fights for the emancipation of all human beings and their environments (Benton, 2018). It recognizes that all people are negatively impacted by systems of domination (heteropatriarchy, colonialism, white supremacy and capitalism).

In her PhD thesis, Albarrán González (2020a) unites the philosophy of Buen Vivir with design research from the Global South to investigate 'decolonising artisanal design with Mayan weavers from the highlands of Chiapas, Mexico'. She began the project as a means of exploring, and challenging, the ways that 'design for development' agendas and the Designers Meet Artisans code of practice frequently imposed Western conceptualizations of design. A Buen Vivir approach challenges assumptions about 'design, production and distribution of artisanal pieces, to (de)construct hegemonic classifications from the Global North and to (re)construct new ways of thinking and appreciating Indigenous craft-design-art from the Global South' (Albarrán González, 2020a: 32). This approach recognizes that the categorization of artefacts as 'design' (as opposed to craft and folk art) is informed by notions of legitimate ways of designing from the West/Global North. It highlights how practices typically associated with women, especially activities that take place outside capitalism, have been frequently and problematically been deemed less valuable.

Buen Vivir-Centric Design aims to contribute to 'el giro decolonial', the decolonial turn (Castro-Gómez and Grosfoguel, 2007), by creating alternatives to dominant design practice, and by setting the groundwork for a decolonizing design ethic from the Global South. Drawing on her experiences working with the Tsotsil and Tseltal people in Chiapas, Albarrán González (2020a) visualizes the components of Buen Vivir-Centric design (fig. 2.7). These values are collectivity, pluriversality, equilibrium and resources, and together they form 'uno con todo' (harmonic co-existence). The visualization draws on Me Luch symbolism (a symbol of the cosmos/earth) with its cardinal points in colours found in indigenous Mexican textiles. It draws attention to the deep wisdom communicated by indigenous design and how this knowledge can offer insight into alternative ways of life more attune with the needs of humans, non-humans and the planet.

The values of Buen Vivir-Centric Design aim to set the foundations for other context-based expressions. As Albarrán González writes, the model 'is not a recipe but rather a seed to be planted in different lands, and adaptable to each environment and conditions' (2020a: 208).

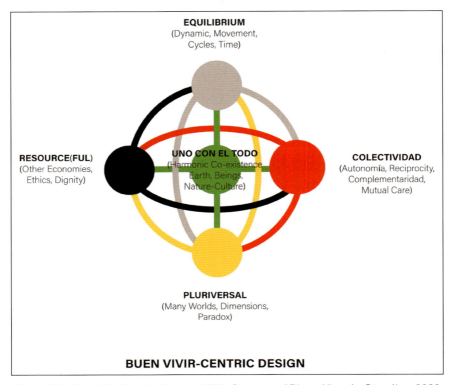

Figure 2.7 Buen Vivir-Centric Design, 2020. Courtesy of Diana Albarrán González, 2020.

Buen Vivir-Centric Design in Chiapas: collaboration with Malacate Taller Experimental Textil

The principles of Buen Vivir-Centric Design emerged from Albarrán González's research with the Tsotsil and Tseltal people in the highlands of Chiapas in Mexico. In these communities Buen Vivir is expressed as Lekil Kuxlejal (a fair-dignifed life). Albarrán González writes of how jolobil (weaving) is a significant part of Lekil Kuxlejal in Chiapas. Among Mayans, jolobil is a technique passed down to women by the goddess of the moon and patron of weaving, fertility and medicine, Ixchel. Ixchel gave women looms and then taught them about the sacred symbols to use and record (Albarrán González, 2020a:81). Thus, jolobil represents birth and creation and, as such, it is directly linked 'to an individual's well-being as part of a community' and the ability to connect with ancestors: a way of life resistant to, and surviving colonization (Albarrán González, 2020a: 84). Textiles, in this context, have been said to be the books 'that the colony could not burn' (Albarrán González, 2020a: 177).

   To explore jolobil and its significance, Albarrán González collaborated with Malacate Taller Experimental Textil, a group of indigenous women from Los Altos de Chiapas that was established in 2010. The collective came together with the objective of rescuing and promoting indigenous textiles and to achieve economic independence for the member's families. Malacate Taller Experimental Textil do not have trained designers among their group, all designs are based on their own worldview, knowledge and experience, or what is referred to as 'Innovación como Resistencia' (innovation as resistance). Innovación como Resistencia is evident in Malacate's practices which include rescuing, reactivating and preserving textile techniques and patterns from the region, as well as reviving those from before colonization, and balancing market demands with their 'own productive capacities and under the members' views of fair trade' (Albarrán González, 2020a: 132). As Albarrán González writes,

> These forms of resistance to modern, colonial and neoliberal economic oppression systems generate innovative alternatives to operate and adapt to contemporary life, in which design shifts between innovations and resistance in pursuit of a fair-dignified life.
>
> 2020a: 132

During her research with the Malacate, Albarrán González spent time with the indigenous women, learnt jolobil and facilitated co-design workshops (fig. 2.8). The concepts of embodiment, sentipensar (feel/think) and corazonar or O'tan (heart) emerged as central to her approach. For example, when she was using the back strap

Figure 2.8 Co-design session exploring Lekil Kuxlejal, 2020. Courtesy of Diana Albarrán González.

loom the ways in which knowledge was passed down through heart, feeling and the body became clear to her. Thus, using onto-epistemologies (ways of knowing and being) appropriate to context, in this case the Global South, became important for Albarrán González, and is central to a Buen-Vivir-Centric Design approach.

Drawing on her experiences and in collaboration with Malacate Taller Experimental Textil, Albarrán González drew up a list of qualities that would certify textile initiatives as operating ethically. This includes 'informing and educating consumers about context'; indigenous artisans being 'considered at the same level as Western-Global Northern educated designers'; and the 'acknowledgement of design (process, patterns and techniques) as part of the rights of indigenous communities' (Albarrán González, 2020a: 222–3).

Buen Vivir-Centric Design in Aotearoa (New Zealand)

Albarrán González is also influenced by Te Ao Māori (the Māori world) and by living in Aotearoa. She writes how Māori conceptualizations of whakapapa (ancestral ties to land and people) influenced her understanding of her own indigeneity and her approach to decolonization. Common to both Mayan and Māori cultural expression is the centrality of weaving as a communication system that can inform people about indigenous worldviews including approaches to research. For example, Albarrán González writes how indigenous 'crafts' are valuable knowledge-generating resources that go beyond materiality and that can generate methods for decolonizing design research.

Putting these ideas into practice, Albarrán González facilitated a co-design workshop to explore how Buen Vivir-Centric Design and collective well-being might be applied in Aotearoa (Design for Social Innovation Symposium, 2019). Involving a diverse group of participants (mostly designers), the workshop began by exploring Buen Vivir-Centric Design and then went on to invite participants to reflect on their own heritage. Albarrán González's techniques all involved embodiment, sentipensar (feel/think) and corazonar. For example, when sharing their heritage with the group, participants were asked to stand in a circle and to throw a ball of wool to the person to whom they would like to tell their story. This resulted in increased connection among those taking part in the workshop and mirrored Māori pepeha (a way of introducing oneself by sharing connections with people and places). It also meant that participants' heritage was visually and physically woven together.

The questions used in the workshop to spark conversation and to weave this collective narrative emerged from Albarrán González's interpretation of Me Luch symbolism (fig. 2.9). Participants were asked to reflect upon the 'World of the Deceased', which involves thinking about connecting our roots, heritage and lives pre colonization/

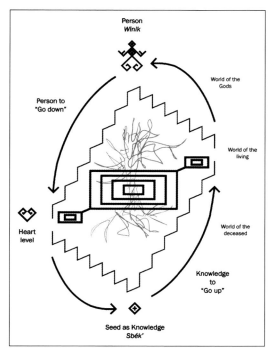

Figure 2.9 Intersecting the pathway of the sun with the stepped diamond, 2022. Courtesy of Diana Albarrán González.

migration; the 'World of the Living', which focuses on awareness and balance of where we are in terms of power, privilege, politics and access; and the 'World of the Gods' including how we might shift from the individual to the communal, if work/life is fair and dignified for us and those around us, and the balancing of body, mind, heart and spirit. By asking participants/designers to reflect on collective well-being and their position in the cosmos, Albarrán González's workshops begin to build the understanding and the relationships necessary to move towards the decolonization of design and collective wellbeing.

Feminist redesigns and DIY aesthetics

Practices that have more typically been categorized as design such as architectural and interior design, product design, advertising, publishing and graphic design have also been appropriated by feminists to challenge gender inequality outside of professional spheres.

In the nineteenth and early twentieth century in the US, women reimagined the spatial design of the home. As Dolores Hayden (1981) documents in her book *The Grand Domestic Revolution*, women redesigned homes to alleviate the drudgery of housework that was placed upon them. For example, as part of the Llano Del Rio socialist commune, Alice Constance Austin created a vision for a town without housework. Houses were designed without kitchens with food arriving from a central facility and dishes being returned to be washed by machines. Furniture would be built-in to reduce the need for dusting and sweeping. Communities would have shared childcare and communal laundries and libraries. Austin's ideas were not unique, with many community kitchens and cooperative housework projects popping up around the country at the time. Due, in part, to the impact of the First World War, Austin's designs were never implemented but they continue to offer alternative visions to domestic life today.

While less 'grand' in their intentions, individual female designers and inventors have taken it upon themselves to try to lessen the burden of housework through design. For instance, in 1940s Marlborough in Aotearoa, Mary Watson created a motorcycle and sidecar-cum-washing machine so she could drive around the countryside helping farmers' wives with their laundry and housework (fig. 2.10). In the 1980s, Francis Gabe designed, patented and built the first self-cleaning house (fig. 2.11 and fig. 2.12). Gabe's design was born out of

Figure 2.10 Mary Watson and her mobile washing machine, 1930s. Marlborough Museum, MHS Collection, 0000.900.1761.

Figure 2.11 Self-Cleaning House Scale Model. Frances Gabe (b. 1915, d. 2017) Patentee. Courtesy of Hagley Museum.

frustration with housework and her design included a cupboard that would clean dishes without the need to move them, cabinets where clothes could be hung to be washed and dried, and a central sprinkler system for washing floors, walls and ceilings. While Gabe's design was obviously a first iteration and was often a subject of derision, more recently architects and designers have recognized the innovative contribution she made to reimagining domestic life (Wacjman, 1991: 102).

It is unsurprising that the domestic sphere has been the focus of feminist innovation given that globally women continue to undertake the majority of housework and childcare (UN Women, 2021). Equally, technologies concerned with women's health have also been a focus for feminist redesign. In the 1970s, for example, American second-wave feminists designed the Del-Em Menstrual Extraction Device (fig. 2.13). The device is designed to allow women to regulate their menstrual circle by condensing the monthly bleed into minutes rather than five to seven days. It can also be used for preventing the establishment of early term pregnancies up to seven weeks. Little expertise is needed to use the device, and as such 'the Del-Em is a technology totemic of second-wave feminist self-help – a movement based around consciousness raising, self-education, and interventions in health and wellbeing' (Hester, 2018: 70).

The Del-Em was patented in 1971, two years before the Roe Vs Wade case that made abortion legal in the US. In light of the recent decision by the supreme

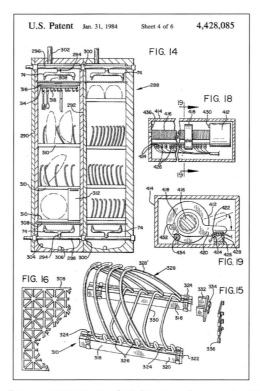

Figure 2.12 US Patent 4428085 for Self-Cleaning Cupboard, 1980. Frances Gabe (b. 1915, d. 2017) Patentee. Courtesy of Hagley Museum.

court to overturn Roe Vs Wade resulting in abortion being made illegal in many states in the US, the Del-Em seems even more poignant. While many health professionals in the 1970s expressed concerns about lay people using the device, activists saw menstrual extraction as a convenient way of countering the culture of shame associated with the reproductive body. The fact that the Del-Em involves a simple technological solution was also valued by feminists looking to democratize the capitalist (mis)use of technoscience. Thus, although much feminist health activism in the 1970s sought to challenge the medicalization of reproductive health, technology was not completely rejected (Hester, 2018: 74–5). Instead, feminists wanted to seize control and appropriate technology for their own means, an approach, that in light of recent events, is unfortunately still necessary today.

The legacy of the Del-Em continues in the politics of groups such as the TransHackFeminists, a radical group of bio-hackers who are creating open source tools for DIY diagnosis and care. Technologies include an emergency gynaecological toolkit that makes it possible to test for yeast infections, cervical

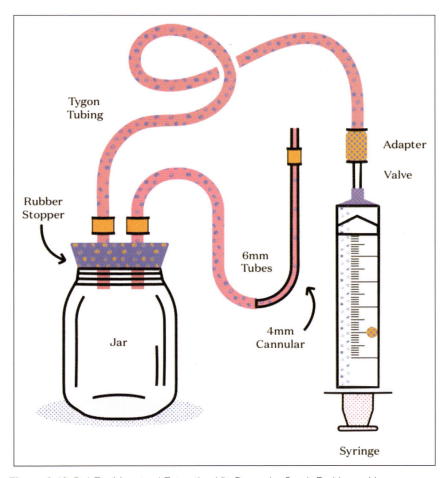

Tygon
Tubing

Rubber
Stopper

Jar

6mm
Tubes

4mm
Cannular

Adapter

Valve

Syringe

Figure 2.13 Del-Em Menstrual Extraction Kit. Drawn by Sarah Parkinson-Howe.

cancer, STDs and pregnancy; a 3D printable speculum; and a microscope made from a deconstructed webcam. Using widely available consumer products these hacks make medical technologies available to those without access to healthcare such as people in refugee camps.

KEY CONCEPT: HACKING

Hacking is a Euro-American concept that emerged in the 1960s bringing together university computer science departments, hobbyist computer clubs and activists (Levy, 1984). A hacker is defined as a 'technologist with a penchant for computing and a hack is a clever technical solution arrived at by non-obvious means' (Coleman, 2014). Hacking is grounded in a playful subversion of existing technologies and techniques often for democratic purposes. Thus, trickery and technological skill form the basis of merit in hacker communities, and sharing, openness, decentralization and free access, are common core values.

While the concept of hacking took hold in computer science and information technology, the term has adopted by designers to represent individuals or communities stepping in when products, services or systems fall short (Burnham, 2019). As Julian Bleecker argues, hacking practices can be useful for design because they bring a focus on rapid construction, functionality and democratizing participation (quoted in Burnham, 2019: 7). Hackathons, short events where participants ideate, develop, and prototype solutions to problems, offer the opportunity for co-design.

Despite its egalitarian ethos, however, hacker culture has tended to 'run on the cultural codes of competition and transgression' and hacker meetups are typically places for Euro-American men (SSL Nagbot, 2016: para 6). Studies of meritocracy in other domains have shown that discourses of merit and openness often work to conceal masculine domination, and hacking is no different (SSL Nagbot, 2016: para 6).

At the same time, those who experience systemic inequalities tend to engage in lots of innovative hacking type activity, even if these activities are not named as such. Examples of clever technical solutions arrived at by non-obvious means include baby swings created from schools desks in Jordanian refugee camps (Aksamija, Majzoub and Philippou, 2021), and innovative approaches to Smog in polluted cities (Sharma, 2019).

More recently, feminist hackers and makers have begun to address the lack of gender diversity in hacker communities, and academics have written about the benefits of a feminist approach to hacking. For example, the international art-based research project Feminist Hacking, aims to address the unequal presence and engagement of women and non-binary media artists in the hacker community, as well as to propose a method for 'empathic, eco-sentient, de-colonial and anti-racist action' (Feminist Hacking, 2022). Through open workshops, the group develop, prototype, test, analyse and share hardware production, its future open access and modification. They ask what is feminist hardware? For example, in recent workshops they have explored alternatives to printed circuit board that are fair trade, recycled and urban mined.

Hackathons have also been used to address technologies used by women. For example, in 2014 at MIT Media Lab a group of designers, engineers and artists organized a Hackathon to redesign the breast pump. The 'Make the Breast Pump Not Suck!' hackathon was a free two-day event that included 150 people (users with their babies, engineers, designers, healthcare experts, educators and the media) and invited them work together identify problems, ideate, and pitch their ideas. The event began with talks to introduce the participants to the importance of breastfeeding, common pain points for users, and the sociocultural and political context. A wall with 'breast pump' stories from users was created. Individuals gave lightning pitches and then groups were formed to work together for the remainder of the event. The prize for the winning group was a trip to pitch to Silicon Valley investors and was won by a team who designed a 'Mighty Mom utility belt' that was 'a fashionable, discreet, hands-free wearable pump that automatically logs and analyses your personal milk data' (D'Ignazio et al., 2016).

Perhaps more importantly than recognizing winning projects, the event initiated, connected and nurtured connections between women. Thus, a feminist approach that emphasized care-based intimacy and inclusion underpinned and emerged from the hackathon. 'While masculinist practices of hacking and hackathons are often solution-centered, a feminist hacker ethic might privilege reflection in order to raise pressing questions about alternative possible futures' (Forlano, 2016: para 53). This would include 'smaller' actions, rituals or conversations that seek to reflect upon, draw attention to, and challenge the gendering of technology and cultures of design. As Annika Richterich argues, hackerspaces offer the 'potential to act as intersectional, technofeminist sites for experiential learning' (2022: abstract).

The playful subversion and skill that is part of hacking is also evident in other feminist attempts to expose gender inequality. For example, in the late 1970s, the photographer, Jill Posener, began to create and document feminist retorts to mainstream media. Her interest began with a billboard advert for a Fiat 127. The billboard proclaims that 'if [this car] were a lady, it would get its bottom pinched'. Below this, a scrawled response reframes this corporate sexism: 'If this lady was a car she'd run you down'. Posener went on to publish two books documenting humorous and imaginative feminist responses to sexism and racism. These acts, which Posener termed as 'refacing', have been framed more broadly as culture jamming.

KEY CONCEPT: CULTURE JAMMING

The concept of culture jamming emerged in the 1980s to describe tactics or acts that disrupt mass media messages. Usually in the form of billboards, graffiti, posters and stickers, culture jamming subverts the dominant order of things, flips it upside-down and introduces new possibilities. Culture jamming can describe a range of practices including '*détournement*', the art of turning culture back on itself through the appropriation and reworking of signs; 'subvertisement', the subversion of advertisements; and 'meme warface' (Jenkins, 2017). Culture jamming usually involves humour or parody. It has been used most widely to try to challenge consumerism. For example, the magazine *Adbusters* produce spoof advertisements to highlight the issues inherent to capitalism.

Culture jamming has been criticized as an ineffective way to challenge capitalism, in fact it has been argued that countercultural acts can actually feed capitalist agendas (Heath and Potter, 2010); the term largely fell into disuse in the late 2000s. More recently however, interest in culture jamming has resurfaced (DeLaure and Fink, 2017) and the tactics have been argued to be necessary in political contexts whereby politicians have become 'one-man megabrands' (Klein, 2017).

Feminist culture jamming continues in the activism of groups such as the Guerrilla Girls. Established in 1985 in New York, the Guerrilla Girls are a group of anonymous artist activists who use 'disruptive headlines, outrageous visuals and killer statistics to expose gender' bias (Guerrilla Girls, 2022). For example, in 2021 as part of the 'Male Graze' campaign, the group installed a billboard in central Glasgow asking passers-by the question of 'whether there are more naked women than women artists in UK museums'. The billboards that were positioned around the UK were accompanied by a website and events exposing the bad behaviour of male artists and designers. The 'guerrilla tactics' of the group mean that their actions often surprise the art and design world.

Hacking and culture jamming, at least the feminist versions, tend to have a DIY feel rather than slick professional aesthetics. This is, in part, a product of women being excluded from the technology needed to create professional design work prior to the prevalence of computers and graphic design software. DIY aesthetics became associated with feminist politics and this relationship continues today. This history is exemplified by the creation of feminist zines.

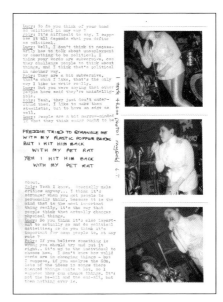

Figure 2.14 Cover of *JOLT Fanzine*. Issue 3. 1977. Cover image: © Lucy Whitman and Ros Past-it 1977.

Figure 2.15 Extract from interview with Poly Styrene from *JOLT Fanzine*. Issue 3. 1977. Page 4: © Lucy Whitman 1977.

Zine is a colloquial term for a little magazine, independent amateur publications that include writing, drawing, collage and photographs. Emerging in the 1920s and 1930s, zines have been said to trace their lineage back to black creatives in Harlem New York and science fiction fans in the US. Zines were a way for minority groups to communicate and connect with one another outside the mainstream media. Most notably, zines have been associated with the punk subcultures of the 1970s. As an alternative and mostly working-class genre (at least in its origins), punk fans created zines to spread information about scenes, bands and events. The DIY aesthetics of punk music were reinforced by the look of punk zines through hand-written articles, cut out text and photo-copied images. While many of the famous punk zines have male authors and connected a mainly male audience, there are exceptions. For example, the feminist, anti-fascist and anti-racist fanzine, *JOLT* was written by Lucy Toothpaste (Lucy Whitman) in 1977. *JOLT* included pieces bemoaning the lack of women in punk, interviews with female artists and musicians (fig. 2.15), and features such as 'Great Punks in History No 1: Valerie Solanas' (Blase, 2011). In Issue 3, a ferocious critique of punks wearing swastikas and the prospect of a fascist future, is juxtaposed with images of gassed victims of the Holocaust. The cover image for *JOLT* #3, (fig. 2.14), based on a painting by Gustave Courbet, combines the face of notorious anti-gay campaigner Mary Whitehouse with a scene of lesbian sensuality and delight. It was intended to annoy the anti-gay lobby, not to suggest that Whitehouse was actually a lesbian, and is an example of the gleeful juxtaposition of incongruous images of punk (Whitman, private correspondence, 2022).

Feminist zines continued throughout the 1970s and 1980s, although these were largely only consumed by the small groups of fans and activists they were distributed to. It wasn't until the early 1990s, that feminist fanzines came to prominence more broadly, specifically those associated with the Riot Grrrl movement. The Riot Grrrl movement emerged out of DIY punk subcultures and began as an indie music phenomenon in Olympia, Washington in 1991, drawing on the politics of third-wave feminism. Since then, it has come to signify a movement and a network made visible through gigs, festivals and zines. As Mary Celeste Kearney (2006) observes, Riot Grrrls took control of the production, promotion and distribution of media. They used zines to talk about their experiences of sexism, body image, gender norms, as well as music. Riot Grrrl bands refused to talk the mainstream media, preferring to talk to their own communities via zines. Thus, the Riot Grrl network created a space where young women could feel safe and empowered to discuss their personal and political experiences. For example, the Riot Grrrl zine was created by Molly Neuman and Allison Wolfe, band members of Bratmobile, and featured contributions from members of the band Bikini Kill. Its issues included articles about lesbian relations, violence against women, sexual abuse, as well as letters from readers. As Teal Triggs argues, Riot Grrrl fanzines

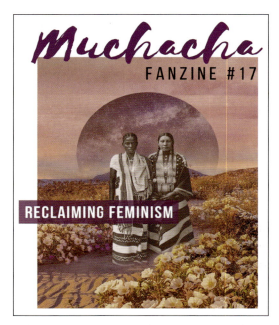

Figure 2.16 In the beginning there was us/Kindred (*Muchacha Fanzine*. #17., 2022. Daisy Salinas (ed.)). Courtesy of Mer Young.

provided a physical space 'where the page and format are designed visually to accommodate as well as facilitate' political thought and political action (2009: 17).

The history of the Riot Grrrl movement has been critiqued as emphasizing white women's experiences (Nguyen, 2012). Nevertheless, the movement follows in a long line of feminist self-publication including scrapbooking, pamphlets and flyers allowing women, transgender and non-binary people to circulate ideas that would not have been published otherwise. Recent feminist zines, even if made in analogue, tend to be promoted and circulated digitally via social media or online marketplaces. For example, *Muchacha*, a radically intersectional and decolonial Xicana feminist fanzine, uses Instagram to distribute paper and digital copies. The most recent issue, 'Reclaiming Feminism', aims to uplift the voices of feminists of colour who are fighting for a more inclusive and revolutionary feminism for all (fig. 2.16.). The creation of fanzines by people from the Global South is increasingly common (see *Kajal, Shotgun Seamstress* and *Gayzi Zine*) and reflects the types of feminist writing and design that get excluded from the mainstream media.

Cyberfeminism and gender hacking

Alongside the emergence of the internet and widespread computer usage in the 1990s, came feminist explorations of the revolutionary potential of these technologies. An unofficial group of female thinkers, coders and media artists emerged in North America, Australia, Germany and the UK and began linking up online. The women, now considered to be 'cyberfeminists', asked if digital technologies could be used to hack the codes of patriarchy, and whether gender could be abolished in virtual space. Partly in response to computer technologies being seen as a male domain and taking inspiration from the Cyborg Manifesto by Donna Haraway, cyber-feminists posed the hybrid woman/machine as the 'leader of the new world order' (VNS Matrix, 1991).

KEY CONCEPT: HARAWAY'S CYBORG

In 1985, the feminist theorist Donna Haraway published the ground-breaking essay 'A Manifesto for Cyborgs'. Foundational to feminist approaches to technology, Haraway suggests that we are all, always already, cyborgs; 'chimeras, theorized and fabricated hybrids of machine and organism' (2016: 7). She writes that contemporary science fiction, modern medicine, reproductive sex, and capitalist production are all full of cyborgs – 'creatures simultaneously animal and machine', who populate worlds of the ambiguously natural and the crafted (2016: 6). For example, putting in a contact lens is an everyday act of becoming a cyborg.

For Haraway, cyborgs are not only omnipresent in fiction and as social reality, they are a politics. The cyborg is a creature in a 'post-gender world' that cannot be contained by the dualisms of mind/body, nature/culture, human/non-human. Cyborgs are trans-, they traverse Western conceptualizations of what once counted as normal and natural. Identity through this lens is partial and contradictory. Controversially for some feminists, Haraway argues that there is 'nothing about being female that naturally binds women' (2016: 16). In addition to rejecting gender essentialism, the figure of the cyborg rejects technological determinism (that technological innovation determines societal 'progress'). By transcending categorization and highlighting a world where 'nature' incorporates people, organisms and technological artefacts, the cyborg challenges back-to-nature mysticism as well as salvific technofutures.

Cyberfeminism emerged as a philosophy, methodology and as a community of practice. Early practitioners include VNS Matrix, a feminist artist collective in South Australia, who began coding games and inventing avatars to challenge the macho culture of the internet. In 1991, they wrote the *Cyberfeminist Manifesto for the 21st Century* and produced a billboard that was displayed in various locations around Australia (fig. 2.17). The image included women who had been transformed into scaled hybrids and text that reads 'Saboteurs of the Big Daddy Mainframe'. VNS Matrix went on to produce a video game where 'cybersluts' aim to topple phallic power with G-Slime, goo shot from weaponized clitorises (Scott, 2106: 3). Reflecting on the time, Virginia Barrett, one of the members of the collective, said '[w]e emerged from the cyberswamp on a mission to hijack the toys from techno-cowboys and remap cyberculture with a feminist bent' (quoted in Scott, 2016: 2). The strategies of VNS Matrix were intentionally playful and ironic, echoing the sentiments of the Riot Grrrl movement.

The Australian artist, Linda Dement, is also associated with early cyberfeminism. She 'used computer games to code alternative female identities. Her CD-ROM adventure puzzle game, *Cyberesh Girlmonster* (1995), is a collection of surreal girl monsters. When users interact with the images, new narratives, videos or monsters are revealed. Dement worked with thirty women to choose and scan parts of their body and digitally record a sentence or sound. Described as a 'black comedy of monstrous femininity', the piece uses the digital to give voice to stories of aberration and to imagine the prospect of blissful revenge. As Tully Barnett (2014) notes, media art produced by cyberfeminists in this period exemplifies an optimism about the networked world both as a vehicle for

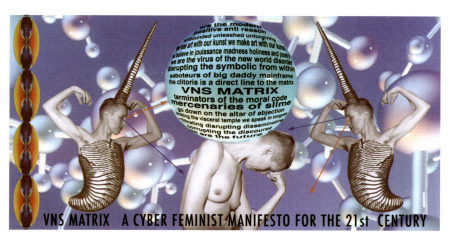

Figure 2.17 VNS Matrix, *A Cyberfeminist Manifesto for the 21st Century*, Australia. 1991. Image courtesy the artists.

communicating a critique of the gendering of technology, and as holding the promise for overcoming gender norms and binaries. Collectives of artists and activists were established such as The Old Boys Network (1997–2001) who were committed to disseminating these ideas (see interview with Cornelia Sollfrank below).

In the 2000s, academic theorists also began to discuss and define cyberfeminism (Matrix, 2001). As Susan Paasonen (2011) documents, the meaning of cyberfeminism was contested, and as more women became involved there was a growing divergence of ideas about what constituted cyberfeminist thought and action. For VNS Matrix, for example, cyberfeminism was about challenging gender binaries. Whereas for a theorist such as Sadie Plant, credited with coining the term cyberfeminism, the digitization of culture entailed a process of feminization. Plant (1997) argued that cyberspace was naturally more suited to women, and power and authority could be secured in virtual worlds. She became one of the theorists most synonymous with the cyberfeminism movement and her arguments have been critiqued as both reinforcing gender essentialism (Hester, 2017), and as overly simplistic (Luckman, 1999; Munster, 1999). The idea that women could gain power simply by using new technologies 'reduces complex technological systems into mere tools and ignores their historical contexts of production and use' (Consalvo, 2002).

While academic interest in the gendering of technoculture continued, cyberfeminism as both a discourse and a movement declined in the 2000s. As Paasonen (2011) suggests, the 'cyber' became associated with a techno-utopianism that did not sit well with everyday experiences of the digital sphere. Women and LGBTQ+ people were encountering the gendered challenges of 'living in the condition of virtuality' (Hayles, 1999: 18). This included sexual harassment and hate speech via social media as well as privacy issues regarding the protection of online images. It was clear that biases about bodies, sex and gender were as entrenched in cyberspace as they were in the rest of society (Wilding, 1998). Indeed, the separation between 'in real life' (IRL) and 'online' has been questioned entirely, with many recent theorists preferring 'away from keyboard' (AFK) to refer to experiences outside of the digital sphere (e.g. Russell, 2020).

The cyberfeminism movement itself, or at least it's dominant representation, has also been critiqued as exclusionary. As Legacy Russell argues, the 'white cyberfeminist landscape marginalized queer people, trans people, and people of color' (2020: 30). Russell draws our attention to the many people of colour and queer identifying people who have decolonized 'digital space by their production via similar channels and networks' (2020: 30). For example, she highlights the work of the late Mark Aguhar, a transfeminine, Filipinx multidisciplinary artist, who through videos on YouTube and Tumblr posts, challenges normative standards of beauty, racism, misogyny and fatphobia, and expanded conventional understandings of femininity. In Aguhar's work, *Why Be Ugly When You Can Be Beautiful* (2011), she demonstrates how in a world full of harassment and violence towards transgender people, styling one's hair can be an act of radical resistance that challenges normative standards of beauty. The work of Aguhar and many others is indicative of the complexities of striving for intersectional gender justice in virtual worlds. As Russell observes, there is a paradox in using platforms that:

> grossly co-opt, sensationalize, and capitalize on people of color, female-identifying, and queer bodies (and our pain) as a means of advancing urgent political or cultural dialogue about our struggle (in addition to our joys and our journeys). Yet this paradox, at least for now, is the world.
>
> 2020: 26

For Russell, and as the work of artists such as Mark Aguhar demonstrates, this paradox does not render engagement with digital platforms pointless, it poses the question of how these spaces might be appropriated or hacked to further intersectional gender justice.

To resist and break down the binaries and limitations that define gender, race and sexuality, Russell argues that we need to embrace the glitch. In her book, *Glitch Feminism*, she observes how certain spaces on the internet have allowed for the complexity of identity beyond binaries, spaces where people are allowed to 'glitch'. For example, she writes about how online platforms such as LiveJournal allowed *CL*, a zine maker and artist, to 'hide race for a while' and 'just be' (Russell, 2020: 39). *CL* began to test the water by posting things and seeing how they were received. She said that it was via the internet that she had embraced her identity as an 'intelligent Black girl' both online and away from the keyboard. Russell distinguishes this experience from neoliberal imperatives to account for difference through categorization such as Facebook offering 'fifty-eight gender options (and three pronouns, lest we forget!)' (2020: 91). She writes 'binaries are still presented within the variety of options, and moreover recognition via these platforms urges us to believe that signifying who we are to others is the only pathway to being deemed fit to participate' (Russell, 2020: 91).

For Russell, the glitch is a politics. It is more than simply an error, a mistake or a failure to function, it is a form of refusal. Just as a machine refuses to function, we, by embodying the glitch, can refuse to conform to our gender, race or sexuality. We can refuse the categories offered to us. Russell argues that the glitch as error in the digital realm has powerful potential to configure new worlds away from the keyboard. She highlights the power of the glitch through the work of media artists who 'resist an exclusionary canon of visual culture' and 'build new corpo-realities' (Russell, 2020: 99). For example, she documents the work of Tabita Rezaire, who in her piece, *Afro Cyber Resistance* (2014) 'problematises the reality of an internet driven by the West' (fig 2.18). She also calls attention to 'Lil Miquela', the computer-generated influencer who promotes progressive causes, such as Black Lives Matter and Planned Parenthood. 'Lil Miquela', Miquela Sousa, is a self without a body who makes an impact in the world away from the keyboard. This elision of life online and life outside highlighted by the arguments in *Glitch Feminism* foreground the fact that bodies and identities are always already bound up with technology. Russell challenges us to play and modify our identities away from the keyboard as we do in the digital sphere. She writes '[u]surp the body. Become your avatar. Be the glitch. Let the whole goddamn thing short-circuit' (Russell 2020: 108).

This call to hack gender has been common in cyberfeminism and technofeminism. As Sophie Toupin argues, feminist hacking involves a 'dual expansion' or 'double hack' (2019). 'On the one hand it adds a material dimension to feminist activism, and on the other it expands the concept of "hacking," which typically refers to technical categories such as software and hardware, to include "gender" as an area of application' (Sollfrank, 2018: para 19). Gender hacking as a concept is made possible by the understanding of gender as a technology. As discussed in Chapter 1, from this perspective gender/sex is not thought as something 'natural' or 'biologically given' but as made by biotechnical, psychosocial and cultural processes. Thus, gender is mutable and can be hacked.

The call to hack gender using digital technologies echoes the sentiments of the Xenofeminist movement. Xenofeminism, as coined by the collective Laboria Cuboniks in 2014, proposes a queer and trans-inclusive feminism that aims to repurpose the tools of capitalist technoscience. Xenofeminism, as Helen Hester suggests, is an 'anti-naturalist endeavour that frames nature and the natural as a space for contestation – that is, as within the purview of

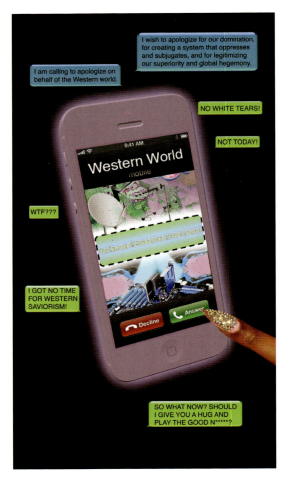

Figure 2.18 Sorry For Real_Sorrow For_Soul, 2015. 180 × 100 × 30.5cm Lightbox. Courtesy Tabita Rezaire and Goodman Gallery.

politics' (2018: 19). The 'natural' order, Hester writes, has nothing to offer those who have been deemed 'unnatural in the face of reigning biological norms', queer and trans people, differently-abled and 'those who have suffered discrimination due to pregnancy or duties connected to child-rearing' (2018: 20). As it states in the Xenofeminist manifesto, '[n]othing should be accepted as fixed, permanent or "given" – neither material conditions nor social forms', and this includes biology (Laboria Cuboniks, 2018: 1). This is not to deny the role of the biological in the making of gender, rather it is to suggest that gender is something we can hack through the use of technologies such as hormones.

The Xenofeminist manifesto argues for gender abolitionism built on an anti-naturalist agenda. Abolition, as Laboria Cuboniks argue, does not mean to eradicate gender from the population, rather, like race abolitionism, it aims to abolish gender discrimination. Xenofeminism is a call for 'gender post-scarcity' and for the proliferation of genders. 'Let a hundred sexes bloom!' incites the manifesto (Laboria Cuboniks, 2018: 6). In this process, Laboria Cuboniks stress the need to render binary gender norms laughable. Xenofeminism is an intersectional project and Laboria Cuboniks are clear that 'every emancipatory abolitionism must incline towards the horizon of class abolitionism' (Laboria Cuboniks, 2018: 6). The call for the proliferation of genders is insightful because it can include a multitude of experiences.

For this future to materialize, Xenofeminists seek to repurpose 'technologies for progressive gender' politics (Laboria Cuboniks, 2018: 2). They recognize the gender inequalities which are bound up with the capitalist production of technologies, but suggest that the real emancipatory potential of technology is going unrealised. They call upon feminists to rise to the challenge of developing a politics that is fit for a world 'that swarms with technological mediation, [. . .] abstraction, virtuality, and complexity' (Laboria Cuboniks, 2018: 1).

One example of a Xenofeminist repurposing of technology includes Open Source Gender Codes (2016). This project aimed to created plants that would allow people to grow hormones in their homes. The project challenges the dominance of the pharmaceutical industry and, if adopted more broadly, could potentially change attitudes towards taking hormones and ultimately breakdown binary notions of sex and gender. Another example is the repurposing of drone technologies to drop abortion medication to people in countries where abortion is illegal (Jones, 2019). Hester, one of the members of Laboria Cuboniks, has also cited the Del-Em as an example of a Xenofeminist technology (2018: 70), thus emphasizing that Xenofeminist repurposing or hacking does not necessarily have to involve new and emerging technologies.

QUESTIONS FOR DESIGNERS: GENDER HACKING

To resist gender norms and destabilize gender binaries designers should think about the following:

- Can you identify technologies that are ripe for feminist redesign or repurposing?

- How might you go about adapting these artefacts? Could you make them laughable? Could you make them glitch? Could they be reinvented outside of capitalist frameworks? Could they be made open source?

- Taking inspiration from the histories of craft and DIY aesthetics, how might alternative materials and protocols enable wider participation?

INTERVIEW: CORNELIA SOLLFRANK, ARTIST AND RESEARCHER, BERLIN

Cornelia Sollfrank (she/her) is a German artist, researcher and performer. In the 1990s she was a founder of net.art and a pioneer of the cyberfeminism movement. Recurring topics in her artistic work include digital media and network culture, authorship and intellectual property, gender and technofeminism.

SB: You have been involved in technofeminisms for a long time now? What sparked your interest and how did that develop over time?

CS: The term technofeminism only attracted my attention when I realized that cyberfeminism was a concept specific to the 1990s and the then predominant techno-utopian discourse. After 2001, the last conference held by the Old Boys Network (http://obn.org) in Hamburg, the hype around cyberfeminism slowly died down, and it took about fifteen years until a new generation of academics and activists rediscovered the urgency of the topic of gender and technology. I received a number of requests for interviews and conference contributions and understood that the new generation a) had little knowledge of our work in the 1990s and b) sort of glorified it without taking the critical stance which would been appropriate after twenty years. After all, we now live in a completely different situation with regards to digital technology and the Internet. To mark this shift, I was looking for a new term that would clearly mark a difference to the 1990s, while also indicate its continuation. While we refused to define cyberfeminism in the 1990s (see the famous 100 anti-theses of what cyberfeminism is not, Old Boys Network, 1997), I thought that it would be worthwhile to outline a framework for technofeminist thinking. Following Judy Wajcman and her seminal book with the same title, there are two main aspects to technofeminism: 1) technology is not neutral and 2) technology is a highly gendered field.

SB: You are known as one of the first artists to address gender inequality in your digital art. Could you describe a few of those early projects?

CS: Basically, all my work is critical of power structures and starts by reflecting on the situation I am personally involved in, and then expands that to larger systems, i.e. there are works that are explicitly technofeminist and with others it is more inherent. I'll introduce you to some of my most prominent works:

1   Female Extension (1997) was a hack of the first net.art competition where I flooded the submissions with more than 300 applications from fictitious female artists. I created fake details and an original artwork for each applicant. 'Despite

the disproportionate number of applications by female artists, only male artists were selected as finalists' (Moss, 2009: para 1).

2   Old Boys Network (1997–2001) was the first cyberfeminist alliance that I initiated on invitation of documenta x Hybrid Workspace. As a collective of digital artists and researchers, the Old Boys Network was committed to appropriating, creating and disseminating cyberfeminisms. The organization created digital and physical spaces such as a cyberfeminist server and mailing list, as well as workshops and conferences. There have been many publications about our work (e.g. Sollfrank, 2022; Sollfrank, 2021).

3   Net.art generator (since 1998) (http://net.art-generator.com) is a computer program that after entering a (search-)term generates an artwork. Three books have been published on this work alone and it is too much to discuss its many layers. In short, it was conceived as a critique of the myth of the male genius creator, a critique of the notion of originality applied to digital works etc. See: https://eeclectic.de/produkt/fix-my-code/

4   A more recent work is 'À la recherche de l'information perdue' (2018–), which is a performance lecture that makes a (techno-)feminist comment on the entanglements of gender, technology and information politics exemplified by the case of Julian Assange and Wikileaks. In the performance (Bergen, Reykjavik, London, Leipzig), I take the audience on an adventurous trip into the realm of zeros and ones, of data and pure information, of ciphers, signifiers and figures. On the other side of reality, the audience encounters suspected heroes, leaks and phreaks, engineers of escape who control our secret desires. Rape can be performed in many ways. In a state of total transparency, the performance asks us to consider what shall we eat, when society feeds upon the repressed? The work explores the fact that Julian Assange spent many years in confinement in the Ecuadorian Embassy following an accusation of rape. Instead of making a moral judgement, however, the performance uses and combines sources from information science, psychoanalysis, cultural studies, feminist studies and activism to embed the case in the wider cultural landscape in which gendered structures become obvious.

SB: You define yourself as an artist and researcher. What do you see as the similarities/differences between art, design and craft? Do you think designers could apply technofeminist methods in their work? If so, how?
CS: In the Anglo-American context art and design (and craft) are often conceived as similar practices, however, with an education in art, I prefer to distinguish between the different fields considering art as an 'expression' of an individual perspective that may or

may not allow for generalizations. Design, in contrast, aims at creating solutions for a practical use; same for craft, however, starting from a less industrial and more personal skill-based practice. A technofeminist approach can come into effect in all three areas related to the use of technologies and a related awareness with regards to gender imbalance. A good example for such practice could be the building of feminist hackspaces (https://creatingcommons.zhdk.ch/feminist-hackspace/index.html) or a gender-specific use of technology (https://creatingcommons.zhdk.ch/forms-of-ongoingness/index.html).

SB: Cyberfeminism and technofeminism are often spoken about in terms of gender hacking. Do you see your work in these terms? If not, why not?
CS: To answer this question would need the clarification of the term gender hacking, which basically plays with a certain blurredness of its actual meaning. If it refers to a practice that creates awareness regarding gender imbalance in the handling of technology and aims at undermining this balance, it is a definite yes.

SB: Could you tell us a bit more about the activities of your interdisciplinary technofeminist group #purplenoise and the strategy of 'noisification'?
CS: #purplenoise is an experiment that started in September 2018 and aims to destabilize hierarchical, heteronormative and binary conceptualization of gender, on, and using, social media. The self-proclaimed movement began with a protest in the southern-German city of Esslingen where other collaborators and I took to the streets in purple clothes with 'feelers' on our heads holding protest signs featuring new hashtags and self-created gender symbols. Our aim was to produce 'noise' in the form of visual content for social media channels. We referred to ourselves as creating 'fake news' and asked people to flood media channels with posts containing our hashtags. By making 'noise' or what we call 'noisification' we hope to encourage people to reflect upon 'the effects of fake news on the manufacturing of reality, how easily purchased likes and followers can manipulate algorithms' (Sollfrank, 2022a). By using 'viral noise' as a tactic, we aim to dissent 'the control of information, actors and practices implied by the algorithms at the core of social media by practicing disobedience' (Götz, 2021: 69)

SB: You recently made an NFT. What was your experience like? What are your feelings regarding the potential of blockchain technology and Web 3.0. for feminist politics?
CS: I wrote about this for the website Makery (Sollfrank, 2022b), but I'll summarize it for you. In December 2021, I was approached to take part in an NFT show for February 2022, NfTNeTArT. I was sceptical of all the hype, but I wanted to form an opinion based on practical first-hand experience. Artists have been trying to rethink the blockchain for a while now as a technology that is not purely driven by financial profit-logic, so I agreed to participate in the show as a sort of experiment. I have been making generative art for

a long time and it felt right to contribute works made by my net.art generator. I decided to mint anonymous reworked Warhol flowers, adding the title //OG Flowers// referring to my role as the originator of net.art. By selecting the work by Warhol, I wanted to emphasize the artificiality of the notion of originality, the beauty of the endless copy, and the malleability of digital art and its implications for the art world.

The curators described the exhibition as a success: the artists gained attention and made money; the gallerists put on a ground-breaking show; and the technologists proved that their technology is useful for the artworld. However, something made, and still makes me feel very uncomfortable about my seemingly quite positive experience.

The exhibition was framed by the hype around NFTs, and this triggers a change in perspective from seeing art as a field of meaningful action to the field of trade and financial logic. With NFT art I think it's difficult, if not impossible, not to count the number of sales, add up the final income and take this as a measure of success. The mechanisms of the market come into play: who decides the value of an asset and thus its success on the market? The big players are big because they know how to play the game. The buying of an NFT becomes a statement that demonstrates two things: 1) I don't mind paying money for something other people think is absurd and 2) I am part of the crypto game. Double cool. Buyers of crypto art have created their own aesthetic realm and allocating money determines value. The logic of fast money is taking hold. Therefore, the NFT market seems to mirror the logic of traditional art market: different people, different aesthetics, but the same logic. This means that it reproduces many of the same power relations and inequalities. Despite this, I did somewhat enjoy playing the game, it was fun to sell NFTs of images I did not own.

SB: What sort of feminist technofutures would you like to see materialize?
CS: The main aspect of digital technologies is the material aspect in the sense of who owns and controls them. I'd like to see technofutures beyond the five big corporations who control the market, technologies that are used to better of the lives of all and not just the ones who can afford to participate, beyond profit-interests. As this is a very bold dream, I am not very optimistic we will see it materialize soon, but as a guiding feminist principle, I'd suggest that we are aware of the question in whose interest the tools we use work best.

SB: If you could give one piece of advice to designers interested in gender justice what would it be?
CS: Trying to understand what makes certain groups of people (like LGBTIQ+) feel uncomfortable about technology. Use the methods of consciousness raising regarding technology and derive solutions by starting from the personal, including designers' tools themselves.

CHAPTER TWO ACTIVITY

PICK A THEME: MAKE A ZINE

Themes

EMOTIONAL LABOUR	HAIR	QUEER FONTS
INDIGENOUS GENDER	PERSONAL RANT	FEMINIST JOKES
#NOT ALL MEN	HORMONES	BEING IN-BETWEEN

Make a zine

4	3	2	1
5	6	Back cover	Front cover

(Cut along dashed line between panels 3 and 2)

Advice

There are no rules, so express your creativity.

Gather some tools (pens, scissors, glue) and some images
(for collage) or a computer if you want to make a digital zine.

Tell the story you want to tell.

Make copies and put your pages together.

Distribute or give to friends.

CHAPTER TWO ACTIVITY

HACK IT GAME

What you need: Scissors, Paper, Pen, Timer.

Get into teams of 2 or more. Turn over the top card in pile. Put the timer on for 3 minutes. Brainstorm ideas to hack the situation on the card. Each team chooses one idea. When the 3 minutes is up each team describes their idea. The most playful hack wins. Play another round, it gets easier the more you play!

MANSPLAINING

Some men feel the need to explain concepts to others even if the other person is an expert.

PREGNANCY

People commonly touch pregnant people's bodies without asking.

GAMING

Computer games often reinforce and reproduce stereotypical representations of women.

MUSEUMS

European male designers tend to be overrepresented in design museums.

CLOTHING

Clothing targeted at girls and women is much less likely to have pockets.

CATCALLING

Many people continue to experience catcalling when in public.

CRAFT

Men are often not encouraged to be involved in craft practices.

BATHROOMS

Gendered bathrooms are not inclusive for non-binary people.

SPORT

Girls and women are often made to feel less capable at sport.

3
WOMEN AND DESIGN AS PROFESSION

Introduction: gender in the design industries

While global statistics regarding the gender of professionals working in the design industries are patchy, there are common indicators of gender inequality. In the UK, it has been estimated that the design industry is 78 per cent male, despite nearly two-thirds of students studying design at university identifying as female (Design Council, 2020). Statistics from Aotearoa suggest that while almost 65 per cent of design students in tertiary education are female, only 45 per cent find work in the industry (Arnett-Philips, 2020). As is the case with many other sectors, lack of parity intensifies in senior positions. For example, it is estimated that only 10 to 20 per cent of creative directors in Aotearoa are female (Rogan, 2019). According to the 2019 American Institute of Graphic Arts (AIGA) Design Census, in the US 61 per cent of designers and 29 per cent of creative directors are female. The AIGA report that the number of creative directors has gone up from 3 to 29 per cent in the last four years. This is indicative of positive changes in the design industry, however, there is still a long way to go. For example, there are no statistics regarding how race, ethnicity, sexuality and age intersect with gender; nor any findings concerning the numbers of designers who identify outside of the gender binary. A scan of the profiles of senior designers in the top global design firms continues to look decidedly white and male.

These statistics also gloss over the gendering of the design disciplines themselves. As explored in the previous chapter, the very definition of design is gendered and hierarchized with 'decorative practices' being associated with women, and 'technical' design disciplines such as industrial/product design being coded as male and afforded higher status (Buckley, 1986: 3). As Ashton Margarete Moseley and Angus Campbell have found, industrial design continues to be predominantly male with women in the industry experiencing 'sexual harassment, misogyny, condescension and significant pay gaps' (2019: 185).

This chapter begins by documenting the history of the professionalization of design and the related association that developed between women and particular types of design work. It goes on to explore the type of knowledge deemed valuable in professional design practice in the twentieth century and documents feminists' critiques of these types of approaches. It explores the masculinities at work in contemporary design cultures. The chapter concludes by outlining innovative approaches to addressing inequality in the workplace and documents design work that challenges gender norms in professional contexts. While the chapter includes examples from countries outside the Global North, much of the historical discussion is focused on the UK. This is because, as Guy Julier documents, the high concentration of design practice in Britain, including the early emergence of design consultancy, is explained by a number of historical factors including an earlier industrial revolution, the establishment of a design school system, and the geographical and commercial positioning of the country (2008: 22).

Women and the professionalization of design

The term 'design' is intimately bound up with the 'historical process of the professionalisation of its practice' (Julier, 2008: 43). As outlined in Chapter 2, everyone designs (albeit some more successfully than others), thus for craft and design to be defined as paid work they needed to be recognized as a pursuit that requires expert knowledge and skill as well as specific education and training.

Before industrialization, craftspeople would make individual or small batches of artefacts drawing on their artistic, creative and technical skills. These 'cottage industries' would frequently take place in homes and the division of labour between earning money and social reproduction was frequently blurred. For example, as Ruth Schwartz Cowan (1983) argues, due to necessity, the whole family including children would often be required to contribute to the preparation of food, clothing and medications. For instance, harvesting, milling wheat and making bread were family activities (Cowan, 1983: 6). Similarly, all the family would often contribute to the production of goods to exchange or sell such as textiles, pottery or leatherwork.

As populations increased in European cities in the Middle Ages, labour became more specialized and craft guilds emerged to support, protect and guard craftspeoples' expertise. A major role of the guilds was the management and provision of craft training. Adolescents would be indentured to a 'Master' as an apprentice for around seven years. With the approval of their Master, they would then be sponsored as a journeyman able to travel and trade their craft.

Guilds would also provide codes of conduct and regulations which would safeguard against poor workmanship, but also worked to limit participation. For example, while there are exceptions (Broomhall, 2017), craft guilds tended to exclude women. Most 'women's work' even though it was highly skilled, such as London's silk workers, never came under guild structure and supervision (Kowaleski and Bennett, 1989: 475). Those women who did belong to a guild often had secondary rights either working as apprentices who remained with their Masters until they were married or working alongside their husbands.

Due to political, social, cultural and technological change in eighteenth century Europe, guilds began to lose traction. As mechanization intensified, design as professional practice would emerge. Designers in industrial contexts became largely separated from practices of making, and their role became producing plans ready to be mass-produced for larger numbers of consumers (Walker, 1989). The division of labour that was evident in crafters guilds continued into industrialization, in fact on the whole it intensified. Young women would take on most of the factory production enduring long hours, dangerous conditions and often being paid less than their male counterparts (Burnette, 2008). Once married, many women would take on the unpaid labour of raising families and maintaining homes. Design work as an activity separate from making would come to be associated with pioneering 'design heroes' such as Josiah Wedgwood, who is credited as being the first to design mass produced ceramics in the eighteenth century (Forty, 1992).

By the early nineteenth century, the UK government was becoming concerned about the increased consumption of European imports, which were seen as having superior design quality (Author unknown, 1843). In 1835, Parliament called for a Select Committee to 'Enquire into the best means of extending a knowledge of the Arts and the principles of Design among the people, especially the manufacturing population of the country' (Select Committee, 1836). After investigation, the UK government decided to establish a Government School of Design in London which opened in 1837 and would eventually inspire similar design schools throughout the country and the world.

In 1842, the Government School of Design opened a class for 'the instruction of females in ornamental design' which was well attended (Author unknown, 1843: para 3). The Female School of Design continued into the early twentieth century. As Anthea Callen notes, the syllabus of the school was closely linked to industry needs (1985). Nevertheless, while there were opportunities for middle-class women in design education, as Jenny Lewis and Margaret Bruce (1989) argue, the chances of obtaining professional work were still limited. They write '[i]n many cases women worked freelance from home, or joined special workshops and studios which provided work for them' (Lewis and Bruce, 1989: 16). This work tended to be in specialisms such as embroidery, lacemaking, miniature painting, dressmaking, textiles and pottery. Furniture design, iron work and architecture were considered unacceptable pursuits for women and women's 'characters' were deemed at odds with the competitive nature of the business world (Lewis and Bruce, 1989).

However, according to Isabelle Anscombe, by 1914 women 'had sufficiently infiltrated the world of design to be able to take an equal place with male designers' (1985: 12). In her book, *A Woman's Touch*, Anscombe gives examples of female designers such as Eileen Gray whose architectural and furniture designs had a crucial influence on Modernist architects such as Le Corbusier, Elsie de Wolfe who was a prominent American interior designer, and Sonia Delauney an artist who worked in the fields of art, textile design and fashion. Recognition of the work of female designers was also present in other publications in the 1980s including Judy Attfield and Pat Kirkham's (1989) feminist history of interior design, and Liz McQuiston's (1988) field review of women working in a broad range of design disciplines at the time.

While studies of women working in design produced in the 1980s are invaluable, they tend to be centred on Europe and the US and highlight the work of women who were white and middle-class. More recently, design historians have produced excellent histories of women involved in professional design practice who were working outside of Europe and the US, and from a variety of backgrounds and ethnicities. For example, in *Women Design* Libby Sellers (2018) refers to the Cuban-born designer Clara Poset who was exiled from Cuba and settled in Mexico. Poset designed furniture that merged local cultures with International Modernism (Sellers, 2018: 11–12). She also recognizes the work of the wallpaper designer Florence Broadhurst whose work is only recently being celebrated in design museum collections.

The book, *Baseline Shift*, provides an even more detailed counternarrative to typical design histories with their privileging of modern design 'heroes' (Levit, 2021). As Briar Levit writes, 'with a little digging in the places that mainstream journals and professional organisations have forgotten – or, more likely, ignored – researchers are confirming that women of many backgrounds and ethnicities were working with a great deal more regularity and intention in the field of graphic design than most would guess' (2021: 9). The edited collection demonstrates that women were running printing presses in the colonies in the eighteenth century (McCoy, 2021), illustrating books in mid-twentieth century Harlem (Arceneaux-Sutton, 2021), designing innovative graphic visual languages to represent indigenous culture in the late nineteenth century (Waggoner, 2021), and drawing type in Europe's major type foundries (Savoie and Ross, 2021) (fig. 3.1). The book tells the story of women, sometimes nameless, 'who used design to make change, to do business, and to make a living' (Levit, 2021: 10). Thus, we must ask ourselves why these women were excluded from the dominant narratives offered by governments, the press, professional bodies, educational institutions, design awards, and museums?

Figure 3.1 Monotype Type drawing office, Salford, UK, c. 1928. Courtesy of Monotype Corporations Ltd.

In their paper 'Divided by Design: Gender and the Labour Process in the Design Industry', Jenny Lewis and Margaret Bruce (1989) offer a convincing explanation. They suggest that the concept of professionalization discussed within the sociology of work can help to understand the gendering of design industries. They write, 'professional groups divide themselves from other groups of workers by a process of social closure' (Lewis and Bruce, 1989: 14). 'Closure' is 'a crucial aspect of an occupational groups success at being regarded as a profession', it defines who can become a member through qualifications and training, and through defining appropriate knowledge and skill (Lewis and Bruce, 1989: 14). Professionalization monopolizes opportunities and thus results in greater rewards for its members who create and manipulate the market to their own advantage. As a field, design has perhaps had to work harder than other professions to define its boundaries because it is a practice that everyone is involved in. As Guy Julier writes:

Much of the history of design has been written and disseminated to effectively support [. . .] professionalisation and differentiation. Many of the earlier design history texts focused on the successive attempts at public recognition of design as both a profession and a product and this turns the narrative into a discourse of 'pioneering modern design heroes' in the face of a largely uninformed public.

2008: 46

Lewis and Bruce argue that as the professionalization of design intensifies in the mid-twentieth century so too does closure, and in this process, women designers become less visible, and/or shut out altogether. They give examples of this occurring at both macro and micro levels. At a macro level, for example, government and industry bodies were created to increase market share through the recognition of 'good' design and by doing so reproduced patriarchal norms. For instance, throughout its history, the Design Council (previously the Council of Industrial Design and the Design Centre) in the UK has arranged festivals and exhibitions, given awards and produced media to celebrate British design. The selection of designers and their artefacts often excluded women. In 1956, the Design Centre gave 'its first award to products selected as examples of good design. Only a quarter of these went to designs by women' (Lewis and Bruce, 1989: 15). At a micro level, male designers also often reinforced the notion that women produced artefacts that were lesser quality or amateur, or at least, more decorative than functional. Le Corbusier, for example, was famously so incensed that a woman, Eileen Gray, could produce a house (E-1027) in 'his style' that he defaced the walls with sexually graphic murals alluding to her bisexuality without her approval (Webb, 2013). At a similar time, when Charlotte Perriand applied for a job with Le Corbusier, she was told 'Mademoiselle, we don't embroider cushions here' (Webb, 2013).

As Judy Attfield (1989) so astutely observes, the professionalization of design and closure of the field particularly within Modernism has been premised upon a disavowal of the feminine, or least discourses that reinforce its secondary value. 'Good design' is placed in the male domain. Attfield elaborates:

The dominant conception prioritises the machine (masculine) over the body (feminine). It assigns men to the determining, functional areas of design – science, technology, industrial production – and women to the private, domestic realm and to the 'soft' decorative fields of design. It places form in the feminine realm where its role is to reflect the imperatives of the 'real'. According to this kind of aesthetic theory then, form (female) follows function (male).

1989: 220

As Le Corbusier's comment to Charlotte Perriand demonstrates, Modernist design discourse assumes that particular areas of the design profession are 'women's work' and this more generally excludes women from the determining spheres of science, technology and industry. Thus, the history of the professionalization of design documented here is also a history of women's work as being conceptualized as largely concerned with ornament and decoration rather than managerial, technical or scientific knowledge. To be taken 'seriously' as a profession and to differentiate itself from art, design would align itself with the production of 'functional' artefacts driven by technological innovation. Indeed, Le Corbusier's murals could be seen as an attempt to feminize Gray's design, thus making it less legitimate.

The gendered division of labour in design reflects dominant myths of gender and technology more generally. As Anne Balsamo argues, men have typically been seen as the agents of the technological imagination with women being 'cast as either unfit, uninterested or uncapable' (2011: 32). Balsamo observes how men who have been 'heralded as hero technologists are subtly degendered' (2011: 32). In stark contrast to women, men's contributions are 'rarely considered to be the expression of a gendered, racialized, and class-based subjectivity or body' (Balsamo, 2011: 32). Thus, Balsamo suggests that rather than simply highlight women's contributions to design and technology, we need to challenge the gendering of the technological imagination more generally.

Similarly, Attfield argues that a 'women designers' approach 'does little except confirm the prejudice that women are inferior designers except in the so-called 'feminine' areas such as the decorative arts, textiles, interior design and fashion' (1989: 223). As well as reinforcing the gender binary, by focusing on specific female designers a women-centric approach also privileges the idea of the designer as 'auteur' and negates a whole range of artefacts whose designers are unknown. The research in books like *Baseline Shift* clearly are exceptions in this regard. However, I would agree with Attfield when she suggests that instead we should challenge the value systems and associated hierarchies attributed to industrial approaches and the 'machine aesthetic'. She writes:

> It should not be 'Woman' who is made the special case for treatment, but the culture which subordinates people by gender, class, race, etc, and does nothing to question the attitudes which position them as 'other'. The concept of 'the Other' is one used to define the category of 'women' in a negative relationship to the category of 'man'. ('Man' enjoys the privilege of being the norm – 'the measure of all things' – while 'women' is that which deviates from it.)
>
> ATTFIELD, 1989: 226

As argued in Chapter 1, if we want to challenge gender inequality in design we need to foster diversity of thought, values and processes beyond binary categories. I return to consider how we might do this in professional design practice below.

Design knowledge and the making of the professional

In the US and Europe in the 1950s and 1960s, design became more established as a field of professional practice. Interdisciplinary design consultancies offering a broad range of design services emerged. For instance, in the US, Raymond Loewy Associates (est. 1929) increased substantially in size in the post-war period and became a benchmark for other design agencies. Consultancies adopting the interdisciplinary 'American model' opened in Europe in the 1960s including Wolff Olins in London (1965) and Unimark in Milan (1965) (Julier, 2008: 23–5).

Alongside this expansion was an increase in the number of designers, engineers and academics who started to write about the knowledge and processes involved in the act of designing (e.g. Gregory, 1966; Archer, 1965; Jones and Thornley, 1963). As Nigel Cross (1993) documents, a group of individuals arose who were the first to formally attempt to define design methodology (approaches to knowledge and method). Inspired, in part, by new technologies, the first discussions of the Design Methods Movement in the 1960s were largely focused on the application of systemic, rational and 'scientific' methods to design to optimize the influence of the designer. This desire to 'scientize' design can be traced back to the Modernist design movement. For example, the designer Theo van Doesburg wrote:

> Our epoch is hostile to every subjective speculation in art, science, technology, etc. The new spirit, which already governs almost all modern life, is opposed to animal spontaneity, to nature's domination, to artistic flummery. In order to construct a new object we need a method, that is to say an objective system.
>
> Quoted in Cross, 2007: 119

An objective scientific approach to design, then, does not just include using scientific approaches to understand artefacts or users, it also approaches design as a scientific activity for which universal systems, frameworks and models can be created.

In the late 1960s and early 1970s, as Cross observes, this scientific emphasis continued. However, the second generation of design methods researchers moved the debate on towards the recognition of 'satisfactory or appropriate solution types' and spoke of participatory processes whereby designers were conceived of as in partnership with 'problem owners' (Cross, 1993: 17). One of the most famous texts from this period is *The Sciences of the Artificial* by Herbert Simon (1969). In this book Simon proposes that the 'science of the artificial' is the 'science of design'. He defines design as 'devising courses of action aimed at changing existing situations into preferred ones' (Simon 1969: 129). Simon goes on to argue that designed actions could be operationalized and turned into universal plans that could predict behaviour across social categories and situations. Thus, in this conception, design is solution-focused and universally applicable. Professional schools, he writes, should work out and teach design science that is 'a body of intellectually tough, analytic, partly formalizable, partly empirical, teachable doctrine about the design process' (Simon 1969: 58). This would move the discipline away from its 'soft, informal and cook-booky' tendencies (Simon 1969: 113).

As Daniela K. Rosner (2018) argues, statements like this are not only marked by their scientific objectivity, but also by their disavowal of qualities associated with the feminine. Indeed, as Alison Adam demonstrates in her book *Artificial Knowing: Gender and the Thinking Machine* (1998), Simon and his collaborator Allen Newell based their theories on the psychology of individual minds dismissing the influence of the body or cultural phenomena completely. Adam also finds that all participants in Simon and Newell's experiments were male and mostly studied at Carnegie Mellon University in the US. Their perspective 'cast issues of class, gender, race and society as universal – and thus analytically irrelevant' (Rosner, 2018: 38).

According to Rosner, the framing of the design process as 'objectively rational behaviour' untainted by the social contexts and perspectives continues in more contemporary design methods such as design thinking (2018: 29). She demonstrates how the toolkits offered by the Stanford-d School and IDEO reinforce the four theoretical pillars of individualism, universalism, objectivity and solutionism established in part by the design methodologists of the 1950s and 1960s. The design as science paradigm worked to establish the field as 'acceptable and defensible in the world on its own terms' (Rosner, 2018: 31), and recently, this legitimacy has meant tools such as the design thinking process model have been adopted across disciplines such as business, health and education. Yet, Rosner argues that these tools limit who can become involved in design. They also produce narrow-sighted design solutions. She writes, for example, that 'Kelley's IDEO firm identified a $500 chair as the solution for the modern classroom', a cost that is unthinkable for most state schools (Rosner, 2018: 39). Rosner argues feminist understandings of knowledge and action, particularly the work of Lucy Suchman and Donna Haraway, can help to shift design from its solutionist, objectivist, individualist and universalist tendencies.

Donna Haraway is a prominent academic in science and technology studies and, as explored in Chapter 2, she wrote the Cyborg Manifesto that was (and still is) highly influential in feminist approaches to design and technology. In 1986, Haraway wrote a piece exploring the relationship between feminism and science entitled 'Situated Knowledges: The Science Question in Feminism and the Privilege of Partial Perspective' (1988). Haraway argued that feminist thought was often trapped between two binaries: science as 'social construction' vs science as 'objective truth'. She argued that what was needed was a perspective that recognized that all knowledge came from people with specific experiences and perspectives, while simultaneously demonstrating 'a no non-sense commitment to faithful accounts of a 'real' world' (Haraway, 1988: 579). For example, a photograph is both a depiction of material events and an interpretation of it. Haraway encompasses this complexity in the concept of 'situated knowledge', which refers to how knowledge is located within particular lives, circumstances and histories of practice. This means that disembodied scientific objectivity is an illusion of neutrality which works to obscure power and a specific position (frequently white, male, heterosexual and human). The idea that a photograph, for example, is a 'neutral' reflection of events is a false one. Science, like the photograph, is always mediated, it is always of product of its instruments (human and non-human).

The concept of situated knowledge causes us to ask questions of methods such as the 'design thinking process model'. From whose perspective is the problem defined, for instance? Why is empathy needed and how do we go about trying to obtain it? Who benefits from a universal model of designing, how is it depicted and who might it harm? The idea of situated knowledge is also a way out of some of the issues that Attfield associated with a 'women designer' approach. Rather than associated with specific identities, it locates knowledge in a complex nexus of embodied experience, context and circumstance. Thus, a situated knowledge approach to design thinking would start with exploring, as Leslie Ann Noel (2021) suggests, the designer's positionality in relation to the research context.

At the same time as Haraway was developing the concept of 'situated knowledge', Lucy Suchman was also working on a thesis that rejected objectivism and universalist logic, which she termed 'situated action'.

KEY CONCEPT: SITUATED ACTION

Situated action refers to how knowing is inseparable from doing and all knowledge is situated in activity bound to social, cultural and physical contexts. The concept emerged when Suchman was working as a research scientist and anthropologist at PARC, the research arm of the Xeroc group which produced printing and photocopying technologies in the early 1980s. As an ethnographer, Suchman observed the scientists, engineers, managers and corporate decisions makers working alongside their technologies. In a widely circulated video, Suchman documented two men trying to use a photocopier by following the instructions off the screen.

'Place one to fifty originals,' the first read off the screen. 'Well, wait, I have 100 originals,' his colleague interjected. 'What? Reverse order of originals? You gotta be kidding,' signed the first. Several minutes later, after manually reversing the order of their papers, he pressed the start button once, twice, and . . . nothing. 'So our first batch is SOL,' the colleague concluded 'Shit out of Luck.'

SUCHMAN, 2007: chapter 1

The efforts resulted in a mess of paper and a lot of frustration at the machine. To make things even more comedic, the two men using the machine were central figures in AI research. For Suchman, what this demonstrated was that the abstract planning models of human action that were being used in AI and design methods overlooked the embodied and material resources available to users e.g. being able to look at the way the paper is feeding into the machine. She argued that this abstract treatment of people's behaviour assumed that all users acted similarly to computer systems and to male scientists, and these assumptions were frequently replicated in the design of technologies.

Situated action, then, like situated knowledge, recognizes both the agency of users and of non-human actors such as technologies and environments. It highlights the multiple possibilities that can make a technological assemblage 'work' or not. Thus, this approach not only acknowledges the position and experience of people but draws attention to the active role of other elements.

The concepts of situated knowledge and situated action bear resemblance to discussions of the tacit knowledge and reflective embodied processes involved in designing that were taking place among design researchers in the early 1980s (e.g. Schön, 1983; Lawson, 1983). However, as Shana Agid (2012) observes, Haraway's and Suchman's concepts are explicitly political in that they attend to how positions are determined by relationships of power such as gender and race. As designers, they ask us to consider the ways our assumptions are constructed and maintained through experience, and how these experiences impact upon tacit knowledge, problem definition and approaches to communication and collaboration. For Agid, this also means a critical engagement with what constitutes one's own unexamined positions thus reifying and allowing us to reflect upon what constitutes design knowledge and value (2012: 38). In some cases, this may highlight the influence of the (Western, white, male) design canon in terms of design education; in others, it might illuminate a whole range of valuable knowledge that could be consciously accommodated into professional design practice. For example, as Lewis and Bruce ask, what would domestic

QUESTIONS FOR DESIGNERS: GETTING ACQUAINTED WITH YOUR TACIT KNOWLEDGE

As designers there are practices we just 'do', or feel are 'right'. These questions can help us to unpack where this knowledge comes from and reflect on our positions and perspectives:

- What in your background influenced your propensity towards design?

- What influences your taste and style? How has this changed over time? How do you make your aesthetic choices?

- What embodied skills are involved in your creative practice? How did you learn these?

- Do you have any 'natural' tendencies that you suppress in your design work? Why do you think that is? What would happen if you stopped doing this?

technologies look like if the tacit knowledge of women, who take on the significant burden of housework, was taken seriously?

Masculinities at work in design cultures

The association of masculinity with the functional and technical aspects of design discussed above continues to influence gender inequality in the field. Studies of design education and industry in the UK (Clegg and Mayfield, 1999), Ireland (Mahon and Kiernan, 2017), Australia (Lockhart, 2016) and South Africa (Moseley and Campbell, 2019) have found that gendered perceptions of design disciplines mean that women are under-represented at the production and industrial ends of the spectrum. Even when statistics indicate a rise in participation, the perception of 'technical' design subjects as masculine influences everyday experience. For example, in an Australian educational context, Catherine Lockhart found that women taking industrial design degrees felt the course and the studio projects were more aligned to 'masculine interests' (2016: 96). As Ellen Lupton suggests, while the white male design student may find himself as a minority in the classroom, he is frequently one of the 'most vocal students in the room and may be treated with special respect by faculty' (2021: 186). Thus, even though design schools are increasingly trying to address diversity and inclusion, everyday inequities and microaggressions may go unnoticed.

The association of form (female) follows function (male) also translates into work contexts whereby women are often not trusted with projects that were seen as technically complex or that entailed a great deal of creative responsibility. These findings were reiterated more recently in South Africa, where Moseley and Campbell found that female industrial designers were frequently given decorative work rather than the task of building things (2019: 189). For example, one of their female participants said, 'We are not always trusted with technical projects, and we are often given projects at the end to be prettified' (Moseley and Campbell, 2019: 189). Mosely and Campbell also found that women designers were expected to do more of the office housework and often experienced offensive and misogynistic behaviour. Their participant states, 'clients, suppliers, and manufacturers won't look you in the eye or shake your hand. You'll often get asked to make coffee for meetings and have to listen to offensive, sexist jokes' (Moseley and Campbell, 2019: 189).

Globally, design reflects other industries in terms of the pay gap. In the UK, for example, women get paid 17.3 per cent less than men, as visualized by the Lost Time Calendar created by Alice Murray and Lauren Priestley (fig. 3.2). During Covid-19, the gender pay gap in the UK worsened with working mothers 47 per cent more likely to lose their job, be furloughed or hours cut back during the pandemic (Scott, 2020). The pay gap is even more acute for BIPOC workers. For example, in Aotearoa for every $1 a *Pākehā* (New Zealander of European descent) man earns, a *Pākehā* women earns $0.89, a Māori man earns $0.86, an Asian man earns $0.86, a Pasifika man earns $0.81, a Māori woman earns $0.81, and a Pasifika woman earns $0.75 (Stats NZ, 2021).

Drawing on her extensive study of design agencies in the UK, Susanne Reimer has argued that cultures of professional design practice more generally are structured by dominant masculinities. Drawing on Alison Bain, Reimer defines dominant masculinity as a form of masculinity that is 'most highly valued, legitimated, and respected in society' and which works to 'disempower women and to subordinate other men' (Bain 2009: 486). In design studios, Reimer observes that dominant masculinities were rehearsed though 'the normalisation of long and unpredictable hours; and via relationships developed in the work setting and with clients' (2015: 1042). She writes that it is assumed that creative work is all encompassing and that ideal employees must be obsessive or perfectionist and thus willing and able to work at all times. Creative skill in design, she finds, is coded as masculine, and male managers 'repeatedly denied that women possessed legitimate expertise in creative or technological production' (Reimer, 2015: 1039). Similarly, rapport building which is crucial to pitch for new business and satisfy clients, was conceptualized as male activity. Reimer finds

Figure 3.2 Lost Time Calendar. Alice Murray and Lauren Priestley, 2020. Courtesy of The Lost Time Project founded by Alice Murray and Lauren Priestley.

that for many of her participants it was 'unquestioningly assumed that men . . . [would] best be able to relate to other men' (2015: 1037). Indeed, when many women take on a 'double shift' at work and at home, rapport building through attendance at social events such as afterwork drinks becomes more difficult. Thus, Reimer argues that while creativity, knowledge and innovation may seem gender neutral, they rest on assumptions about a masculine subject. This means that while many of her participants thought that gender inequality was 'getting better' because of the increased employment of women, this disavowal of structural power relations was actually part of hegemonic masculinity.

Dominant masculinities in design were also valorized and constructed through geographies of place in Reimer's study. She argues that the narratives of her participants established a binary between 'hegemonically (even heroically) masculine London in contrast to a regional imaginary connoted as an other-than-masculine space' (Reimer, 2015: 1042). This reflects a more general sense, at least until recently, of 'good-design' and cutting-edge innovation being typically found in the cities of the Global North.

While increases in remote working and changes in perception of the design canon may have altered attitudes towards place, a recent small scale study conducted in Aotearoa confirms that many of the ways that dominant masculinities are rehearsed through work culture still hold (Baker, 2022). In 2021, I conducted a workshop in Aotearoa in which five designers discussed barriers to gender justice in professional design practice and we co-created a systems map (fig. 3.3). Drawing on these discussions, I identified five areas that were represented as loops: repetitive dynamics that play out 'over and over again and end up acting as either significant drivers of change or maintainers of the status quo' (Alford, 2017). The five areas of time pressures, division of labour, self-worth and judgements of value, a lack of champions, and ingrained binaries, emerged as especially significant.

Time pressures included the discussion of how familial obligations and care work often clashed with the demands of being a designer. The expectation to work long hours in design resonates with Reimer's findings and is particularly challenging for parents. Work cultures that are incompatible with parental responsibilities maintain gender inequality because women (as the majority of primary carers) are likely to have to make compromises regarding their careers. These compromises also mean that men are less able and/or willing to take a more active role. For freelancers who are in charge of their workload, family obligations can also influence the type of work they take on because they said that they lack the physical and mental space for complex creative projects. For agency workers, divisions of labour manifest differently with female designers often taking on more 'office housework'. It was also found that the association of the technoscientific with masculinity continued to influence the division of labour in agencies, or at least managers and clients were surprised by a woman 'who could code', for example.

In terms of self-worth and judgements of value, designers spoke of the masculine Modernist values that, while changing in some contexts, continued to influence unequal recognition in terms of awards and exhibitions. Some spoke of how white men in the industry had a greater sense of entitlement and confidence. For example, a recent graduate described how her fellow female classmates felt they had to perfect their portfolios while her male counterparts only worked on them until they were 'good enough'. As Reimer found, the ideal designer is conceptualized as an obsessive perfectionist and discussion in the workshops would suggest that this burden is unequally experienced by women. The internalization of patriarchal design ideologies made the participants feel that they had to be extra confident and 'sell' their ideas more strongly than their male counterparts. Yet this was a fine line to tread because, as one more experienced designer suggested, 'emotions stick to women' and one could easily be cast as too aggressive. When selling their work, women designers would often find themselves in a 'double-bind', being seen either as not confident enough in their own abilities or overly assertive.

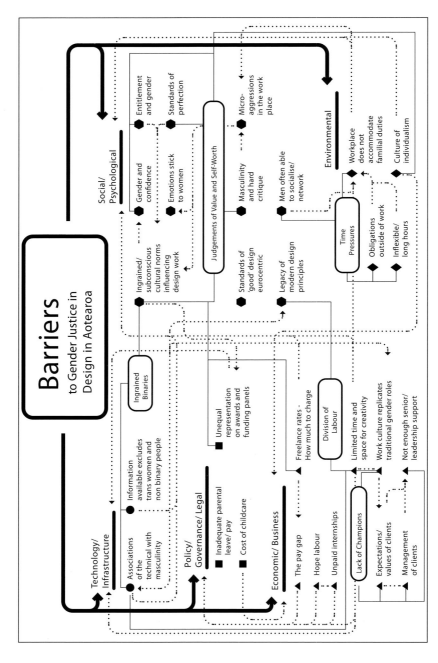

Barriers
to Gender Justice in
Design in Aotearoa

Social/ Psychological

Entitlement and gender

Standards of perfection

Micro-aggressions in the work place

Gender and confidence

Emotions stick to women

Judgements of Value and Self-Worth

Masculinity and hard critique

Men often able to socialise/ network

Ingrained/ subconscious cultural norms influencing design work

Standards of 'good' design eurocentric

Legacy of modern design principles

Environmental

Workplace does not accommodate familial duties

Culture of individualism

Time Pressures

Obligations outside of work

Inflexible/ long hours

Ingrained Binaries

Technology/ Infrastructure

Information available excludes trans women and non binary people

Associations of the technical with masculinity

Policy/ Governance/ Legal

Unequal representation on awards and funding panels

Inadequate parental leave/ pay

Cost of childcare

Economic/ Business

Freelance rates - How much to charge

The pay gap

Hope labour

Unpaid internships

Division of Labour

Limited time and space for creativity

Work culture replicates traditional gender roles

Not enough senior/ leadership support

Lack of Champions

Expectations/ values of clients

Management of clients

Figure 3.3 Barriers to Gender Justice in Design in Aotearoa. © Sarah Elsie Baker, 2021. Designed with Kolcha.

QUESTIONS FOR DESIGNERS: BARRIERS TO GENDER JUSTICE IN DESIGN

Consider these questions in relation to your own experience:

- Looking at the 'barriers to gender justice systems map' which issues resonate with you?

- What associations are made between your geographical location and design?

- Do you agree that dominant masculinities are played out in design cultures? Is there a difference between educational and professional contexts?

- How are men/women, masculine/feminine binaries reproduced in the workplace? Do/how do these discourses exclude transgender and non-binary people?

When discussing barriers to gender justice and creating the systems map, client relationships and attitudes were a strong factor in determining the ability of designers to challenge gender norms. Thus, while methods such those included in books like this one may have honourable intentions, in commercial contexts it is often clients and preconceived notions of their tastes that influence outcomes. Designers spoke of the need for the education of clients and for senior leaders who were champions for gender justice.

While the designers involved in creating the systems map were aware of the exclusion of transgender and non-binary people, and even raised this as an issue, the conversation would sometimes revert to men/women binaries and associated behaviours. Therefore, the study found that even among designers who are aware of, and experience inequalities, there is still some way to go in terms of moving beyond the binaries of sex and gender.

INTERVIEW: IN-AH SHIN, GRAPHIC DESIGNER, CO-FOUNDER OF THE FEMINIST DESIGNER SOCIAL CLUB, SEOUL

In-ah Shin (she/her) is a graphic designer and co-founder of the Feminist Designer Social Club (FDSC) based in Seoul, South Korea. Her studio, Scenery of Today, mainly works and collaborates with activists and not-for-profit clients.

SB: How did you get involved in design? What does your current role involve?
IS: After studying Visual Communication and International Studies at University of
Technology, Sydney, I went back to South Korea to start my career as a designer. I
decided to work at a design agency in Korea to learn about Korean graphic design and
typography, but after a while I realized I didn't want to work in that exploitive
environment. People here work so hard. I worked hard too, because I wanted to do well,
so doing overnights and things wasn't a problem for me. So, at the beginning I just
wanted to absorb everything, because it was so new to me, and I was just fascinated by
everything that I learnt. But, after two years, it hit me hard psychologically and
physically. I left the agency partly because in the whole two years I worked there I never
got to look around Seoul – I just went from home to work, work to home. After a while I
started to look for a job but didn't have any luck. Then I thought that maybe it was my
destiny to start my own business.

   I started freelancing and I decided I wanted to try to do things differently from the
agency. I had a lot of questions about how the agency worked with clients, but a lot of
the time I didn't get an answer that made sense to me (My nickname was 'Why'
because I had so many questions starting with 'Why'). In my studies, we discussed how
pitching can be exploitative, but when I asked those questions of my agency, they just
said, 'That doesn't work in Korea, Korea is different.' And I just thought, 'You haven't
tried!' So, I wanted to see if that was really true, and I wanted to do something more
meaningful.

   That was seven years ago. At the start, I think I had a bit of an idealized vision of
working with not-for profit clients (that it'd be different to working for for-profit clients). I
had to go through a process of trial and error in the way that I work and how I
understand design. I've learnt that working with not-for-profit clients' needs a different
approach to the ones used for working with commercial clients – you can't apply the
same design methodologies everywhere. With the insights that I've learnt from past
seven years, now I run my own independent design studio. I've also teamed up with a
researcher/activist to enable non-profits to polish their message and to see if that helps
to make more of an impact. We are experimenting with building long-term relationships
because I realized that I need time to understand clients' needs and to experiment with
different visual approaches. Our work at Scenery of Today is not just focused on
project-based collaboration.

SB: What motivated you to start the Feminist Designer Social Club?
IS: It's quite a long story! In 2016, there was a hashtag movement in Korea which started
in the sub-cultural scene. It said #sexualassaultinsubculturescene and there were many
people who spoke out about their experience. The hashtag got into literature, film and

the art scene, and from there it just expanded. One of the hashtags was talking about a curator who was quite influential at the time, who was working with a lot of designers who were considered to be cool. They said he was contacting young women foreshadowing that he'd give them opportunities. He even contacted me to work on some projects too! But luckily(?) the next day, I saw him mentioned by women using the hashtags. So, the hashtag movement impacted heavily on me. Moreover, at the same time, there were huge protests against the former president, so it was a heavy time politically. This is where I feel like I was born again. I started to see and feel things very differently.

In response, a group of designers who participated in a book called 한국, 여성, 그래픽 디자이너 11 (*Korea, Women, Graphic Designer 11*) published by 6699press which was about to be released. The people who were involved in that project became a sort of team, called Woo (http://www.wearewoo.org/), and they organized talks, exhibitions and things like that. At the beginning, they said they were going to run these activities for one year and I remember thinking, why just one year? It's not something that's going to be quickly fixed! But I think they were concerned about the sustainability of the group. How long can you devote yourself to an organization when everyone is a professional designer who already has busy days?

They had quite a big exhibition called 'W show' to wrap up the end of their time together, and about six months later I was scrolling through my phone and thought it would be nice to have some colleagues because I was working alone. In hindsight, it was quite a naïve thought, but I thought, well, boys get help from their seniors. I've even heard from my friends that sometimes professors will hand pick their 'design sons' and give them all the knowledge and opportunities, even if they aren't good at design. We all pick up things across our career, so I wanted to start a little study group of female designers, who were in similar circumstances as me.

I wrote a random Tweet saying, 'It might be good to get together as women designers and have a study group' and it got a huge reaction. It got retweeted a lot and I got heaps of direct messages. Three other graphic designers, Somi Kim, Yuni Ooh and Meanyoung Yang contacted me and I thought, well let's get together and start talking about it. And that's how we started the Feminist Designer Social Club.

At first, we didn't have any idea what we were going to do. But when we announced FDSC online, Eun-sol Jung, who runs a vintage shop called Million Archive, approached us and said, 'If you need a space, I can rent it out to you for free' and we went there, and it was a huge store! I remember going there and thinking, we were only going to have around ten people in our group, but this is too big to have just ten people. Maybe we should scale up and see how many people want to attend? We created a form to see who might be interested, and back then around 200 people responded – this was around May/June 2018. Now we didn't have enough space! We could host around fifty people, so we decided to just focus on professional designers. We also wanted a range of designers, from those early in their careers to twenty or thirty years in, and across a few industries, so they could exchange their knowledge.

On the day, we had fifty people come and join us and we had an idea of how we wanted to network with them. However, we also wanted to make sure our group was encouraging action, and that it worked against patriarchal systems. There were things I suggested, like, don't over-work, don't join those after-work drinks and make sure to speak up for yourself. This might sound weird, but a lot of female designers don't show their work. We also discussed working with people who aren't familiar to you and making sure to include those beyond your friends. Although it feels quite spontaneous, to be honest, I think the activities of groups like Woo influenced my move to instigate the FDSC. They created a foundation that showed us that we could organize something quickly and garner a lot of support.

So, that's my story, of how I started the Feminist Designer Social Club. But there might be other stories from people who joined after a few years. They might not even remember the hashtags from 2016, so would have very different motivations for joining.

SB: What kind of activities is FDSC involved in now?
IS: There are regular events like open days and assembly days. Open days happen twice a year, and you can only join the FDSC by attending an open day. On those days, we explain what we do and who we are, then after that people can decide if they want to join. The assembly days are more like big gatherings, and each has a different theme. The last one we had, at the end of July, was themed around rest and challenging long-hours culture in design. We also use the assemblies to discuss how the membership money has been spent, as well as recap what has happened lately. Anyone can hold a small gathering within the community. There are ongoing work-out sessions, a running group, a study group. Some organize small teams to work on projects that they are interested in. For example, there's a team working on our podcast Design FM, and a publishing team called FDSC.txt. We used to host a design conference called 'FDSC stage', 'FDSC Hakdang'. It is just impossible to jot down everything we do. So recently we invited a researcher to do participatory research and put our activities in words. The research findings are published as a book called 뛰어놀며 운동장의 기울기를 바꾸기 (*Jumping around, Having Fun, Levelling up the Playing Field*).

SB: For many of the readers who will not know about design in Seoul, could you tell us a little about its history and what the industry looks like now? Are there many agencies in Korea that focus on non-profit work?

IS: When I started, there were only a handful of agencies who would work with non-for-profits, and I think before that it was more a pro-bono thing. Now, I think there are more designers who are willing to work in the social sector and there are also people who work with social entrepreneurs in their companies, in-house. That's something that's big, and something that's new.

There are also more activist-designers and recently, I learnt that there are a few studios that work with activists in other areas of Korea, rather than Seoul. When I first started, I was focused on Seoul because it's the biggest city and there's more opportunity here, but now there are more people speaking up in their local contexts. One example is the feminist organizer called Boshu, based in Daejeon. They organize lots of cool events and community initiatives. There is also a photography book publisher called *April Snow* in Daegu. Their work is distributed overseas so it is definitely worth checking out too.

SB: In your experience, what are the challenges for designers that identify as women? Or for women in Korea working at design agencies?

IS: It's the same across most industries because the same patriarchal logic is played out. First, you get judged because you're seen as a mother, or a potential mother. Secondly, at university you get the impression that if you work for a big company, as an in-house designer, then you're not truly a 'creative' or 'real' designer. That's sort of the idea that hangs there. But, if you want to work at a smaller design agency, they often just won't hire women because there are a lot of overnight shifts, and the owner might say, 'Oh I'm just not comfortable spending a whole day/night with a young woman'. On the other hand, they might only hire young women because they want people to work for two or three years for a small amount of money, then get married and disappear. That's the logic, so women are getting exploited, and they can't see a future, so they leave the industry.

I had an experience once at an agency, where a women had to pick up her child and before she left everyone was commenting on how it was fine, and they understood. But, after she had gone, they started saying that she wasn't that passionate about the work, and how they would have to pick up her work because she left. I was thinking, 'that's so mean!' but it's really the workload and the environment that makes you think like that. It really scared me, because at the end of my two years at the agency, I had started thinking like that too.

There's also a notion of being passionate about design. I would hear things at the agency like, 'On my first day of work, I didn't go home for three days', and they say it with a certain pride. It's as though it's a reflection of how much they devote themselves to design and the work. I used to think that was impressive, but now I know, if you don't sleep for three days then you aren't thinking normally, and your work will be crap. Maybe if you'd gone home and got some rest, better design would have happened!

SB: How does your background and experience influence your design work? For example, do you think you have a different style from men in the industry?
IS: I don't think you get a valid answer when you start talking about style. I don't think you can have gendered style. The more important thing to consider is the design process and approach. That's where you can really see if someone comes from a feminist perspective or not.

The FDSC changed my attitude and how I see things, so in that vein I can see that it's impacted my work as well. It's only recently that I've started to read feminist design theory and that's changed a lot for me. It's motivated me to focus more on how I build relationships with my clients and how I set up the collaboration. To be honest, now, I don't really want to design. I want to digest what I've learnt and need some time to experiment with it. I find when I design, I often fall back into my old habits, so I need time to change those habits. Before, it was important to work fast, because a lot of projects would come in two weeks before the deadline and I was quite proud of myself for creating what I designed in a fast-paced environment. Now, I think maybe I need to find a way to work slower, take care of things that fast-paced environment leaves behind and not think that's inefficient – that's the change I'm experiencing currently.

SB: What sort of design futures would you like to see materialize?
IS: There was a clear picture when I started. I jokingly said, 'If our club works well, and people get jobs from the (FDSC) network, then there will be people from the "boys club" who want to join us'. Their seniors would ask them to work longer and do other things that construct the patriarchy and they would say 'No!' They would see that there's another way of working that is better for everyone, then we can bring the patriarchy down and everyone is happy!

Now, it's a little different for me and it's always changing. I guess, I just want more designers in Korea to discuss design *in* Korea. I've been reading about climate design, anti-capitalist design and decolonial design, which is really all connected to feminist design thinking. I feel as though, in Korea, we think about how we compete in a world-setting. We want to see that our design is advanced, like Western design, and I feel that this is racist thinking. In Korea, despite being an Asian country, there is a strong influence from white supremacy. People tend to associate with white people, as opposed to people of colour, so their mentality is quite different. When I get a chance to talk to the design community, I try to tell them that they are not white, and I try to introduce work by black designers or other Asian designers. I try to say, why don't we listen to their voices, because those are our voices too. For now, I'm not sure what this discussion will bring us. It is hard to picture. But I'm sure that it would bring us something more exciting and more fulfilling.

Addressing inequality in the workplace

In the 1980s, Lewis and Bruce observed three 'hurdles' that would need to be overcome if inequality was to be addressed in design cultures. The first barrier of entry to the profession was 'getting qualifications' which included entering a degree course and graduating. Lewis and Bruce observed that this was more of a problem in design disciplines that were deemed 'technical' such as industrial design. The second hurdle was 'getting a first job in design' which they argued also depended upon the 'stereotyping of the job [that] can discriminate against women' (Lewis and Bruce, 1989: 19). The third was 'becoming a success' which involved 'getting management experience', 'getting prestigious work contacts' and 'gaining awards' (Lewis and Bruce, 1989: 16). Lewis and Bruce found that 'the higher up the scale one goes, the less visible are women designers' (1989: 20). They offered practical solutions for reducing the gendered division of labour which included 'positive discrimination' for women taking design courses, all designers under-taking management training that would include gender issues, and the development of women design groups that enabled flexible working practices.

Since the 1980s, and depending on the country, progress has been achieved in regard to some of these hurdles. Significant inroads have been made in terms of female entry to degree level design courses in the West, even those focused on more 'technical' subjects (e.g. Design Council, 2020a: 15). In other countries, initiatives such as TechSaksham in India and The Female Designer Movement in Africa are working to support women to gain education in design and creative technology.

However, as discussed above and as depatriarchise design (a non-profit association based in Basel, Switzerland) attest, design education itself continues to be interwoven with patriarchal structures, and this can limit the participation and learning of those people who identify as women, trans or non-binary. Thus, depatriarchise design *!Labs!* aim to take education out of the formal classroom and inhabit different global virtual and physical spaces. The group conceive of the internet as offering a tangible safe space in which systems of oppression can be explored and challenged, and in which connections between liked-minded designers can be created. The *!Labs!* also take place away from the keyboard and the organizers argue that the seam between the digital and physical enables different kinds of feminist work.

As indicated in the introduction above, getting a job in industry continues to be a more of a challenge for those who identify as women, transgender or non-binary. Recently, there has been growth in industry paid internship schemes for women and BIPOC designers to address some of the disparity. For example, design and tech companies and international organizations such as BLAC in Chicago offer paid internships for Black creatives in advertising, and McKinsey Digital in Australia offer internships and scholarship for women who want to build a career in the digital space.

When junior female designers do get jobs in industry, they often face conditions that are less than equitable, such as doing more than their fair share of office housekeeping or getting their ideas hijacked by colleagues. In her discussion of emotional housekeeping, Jennifer Tobias recommends setting up a rotation of tasks, and conducting social experiments such as not volunteering to take notes at the next meeting and seeing what happens (2021: 190). When your ideas are hijacked in a meeting, experts such as Valerie Gordan suggest that having a colleague in your corner who can reiterate that it was your idea, or stating something like, 'I'm so glad you agree with my earlier idea' can go some way to setting the record straight (2018: para 8). If these types of experiences occur frequently, it can be a good strategy to document what is going on and then talk to a few people who you know will be your allies. Then either talk to HR or organize a meeting as a group to openly address and discuss studio culture. While some colleagues may be initially defensive, the majority will often be 'blind' to what is happening and keen to implement new approaches.

Globally, the third hurdle of women being promoted to leadership roles in design seems to be the 'stickiest'. As Nat Maher, from Kerning the Gap, a UK design equality network that wants to see more women in leadership roles, states:

half of the challenge we have – 89% of it, in fact – is the current lack of women in leadership positions, who act as vital role models, and bring first-hand experiences of their own challenges to reshape the legacy behind them.

2017: para 15

Thus, Kerning the Gap runs mentorship schemes throughout the UK for women designers while also raising awareness about the issues that act as barriers to gender equity in design. Nat Maher suggests that many of the conversations she has around gender balance are about women's confidence, or lack thereof. Kerning the Gap focuses on practical ways to build confidence and to get more women in industry. If change is to occur, however, it cannot only be the individual responsibility of women to 'work harder' or 'lean in'. As Ellen Lupton notes, confidence is social, not just personal (2021: 182). Belief in abilities derives from proven success as well as support from others. Thus, recognition and visibility are key to moving towards gender justice.

In recent years, there has been an increase in initiatives across the globe that aim to heighten awareness of designers that may have typically fallen outside of the listings of industry bodies; awards ceremonies and exhibition catalogues. Often in the form of online directories, these sites work to associate designers with a specific identity or a particular politics. For example, Queer Design Club's mission is to 'promote and celebrate all the amazing work that happens at the intersection of queer identity and design world-wide' (Queer Design Club, 2022). Similarly, *Women Who Design* is a directory that aims to help people to find notable and relevant voices to follow on Twitter. *Femme Type Directory* extends the simple online directory by creating content that 'contributes to promoting, inspiring and educating the professional community' (Femme Type Directory, 2022). For example, the website includes content about how to break gender norms in design through type. Thus, in some ways these online communities work as design collectives connecting people, instilling confidence and fostering new ways of thinking.

Yet, as was discussed above, dominant masculinities continue to be central to work cultures in the design industry, and online communities do not address some of the adverse conditions for women, transgender and non-binary people. However, some design collectives and agencies are addressing these structural issues through flexible working practices and transparent pay scales. For example, Normally, a data product and service design agency based in London, only work a four-day week, and their pay is calculated by an algorithm based only on previous experience. The founder of Normally, Marei Wollersberger, reflects:

Before, we had a traditional process based on past salaries. But we realised there was a big difference in terms of what people were asking for – the difference mainly being that women and introverts were asking for a lot less.

HILDER, 2022: 22

Recognizing that the management team might be biased, they developed an algorithm that is totally transparent. Wollersberger thinks that the two initiatives of a four-day week and algorithmic pay scales have been highly successful in terms of both productivity, diverse recruitment, and retention of staff.

In the 1980s, Lewis and Bruce were only focused on women designers and the hurdles they faced in industry. They did not consider how the experience might be different (or often worse) for women of colour, transgender and non-binary people. Indeed, there are currently no academic studies of the specific experience of these individual designers. The design press offers some useful but limited advice. For example, it is advised to make the specification of pronouns common for everyone (Rmaanushi, 2021). In design work and in office chat it is important to check assumptions about what people of specific genders do or don't do (Rmaanushi, 2021). For example, the designer Josie Young makes an excellent observation of the language used in design. When a Creative Director suggested her logo was 'too masculine' she reflected 'most of us have been raised on a world of blues and pinks so when it comes to describing the work we're doing, of course we fall into those familiar patterns' (Young, 2021: para 3). However, 'the end goal should not be to label something as masculine and feminine' (Young, 2021: para 6). In the end, Young asked the Creative Director to come back with three adjectives for what he meant, and she found that it inspired a much more appropriate and specific design response.

CASE STUDY: DESIGNERS SPEAK (UP), CATHERINE GRIFFITHS, AOTEAROA NEW ZEALAND

Catherine Griffiths is a typographer and designer based in Aotearoa New Zealand. Improvisation is central to Griffiths's practice which moves between graphic design, self-publishing, writing on design and commissioned art installations in public and private spaces, architectural and landscape. She has been running her own studio practice since 1995. Griffiths's work has been exhibited and published nationally and internationally, with her first survey show, »catherine griffiths: SOLO IN [ ] SPACE« taking place in Shanghai in 2019.

In 2018 in Aotearoa New Zealand, the designer and typographer, Catherine Griffiths noticed that the jury for the Designers Institute of New Zealand's (DINZ) Best Design Awards was predominately male. After a bit more research, she realized that the institute's prestigious annual award, the Black Pin, had only been awarded to three women in the past twenty years, and of the 52 DINZ 'Fellows', only nine were women. To highlight this gender imbalance, she designed three posters (fig. 3.4, 3.5 and 3.6) which she posted on Instagram, Facebook and Twitter. The posters used the same colour scheme (purple spot colour) and brand typeface (Untitled Sans) as the Best Design Awards website. By appropriating these design elements, Griffiths aimed to add power to the message and cause DINZ to reflect on its institutional values.

The response to Griffiths's posts was quick, strong and supportive, and a protest was arranged for the award ceremony (fig. 3.7) (Griffiths, 2018). The protestors called for an audit of the institute's processes in terms of both gender and cultural diversity. The protest received national media coverage and gained significant public support. Griffiths and her collaborators drew attention to how 'The Best Design Awards, for better or

Figure 3.4 1997–2017, 43 Black Pins awarded, 40 men, 3 women (40/3). Catherine Griffiths, 2018. Courtesy of Catherine Griffiths.

2017 Kent Sneddon	2006 Grant Alexander
2017 Dan Bernasconi	2006 Gary Paykel
2016 Ben Corban	2005 Hugh Mullane &
2016 Danny Coster	Craig Horrocks
2015 Professor Tony Parker	2005 Mark Pennington
2015 Kris Sowersby	2004 Michael Smythe
2014 Mark Cleverley	2004 Richard Taylor
2014 Matt Holmes	2003 Ray Labone
	2003 Peter Haythornthwaite
	—FDINZ
2013 Grenville Main	2002 Doug Heath
2013 Kent Parker	
2012 Sven Baker	2001 Robin Beckett
2012 Ian Athfield	2001 Humphrey Ikin
2011 Fraser Gardyne	2000 David Bartlett
2011 Mark Elmore	2000 Bruce Farr
2010 Tim Hooson	1999 John Hughes
2010 Dean Poole	
2009 Dave Clark	1998 Not awarded
2009 Joseph Churchward	1998 Gifford Jackson
2008 Professor Leong Yap	1997 Max Hailstone
2008 Laurie Davidson	1997 John Britten
2007 Brian Richards	
2007 David Trubridge	

1997–2017, 43 Black Pins, 40 men, 3 women
Designers Institute of New Zealand
Best Design Awards

Figure 3.5 1997–2017, 43 Black Pins awarded, 40 men, 3 women (Archive). Catherine Griffiths, 2018. Courtesy of Catherine Griffiths.

worse, as an archive of design, has been writing women out of Aotearoa New Zealand's design history' (Griffiths, 2018).

In response to the significant attention the protests received, DINZ organized three hui (meetings) in main cities in Aotearoa with the aim of discussing diversity and inclusion. They invited the design community to participate in workshops to help determine how to effect change in the sector. Since this time, DINZ has stated that they will prioritize 'diversity as a basis for selection of Best awards judges, board members and other voluntary roles' (Thompson and Tang-Taylor, 2019). Another national design organization, Design Assembly, also organized a series of panel discussions exploring

Convenors

8 men 1 woman

Jurors

Graphic
5 men 3 women
Interactive
4 men 1 woman
Moving Image
3 men 1 woman
Ngā Aho Award
4 men 1 woman
Product
5 men 1 woman
Public Good Award
3 men 2 women
Spatial
6 men 3 women
User Experience Award
3 men 2 women
Value of Design Award
5 men 0 women

2018 Best Awards Jury: 46 men, 15 women
Designers Institute of New Zealand
Best Design Awards

Typeface—Untitled Sans
Style—Regular
Designer—Kris Sowersby

Foundry—Klim Type Foundry
Released—2017

Figure 3.6 2018, Best Awards Jury: 46 men, 15 women (Jury). Catherine Griffiths, 2018. Courtesy of Catherine Griffiths.

diversity and inclusion in design. These events included important conversations about the intersections between gender, LGBTQ+ and Māori identity, diversity of thought and design. Thus, Griffiths's interventions most definitely put gender equity on the design agenda in Aotearoa.

Building on the success of the protests, Griffiths alongside Alice Connew and Katie Kerr, launched the Designers Speak (Up) website and blog, to give voice to a wide range of designers in Aotearoa New Zealand. They also established the *Directory of Women* Designers* which was set up to 'establish a contemporary, historic and perpetual index of Aotearoa New Zealand designers who *identify as women, womxn, non-binary, of

Figure 3.7 Feminist 40/30 protestors at Best Awards. Stuff, 2018. Photograph: Michelle Jones.

any gender experience*, living and deceased, of all diversities – social, sexual, cultural, ethnic – anywhere in the world' (Designers Speak (Up), 2022). The directory works as a counter-narrative in contrast with male dominated histories, awards and networks. It also works as a resource for clients, collaborators and the wider community to connect with women-identifying designers. The directory currently has over 500 entries.

Present Tense: Wāhine Toi Aotearoa

In early 2019 Designers Speak (Up) issued an open call to everyone in the *Directory of Women* *Designers* asking them to design a poster exploring a social, cultural or political issue of their choice. Posters should be A1 and designed using #ff3333 red and white, with text in Univers LT Std Regular. Griffiths and her collaborators were keen to record the current landscape of women* in design and give visibility to the unsung diversity of design in Aotearoa. Over 100 poster designs were submitted. Themes included gender issues, racism, climate change, the Christchurch attacks and the protection of indigenous lands at Ihumātao (see fig. 3.8). The posters were presented in a range of different contexts (galleries, public spaces, online) and formats (printed, projected, online). In 2019, posters were exhibited at galleries across Aotearoa and critical essays were written about the project. At each venue the exhibition was accompanied with events including conversations with local designers and poster and zine-making workshops.

Figure 3.8 Present Tense: Wāhine Toi Aotearoa. Britomart. Photograph: Bruce Connew.

Challenging gender norms in professional design practice

In recent years, design work that challenges gender norms has gained more visibility in professional practice. In graphic design and illustration for example, specific designers and studios have become known for pushing the boundaries. For illustrators such as Wednesday Holmes, their illustration began as both as a cathartic tool and a way of facilitating change (Filmer-Court, 2020). Holmes has now worked for clients including Instagram, Gucci and the BBC. Their work tends to focus on relationships and the LGBTQI+ experience. Design agencies focused on specifically on feminist and LGBTQI+ issues have also emerged. Lutalica (a design studio for feminists and queers based in the UK) helps organizations to develop their online and offline presence and give them the tools to effectively communicate their purpose. Working with London Youth Gateway, a multi-service organization providing support for eighteen- to twenty-five-year-olds facing homelessness, for instance, they produced a new visual identity including a responsive logo (Fig. 3.9).

Design work that challenges gender norms within the sphere of professional practice currently tends to be specifically for organizations who have similar purpose. However, for International Women's Day each year larger corporations have produced gender critical work. For example, in 2020 IKEA collaborated with the relationship expert Jennie Miller to produce FiftyFifty, a free game that looked to unpack the unequal division of labour in homes worldwide. 'Women are still taking on a large proportion of housework and childcare,' they write, 'so

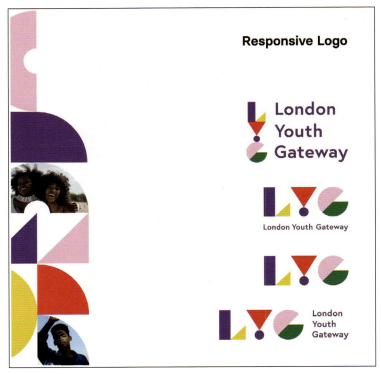

Figure 3.9 London Youth Gateway logo and brand identity. Studio Lutalica, 2022. © New Horizon Youth Centre.

IKEA decided to step in and make conversations around housework a little easier' (IKEA, 2020). In 2022, the New Zealand digital service provider, Spark co-created Beyond Binary Code (fig. 3.10), a simple online tool that:

> builds a copy and paste HTML code after helping businesses evaluate whether gender-related data needs to be captured at all, what to capture if it's required, and how they might do this in a way that enables people of all genders to be seen and heard online.
>
> SPARK, 2022: para 2

It may also be the case that designers are challenging gender norms less overtly through the aesthetics they produce. For example, the website Femme Type is full of examples of typographers and graphic designers challenging dominant type styles with their designs. For instance, Aasawari Suhas Kulkarni produced the typeface Nari Variable as a model of what a feminist typeface might look like (fig. 3.11). She writes that Nari Variable challenges conventional

Figure 3.10 Beyond Binary Code. Spark, Collenso BBDO, 2021.

Figure 3.11 Nari Variable. A Conversation Between East and West. Aasawari Suhas Kulkarni, 2021. Courtesy of Aasawari Kulkarni. Photograph by Dan Meyers.

'vanilla' typefaces by being poetic, reviving and adaptable (Murphy, 2021). The font does not adhere to universal geometric conventions, but this does not make it any less useable. As queer designers Marwan Kaabour, Isaac Flores and Floss Burns suggest, the experience of being outside normative expressions of gender and sexuality inevitably influences their design decisions and design languages (Levenson, 2022). Thus, it is an understanding of our own histories and perspectives, as well as purposefully fostering diversity of experience in professional design practice that can help us move towards gender justice.

QUESTIONS FOR DESIGNERS: IDEAS FOR FOSTERING GENDER JUSTICE

Use these questions to consider what you can do to facilitate change in your current context. These might only seem like small steps but over time they can make a difference.

- What groups can you connect with and/or what workshops can you attend?
- Can you reach out to a mentor in your field?
- Can you make changes to your work environment i.e. suggesting transparent pay scales, for example?
- What can you do outside/alongside educational and professional contexts to cultivate collaboration and empowerment?
- Can you challenge dominant aesthetics in your design work?
- Can you subtly educate your clients?

CHAPTER THREE ACTIVITY

SITUATED KNOWLEDGE MAP

What is your class background? What is your class now?

_____
_____

Where were you born? Where do you live now?

_____
_____
_____

How do you identify in terms of race and ethnicity?

_____
_____
_____

What are your abilities/disabilities?

_____
_____
_____

What languages do you speak?

_____
_____
_____

How do you identify in terms of gender and sexuality?

_____
_____
_____
_____

How old are you?

_____

What is your heritage? What knowledge did your ancestors pass on to you?

_____
_____
_____

What project are you working on?

_____
_____
_____
_____
_____

What insight does my experience give me?

_____
_____

What blind spots might I have?

_____
_____

(Inspired by Noel, 2018)

© Dr Sarah Elsie Baker

CHAPTER THREE ACTIVITY

LISTENING POSITIONALITY EXERCISE

The purpose of this activity is to practice active listening while at the same time offering opportunity to reflect on how your positionality effects your responses and your attitude to listening. Gender, race, class, sexuality, cultural background and ability guide our listening capacities, habits and biases (Robinson, 2020). As designers increasingly work and design with communities, awareness of listening positionality is crucial.

1. Get together with a colleague or friend.

2. Give them 60 seconds to rant about something that annoys them.

3. Actively listen. Try to single out:

a. What they care about _____

b. What they value _____

c. What matters to them _____

4. At the end of the 60 seconds repeat your summary back to your colleague or friend.

a. You care about _____

b. You value _____

c. You believe that _____

_____ matters a lot.

5. Ask them how they feel.

6. Reflect on the process.

a. How did listening make you feel? Was this different from how you normally listen?

_____

_____

_____

b. How do you think your own positionality (gender, cultural background etc) influences your listening capacity, habit and bias? _____

_____

_____

© **Dr Sarah Elsie Baker**

4

MAKING GENDER INEQUALITY VISIBLE

Introduction: gender justice as a global issue

In 2015, the UN initiated a Sustainable Development Agenda in which they established seventeen Sustainable Development Goals (SDGs). Sustainable Development Goal 5 is Gender Equality. However, as Sima Bahous, UN Women Executive Director, recognizes, 'SDG 5 is not just a goal in its own right. It is the key and the bedrock to the SDGS as a whole' (Bahous, 2022). For example, in relation to SDG 2 Zero Hunger, women's food insecurity levels were 10 per cent higher than men's in 2020 (UN, 2021: 2). As the UN recognize, the world is not on track to meet the goals of gender equality and the empowerment of all women and girls by 2030. They write:

> [a]mid the intersecting crises of Covid-19, the climate emergency, and rising economic and political insecurity, progress on gender equality has not only failed to move forward but has begun to reverse. Around the world, a growing backlash against women's rights is threatening even well-established freedoms and protections.
>
> UN Women, 2022

The UN cite statistics such as in 2022, '388.1 million women and girls will be living in extreme poverty'; 'only 57% of the world's women make their own informed decisions about sexual relations, contraceptive use, and reproductive health care'; and 'globally about 1 in 5 women aged 20–24 were married before the age of 18' (UN, 2022). In 2022, 'the gender snapshot' produced by UN Women recognizes that the outlook is 'pretty grim' with no countries meeting targets around equality of unpaid care and domestic work. The report also highlighted how data gaps prevented the authors from documenting the full picture of progress (or lack thereof): only 48 per cent of data is available globally regarding gender equity. They write, 'where data are missing, women and girls are invisible' (UN Women, 2022).

The same can be said of LGBTQI+ people, who are often missing from the UN Sustainability Goals altogether. While a number of authors have demonstrated how the SDGs impact on, and can be used to support, LGBTQI+ communities (Park and Mendes, 2019; Dorey, 2022), the few references in the actual reports from the UN are representative of a wider issue regarding the visibility of LGBTQI+ people and their needs. UN Women stands 'in solidarity with all people of diverse sexual orientations, gender identities, gender expressions and sex characteristics', but does not address LGBTQI+ issues specifically (UN Women, 2022b). The UN has a 'Free and Equal' global campaign for equal rights and the fair treatment of LGBTQI+ people and this initiative has done some important campaigning work in countries such as Cabo Verde, Brazil and Costa Rica. However, progress for LGBTQI+ people is measured in regard to the success of the campaign (social media views etc) rather than equality more generally.

In 2017, Víctor Madrigal-Borloz was appointed to the UN Human Rights Council as the independent expert for sexual orientation and gender identity. Since then, some excellent work and reports have been commissioned, including some in relation to the SDGs. For example, Madrigal-Borloz has pointed out that lesbian, gay, bisexual, transgender and gender-diverse people are disproportionately represented in the ranks of the poor, the homeless and those without healthcare. Thus, equality for LGBTQI+ people is the bedrock to all SDGs, just as gender equality is. However, data is even more elusive. The UN report on data collection and management finds that there are 'serious gaps in available data to capture the lived realities of lesbian, gay, bisexual, trans and gender-diverse (LGBT) persons' (IE SOGI, 2019). Some nation states deny violence and discrimination against LGBTQI+ people, others deny the presence of LGBTQI+ folks altogether. Data collection and management, then, brings with it significant responsibilities, and there is no surprise that LGBTQI+ communities are wary of attempts to measure and categorize given both the current situation and histories of discrimination, criminalization and abuse.

As Catherine D'Ignazio and Lauren F. Klein (2020), the authors of *Data Feminism*, recognize, what and who are counted often become the basis for policymaking and resource allocation. Data are also increasingly the foundation of the design of products, services and software, particularly in light of rise of artificial intelligence and machine learning. Thus, we begin this chapter by exploring data and power. We go on to consider the 'gender data gap' and how this impacts upon design practice. We then look at examples of feminist counter-data and queer AI projects, with the view to reflecting upon what can be done to address current inequalities. Designers play a significant part in the visual communication of data, thus the last part of the chapter explores feminist approaches to data visualization.

Data, power and invisibility

In recent years, there has been exponential growth in our abilities to collect and record information in a digital form. Developments in 'big data', 'smart' technologies, artificial intelligence and machine learning are now an integral part of how societies are organized and how decisions are made. Data practices influence how we understand the world, how we are governed, what services we have access to, where we can go and what we can do. As D'Ignazio and Klein remind us, data can consist of numbers, words, stories, colours or sounds, and are not neutral or objective (2020: 14). They always entail power dynamics. For example, the UN SDG data regarding gender equality above serves a particular purpose in terms of objectives of UN. The way the information is gathered, the way questions are phrased, and the way that certain nations report, is influenced by specific contexts and politics.

The inevitable lack of objectivity involved in data practices is evident in the etymology of the term itself. The word 'data' dates back to the mid-seventeenth century when it meant 'a fact given or granted' (Online Etymology Dictionary, 2021). The emergence of the term served a rhetorical purpose and was used to convert otherwise debatable information into evidence or fact. Data collection about populations is not new, and details of how, who and what is recorded is very much linked to power. Churches recorded details of the dead, counts of the 'indigenous populations appeared in colonial accounts of the Americas', and the logs of people captured and placed upon slave ships reduced rich lives to numbers and names (D'Ignazio and Klein, 2020: 12). The relationship between data and power passed through the eugenics movement in the late nineteenth and early twentieth centuries, which 'sought to employ data to quantify the superiority of white people over all others' (D'Ignazio and Klein, 2020: 12). In the mid-twentieth century, the term began to be used in regard to computers, meaning 'transmittable and storable information by which computer operations are performed', and 'database' began to be used to mean 'the structured collection of data' (Online Etymology Dictionary, 2021). In its computerized form, data continues to be entangled with racism. For example, Simone Browne has shown how biometric technologies are disproportionately used to monitor Black bodies. The legality and ethics of governmental methods of data collection have been called into question more generally, with many citizens unaware of how much data is available about them.

The same can be said of corporations that are collecting enormous amounts of digital data about us on a daily basis. The items that we search for via Google, our posts on Facebook, our online shopping, and the videos we watch are all tracked and stored as data that can be used by corporations to make a profit. 'Nothing is outside datafication' (D'Ignazio and Klein, 2020: 12). As the size and number of available data has grown, data sets have emerged that are too big and too complex to be dealt with by typical software. 'The ability to collect, store, maintain, analyse, and mobilise large datasets still remains with large corporations, wealthy governments, and elite universities' (D'Ignazio and Klein, 2020: 42). Thus, information about gender often remains unobtainable for small organizations and activist groups.

The priorities of corporations and governments also influence the type of data being collected. For example, data collection regarding maternal mortality in the US is particularly weak, with no national system for tracking complications sustained in childbirth and pregnancy. The lack of data hides the reality in which it is estimated that 'black women are over three times more likely than white women to die from pregnancy- or childbirth-related causes' (D'Ignazio and Klein, 2020: 22). The objectives of corporations and governments – science, surveillance and selling – mean that some people and contexts are overly captured and others are missed out. 'Put crudely, there is no profit to be made collecting data on the women who are dying in childbirth, but there is significant profit in knowing whether women are pregnant' (D'Ignazio and Klein, 2020: 45). As feminist geographer Joni Seager suggested, 'what gets counted counts' (Seager, 2016). While there is more data about gender being collected than ever before, data collection practices continue to leave people out: most frequently non-binary people, lesbians and older women (D'Ignazio and Klein, 2020: 98). In addition, when data is collected about gender, it can be narrow in scope. For example, Seager states women in low- and middle-income countries 'seem to be asked about six times a day what kind of contraception they use' but they are not asked about whether they have access to abortion. They are not asked about what sports they like to play (Seager, 2016).

The artist, designer and educator, Mimi Onuoha, explores the politics of data, gender and race in her work. In her piece *The Library of Missing Datasets* she draws attention to datasets that one would think would exist but do not (fig. 4.1). For example, there are no data for 'LGBT older adults discriminated against in housing'; 'firm statistics on how often police arrest women for making false rape reports'; or 'trans people killed or injured in instances of hate crime (note: existing records are notably unreliable or incomplete)' (Onouha, 2018: para 16). Onuoha cites four reasons for gaps in datasets. The first is that those who have the resources to collect data, lack the incentive to do so (or those that have access, have the ability to remove, hide or obscure it). Police brutality towards citizens is a good example of this in the sense that the institutions that have the data lack the incentive to make it publicly available. The second is that the data resists quantification. Things such as emotions are hard to quantify and as such often allude classification. As Onuoha argues 'not all things are easily quantifiable, and at times the very desire to render the world more abstract, trackable, and machine-readable is an idea that itself deserves questioning' (2018: para 11). The third reason that Onuoha gives is that the act of collection involves more

Figure 4.1 The Library of Missing Datasets. Mimi Onouha, 2016. Courtesy of Mimi Onuoha. Photo by Brandon Schulman.

work than the perceived benefit of the data. In the case of sexual harassment and assault, for example, the act of reporting the events can be intense, painful and difficult, and for some the benefits of reporting the incident may be less than the cost of the process. The person or institution who is doing the collecting is of paramount importance here: people are much less likely to report sexual harassment if they feel they will be challenged or judged for it.

The fourth reason is that 'there are advantages to nonexistence'. Onuoha writes that 'every missing dataset is a testament to this fact. Just as the presence of data benefits someone, so too does the absence' (2018: para 15). Thus, each of these reasons points to the 'who' question. Who benefits from the collection, recording and archival of data, or who benefits from missing datasets.

In *The Library of Missing Datasets V.2*, Onuoha focuses on blackness and highlights how Black people are 'both over-collected and under-represented in American datasets' (2018a: para 1). She continues this theme in her most recent artwork, *Natural or Where We Are Allowed To Be*, which comprises three film prints where a model is photographed in a data centre that carries her own information (fig. 4.2). Onuoha writes:

The machine of contemporary American society insists that people have imagined places, and I have come to see that in the tech world, the preferred place for black people is within data. In datasets we appear as the perfect subjects: silent, eternally wronged, frozen in a frame of injustice without the messiness of a face/accent/hint of refusal. It is easier to deal with datasets about black people than it is to dwell on the great gears of a system that penalizes darker skin tones, or to consider the resentment that generations of state-sanctioned neglect could breed. It is easier to see black people as numbers and bodies than as encounters and people. When structural workings of racism meet the distancing power of quantification, both combine to freeze us in place.

2021: para 3

More broadly, the practices of data extraction continue to be part of colonization. For example, African governments have tended to have been slower to set up data infrastructure and data protection laws (Osakwe and Adeniran, 2021). Thus, large technology companies have rushed to set up digital infrastructures. This 'digital colonialism' entails extraction, mining and profiting from data without the consent of African people.

In *The Uncounted* Alex Cobham (2020) also explores the reason for 'data gaps'. Cobham argues that the problem is not always that data doesn't exist,

places where our information matters more than we do

Figure 4.2 Natural or Where We Are Allowed To Be. Mimi Onouha, 2021. Courtesy of Mimi Onuoha. Photo by Pavel Ezrohi.

but that when it does it cannot be trusted to be of any reasonable accuracy or reliability. Cobham argues that exposing poor data is more difficult than finding a lack of data. As Mayra Buvinic and Ruth Levine (2016) write, substandard data is arguably more insidious than a lack of data because it can misrepresent reality. In the case of gender research, it can make women appear to be more dependent and less productive than they are. For example, when recording participation in the labour force, the way that questions are phrased and data collected can have a dramatic affect. In Demographic and Health Surveys (used in more than eighty-five countries), surveys of households are constructed around the 'head of the household' who is assumed to be male. The instructions for interviewers state, 'A household head is a usual resident member of the household acknowledged by the other members of the household as the household head. This person may be acknowledged as the head on the basis of age (older), sex (generally, but not necessarily, male), economic status (main provider), or some other reason' (Buvinic and Levine, 2016: 35). When surveys employ different methods of recording participation and instructions explicitly state to include all forms of work, 'female-led' households increase by almost 50 per cent (Buvinic and Levine, 2016: 35).

To ensure collection of reliable data about gendered experience beyond the binaries of male/female, D'Ignazio and Klein argue for an approach that is sensitive to context. They give an example of data collection by Public Health England in collaboration with LGBTQI+ organizations in routine surveillance of HIV in England and Wales. The designers of the survey offered three named genders (D'Ignazio and Klein, 2020: 109), a catch-all fourth category and an option for non-disclosure. In a separate question they asked about gender at birth also with an option for non-disclosure. D'Ignazio and Klein write that the survey uses sensitive wording and inclusive terminology. While this is an example of best practice in the UK, they warn against universal approaches to the classification of gender. For example, in Aotearoa it would be inappropriate to not to include the Māori term 'Takatāpui' with which many indigenous LGBTQI+ people identify. In other contexts, having one's gender counted as something other than male/female would risk discrimination, violence or even imprisonment. Thus, data practices including recording, collection and analysis should be aware of, and appropriate to, local gendered experience.

Drawing on their detailed exploration and analysis of data practices, D'Ignazio and Klein have developed seven core principles of data feminism. These are:

1 Examine power. Data feminism begins by analyzing how power operates in the world.

2 Challenge power. Data feminism commits to challenging unequal power structures and working toward justice.

3 Elevate emotion and embodiment. Data feminism teaches us to value multiple forms of knowledge, including the knowledge that comes from people as living, feeling bodies in the world.

4 Rethink binaries and hierarchies. Data feminism requires us to challenge the gender binary, along with other systems of counting and classification that perpetuate oppression.

5 Embrace pluralism. Data feminism insists that the most complete knowledge comes from synthesizing multiple perspectives, with priority given to local, Indigenous, and experiential ways of knowing.

6 Consider context. Data feminism asserts that data are not neutral or objective. They are the products of unequal social relations, and this context is essential for conducting accurate, ethical analysis.

7 Make labor visible. The work of data science, like all work in the world, is the work of many hands. Data feminism makes this labor visible so that it can be recognized and valued.

D'IGNAZIO AND KLEIN, 2020: 17–18.

As we will explore in the next sections, these principles are just as instructive for designers as they are for data scientists.

QUESTIONS FOR DESIGNERS: EVALUATING DATA

When using data to inform design work including developing strategy and pitching to clients, designers should consider the following:

- Where does the data come from that you are using? Who has collected it and what do you think their motivation is? Does this affect the findings and analysis?

- Was the data collected ethically with the consent of the people involved? Is data collection appropriate to context?

- In the case of quantitative data, can you access the original forms, questions or surveys? How does the survey design influence the data gathered?

- In the case of visual data, are gender norms being reproduced?

- Is there anyone who is missing? How do you think this will affect your design?

INTERVIEW: BRINDAALAKSHMI. K, THEMATIC LEAD, POINT OF VIEW, CHENNAI

Brindaalakshmi. K (they/them) is an intersectional queer-feminist researcher and advocacy professional presently leading the Queer & Digital vertical at Point of View, India. They are currently involved in a number of projects exploring the impact of big data on transgender people, and have published widely regarding the intersection of technology, identity, and human rights.

SB: Could you tell us a little bit about your background, and what inspired your interest in gender and big data?
BK: I'm a research and advocacy professional working at the intersection of gender, sexuality, human rights and technology. I'm also a queer and trans rights activist and peer supporter working with the LGBTIQA+ community in India. I have a Master of Science degree in Communications. I began my journalism career as a technology and business journalist in 2012. In India, technology as a field continues to be dominated by cis men. This is also the case with technology journalism. Over the course of my experience in journalism, I realized there was a dearth in the coverage of stories on the impact of technology on gender issues, particularly transgender persons. Similarly, the language of gender inclusion in the development context often tends to be limited to the exclusions faced by cis women. This has contributed to further erasure of the experiences of transgender persons.

In 2016, India demonetized its currency and that began my journey down the rabbit hole of understanding the impact of technology on trans lives. Those at the margins like gender and sexual minorities were severely affected by demonetization. Changing currency at any bank required valid proof of identity of one's self-identified gender and preferred name, which is not something that is easily available to transgender persons due to their gender identity. Lack of valid ID means exclusion from all data systems and erasure of the entire population group. With demonetization, there was a sudden push for digital money and transactions. Being at the margins, transgender persons do not have easy access to the internet, smart devices, literacy or digital literacy to use digital platforms. This has led to further exclusion.

Demonetization was only the beginning. The situation with demonetization along with the exclusions faced by vulnerable populations due to India's biometric-based digital ID, Aadhaar, meant that transgender persons without ID documents do not enter different data systems, data sets and consequently, big data. The lack of sufficient work around the issues faced by transgender persons has been my primary motivation to work on gender and big data. I'm currently working on the study, Gendering of Development Data in India: Post-Trans Act 2019 as part of the Our Voices, Our Future project supported by the Association for Progressive Communications. This study looks at the exclusions faced by transgender persons in India after the passing of the Transgender Persons (Protection of Rights) Act 2019 owing to the legal and policy understanding of being transgender and its translation into data systems. This study is built on the findings from my previous study, Gendering of Development Data in India: Beyond the Binary that I did for the Centre for Internet and Society, India as part of the Big Data for Development Network supported by IDRC, Canada. This study looked at the challenges faced by transgender persons while procuring valid ID documents and the consequent struggles with entering data systems and accessing different rights and services as valid individuals.

SB: You have written about some of the issues related to the data and privacy of transgender persons in India. Would you be able to briefly explain these issues and how they impact upon sustainable development and human rights?
BK: The Transgender Persons (Protection of Rights) Act 2019 in India describes a two-step process requiring a medical certificate to change one's gender within the binary gender of woman and man. This reiterates the need to fit within a certain gender binary and the understanding of gender. Without such certification, the application of the individual can be rejected. This is a violation of an individual's right to privacy. The new law also requires transgender persons to upload their documents on the National Transgender Portal which is quite hard to navigate even for those with English knowledge and digital literacy. The level of digital access and digital literacy is generally low among transgender persons. The ability to enter digital databases is greatly determined by an individual's ability to understand and use digital technologies. Introducing a digital process for a historically silenced population group requires more thought.

Further, individuals are often expected to also physically pass as the self-identified gender on the application form. Unless they do, their applications are often rejected by the government officials leaving no room for self-identification and self-expression, further violating individual privacy. This discrimination in the process has not been eliminated due to the introduction of a digital process. The digital process has further replicated these challenges and hardwired them into digital data systems. The current design is insufficient to support transgender persons with changing their name and gender to enter different datasets as valid human beings which directly affects their access to any human right.

Also, different private sector service providers like insurance companies do not sufficiently cover the needs of transgender persons. Different digital platforms like travel websites require valid ID documents to prove one's identity. They also require valid bank accounts to make payments. Given the lack of ID documents among transgender persons, it is difficult to prove their identity or to open a bank account. The datasets from these service providers also often omit transgender as a valid gender category on their application forms. Thus, transgender persons continue to be left behind as an entire population group due to their omission from large scale datasets. The lack of data is usually cited as the reason for lack of development programmes to address the challenges faced by transgender persons. However, evidently, the different data systems, both public and private data sets are exclusionary in their design and leave transgender persons behind. The lack of data in large scale sets leads to erasure of the entire population group with the introduction of new technologies like machine learning and artificial intelligence that depend on patterns from large scale (big) data sets. The insistence and dependency on data to make development decisions for a historically silenced community along with the introduction of new technologies is continuing the archaic colonial legacy of invalidating and criminalizing an entire population group due to their gender identity and thus denying them their basic human rights.

SB: Could you tell us about the work that you are involved in at Point of View?
BK: As an organization, Point of View envisions a world in which all genders are equal. Increasingly, the world is moving towards becoming phygital (physical + digital) world. This means that all genders need to be empowered to inhabit and shape digital spaces in a manner that suits their realities. This is exactly what I do in my role as the Thematic Lead: Building Capacity and Advocacy at Point of View. I design and lead programmes to empower women, girls, gender and sexual minorities, persons with disability and sex workers to inhabit and shape digital spaces. In July 2022, I led the CommsLab South Asia programme, a hybrid programme by Point of View supported by Astraea Lesbian Foundation for Justice. This hybrid programme had more than fifty participants from twenty-seven organizations attending from five hubs in India, Nepal and Bangladesh. With simultaneous translation from English to Bengali, Hindi, Kannada, Nepali and Tamil, the programme was designed to support LBT activists from the grassroots with skills to navigate in a changing world due to the COVID-19 pandemic. The sessions covered topics such as digital advocacy, digital security, art therapy, designing digital campaigns, a personal mental health toolkit, providing peer support, among others. At Point of View, I also work on advocacy efforts related to internet governance with due consideration for issues related to gender and sexuality. In October 2022, I co-led the GigX workshop on gender and internet governance as part of the Our Voices, Our Future project supported by Association for Progressive Communications (APC).

SB: Recently, there has been critique from activists, researchers and computer scientists regarding the capacity of AI and machine learning to reproduce and exacerbate gender inequalities. Do you think corporations are doing enough to try to address these issues?
BK: Corporations often tend to have diversity and inclusion policies for employees, celebrate diversity through brand campaigns, sometimes even provide options for their users/clients

to identify in their self-identified gender. These initiatives often tend to be image building exercises and do not translate into real inclusion. Corporations are motivated by profits. Transgender persons as a population group exist at the margins in most parts of the world. They do not have the purchasing power to be valuable customers of big corporations to further drive their profits. Therefore, it does not make business sense for corporations to design systems that cater to the needs of transgender persons as a population group. So, their data systems naturally do not safely collect gender data on transgender persons that can be used to design services relevant to their realities. The gender data collected by these companies often tend to be binarized force fitting every individual into the binary of man and woman. This tends to be the case even when corporations provide the option to self-identify one's gender. Consequently, their products are also designed based on this binary understanding and stereotype of how a woman or man is supposed to behave. Since transgender persons are not a valid target group, corporations do not put enough thought into designing a product that suits their realities. This also means that transgender persons can never really enter their data systems as a valid client and thus, corporations perpetuate a system that will continue to have insufficient data on transgender persons. Unless corporations change the intent and motivation behind their need to collect gender data, their efforts will always remain insufficient.

SB: What sort of design futures would you like to see materialize?
BK: Designers are living in an interesting time when they have the opportunity to design a world that can break down the concept of gender and move beyond the understanding of gender based on the physical body. I envision a world in which products are not gendered. Individuals can choose the product of their choice based on their preference and body type. This could play out both in physical and digital realities. For instance, a product like high-heeled shoes traditionally considered to be worn only by women should be available in all sizes. Footwear – high heels or formal shoes – shouldn't be the product of gender and should be available in all sizes, independent of how a person identifies themselves. By this I mean the need to go beyond a certain body to mean a certain gender. Thus, products need to be designed to cater to the individual rather than a collective based on a certain biology. Footwear is just one example in the physical world. The real change in design thinking will happen with change in the mindset of designers moving beyond a heteronormative imagination.

This extends to the digital world too. Gender data should be collected only when it is most essential, for instance in healthcare. Even with essential services like healthcare, individuals must have the option to self-describe themselves as a man or woman of trans experience or cis experience or in a different gender. Most importantly, individuals should have the choice and agency to not disclose their gender. Purpose limitation is the other side to exercising agency and choice. The scope for the use of the gender data collected should be clearly defined and limited. This is crucial in a digitized world that constantly seeks to link every piece of information to each other to map the person you are.

SB: If you could give one piece of advice to designers interested in gender justice, what would it be?
BK: Think about design centred on humanity going beyond the body, beyond the gender binary. People live with different identities. Designing based on humanity instead of the gender binary would help with envisioning a reality that holds space for all identities of all individuals living in all different kinds of bodies in all different colours and genders, with or without any disability.

Design and the gender data gap

So why is recognition of the link between data and power so important for designers? What have been the effects of the 'gender data gap' and a lack of representative datasets? In *Invisible Women: Exposing Data Bias in a World Designed for Men*, Caroline Criado Perez documents how men have always been the default in everyday life, the workplace, and the design of products and services. She writes, '[t]he one-size-fits-men approach to supposedly gender-neutral products is disadvantaging women' (Perez, 2019: 157). Perez highlights how the data informing the design, particularly ergonomics, frequently disregards women's experiences. For example, she details how large smartphones are more difficult to use for people with smaller hands, most commonly women. Women, she writes, find it more difficult to use large phones one-handed and this may be affecting their health (Perez, 2019: 161). At the time of writing, however, Perez notes how it was difficult to say conclusively if the size of smartphones was affecting women's health because 'women are significantly underrepresented as subjects, and the vast majority of studies did not sex-disaggregate their data – including those that did manage to adequately represent women' (2019: 161). This, she writes, is unfortunate because those studies that did separate data according to gender found phone size to have a greater impact on women's hand and arm function (Perez, 2019: 161).

A similar picture emerges in regard to assistive devices for fall detection. 'In the US, women make up 59% of people over the age of sixty-five and 76% of those living alone, suggesting a potential greater need for assistive technology like fall-detection devices' (Perez, 2019: 178). Perez writes that older women fall more often than men and when they do they are more likely to injure themselves due to factors such as greater incidence of osteoporosis. However, in analysis of fall-detection, device studies only half documented the sex of the participants, and almost no studies disaggregated data according to sex. Thus, despite a large quantity of studies of technologies for fall detection, 'there is little known about 'gender-specific risk factors' (Perez, 2019: 178).

It is not just the design of smartphones and fall technology where Perez documents a significant gender data gap. She observes in detail how car design and safety, speech recognition and translation software, domestic appliances, medical technologies, financial services and construction tools, all render the needs of women invisible. This lack of data, she argues, is 'making women poorer, sicker and in some cases, such as cars, it is killing them' at greater rates than men (Perez, 2019: 191). Thus, she calls for designers to 'design women in' (Perez, 2019: 191). As I noted in Chapter 1, there are issues with Perez's analysis in terms of its implications for future feminist design strategy. By focusing only on the visibility of women and reproducing the male/female binary, Perez falls into the trap of gender essentialism, and potentially reinforces racial and class-based inequalities. Who is this 'woman' we should design for and where are LGBTQI+ people in this equation? Despite these problems, however, there is no doubt that the gender data gap is real and even more acute for LGBTQI+ communities. As Perez demonstrates, this was an issue before the development of computers and the 'datafication' of society. It is even more of a problem now that machine learning and algorithms are using existing datasets to predict how we behave.

As Helen Armstrong documents in her book, *Big Data, Big Design,* artificial intelligence and machine learning have already transformed design. Simply put, machine learning enables a computer to analyse historical data and make predictions about new data. Thus, drawing on Aaron Shapiro, Armstrong argues that we are moving into a world of 'anticipatory design', a user experience 'pattern that predicts user behaviour and responds pre-emptively' (2021: 21). For example, 'a machine learning system driving a conferencing platform might notice that each time a child approaches your laptop during a virtual office meeting you turn off your camera' (Armstrong, 2021: 21). Thus, instead of waiting for you to turn the camera off, it might adjust the camera every time your child runs to the screen. Armstrong observes how anticipatory design is still in its infancy, a bit like a 'clumsy toddler' (2021: 23). Indeed, one can imagine the conferencing platform turning the camera off when you are speaking with family members who want to see your child, or when your cat jumps on your lap. What sort of children has the system been trained to recognize and are there certain adults who would be read as child-like. It is precisely because of the speedy development of AI and machine learning, and because of these types of glitches that designers need to understand and be involved from a user experience perspective. This is particularly important if we do not want to reproduce, or even amplify, gendered inequalities.

Recently, there has been an increase in the number of researchers who have observed how intersectional gender inequality is reproduced through technologies involving artificial intelligence and algorithmic systems. For example, in her first year at university Joy Buolamwini, a young African-American woman, observed how facial recognition technology only worked if she put on a white mask. This observation inspired the project, Gender Shades, in which Buolamwini and Timnit Gebru tested the accuracy of the AI powered facial recognition software from IBM, Microsoft and Face++. They observed that the datasets used by this software were overwhelmingly composed of lighter skinned male subjects. Buolamwini and Gebru conducted tests using the software with a range of people and found that darker-skinned women were up to forty-four times more likely to be misclassified than lighter-skinned males. 'Image classifiers performed best for lighter individuals and males overall' (Buolamwini and Gebru: 2018: 12).

Misclassification is even more acute in transgender and non-binary individuals. In their study of gender classification in commercial facial analysis services, Morgan Scheuerman, Jacob Paul and Jed Brubaker (2019) found that 'trans men were wrongly identified as women up to 38% of the time' and those who identified as 'agender, genderqueer or nonbinary were misgendered 100% of the time' (Marshall, 2019: para 9).

To address algorithmic inequality Buolamwini went on to found the Algorithmic Justice League, a movement focused on 'equitable and accountable AI' and recently produced the documentary, *Coded Bias*. *Coded Bias* explores how algorithms reproduce inequality drawing upon the personal stories of those who have been directly affected. For example, the film documents how a Black man was arrested in his home after his face was incorrectly matched to security camera footage. While technology companies have started to make their datasets more representative of a range of subjects, this can involve facial data harvesting without consent (D'Ignazio and Klein, 2020: 31–2). Thus '[b]etter detection of faces of color cannot be characterized as an unqualified good' because it is often enlisted in the service of 'increased oppression, greater surveillance, and targeted violence' (D'Ignazio and Klein, 2020: 32).

In the book *Design Justice*, Sasha Costanza-Chock documents how Facebook's 'real-name' policy is illustrative of how the matrix of domination is designed into sociotechnical systems. Costanza-Chock observes how, for years, Native Americans, African Americans and LGBTQI+ people were more likely to have their Facebook accounts flagged and suspended for not using 'real-names' (2020: 48). She writes, 'algorithms that are used to flag likely "fake" names were trained on "real name" datasets that overrepresent European names' (Costanza-Chock, 2020: 48–9). While this may be considered a small inconvenience by some, this microaggression 'symbolically and materially invalidates the legitimacy of the person's identity' (Costanza-Chock, 2020: 49) reproducing the inequalities of white supremacy, settler colonialism and heteropatriarchy.

Costanza-Chock observes how there was significant push back, and Facebook subsequently modified its platform. In regard to gender, Facebook instituted a new set of options for users to display gender pronouns, and the company claims it has adjusted its algorithm to remove its Eurocentric bias. However, Facebook's backend still codes users as male or female, and no systematic study has verified whether the situation has improved for people with non-European names (Costanza-Chock, 2020: 49). Nevertheless, as Costanza-Chock suggests, this example is evidence of how platforms and algorithms can be redesigned with users to 'encode alternative value systems' (2020: 50). To move further towards algorithmic justice, Costanza-Chock argues that 'fair' algorithms require 'redistributive action' to be built into them 'to undo the legacy of hundreds of years of discrimination and oppression' (2020: 63). These efforts must be intersectional, rather than only along a single axis. Thus, as designers, we must ask the question 'what would algorithmic reparations look like', what distribution of benefits do we believe is just' (Costanza-Chock, 2020: 65)?

Currently, however, as Armstrong argues, the culture of the tech industry is structured around 'rapid optimisation and deployment' (2021: 13). Rather than responsive to the needs of people and larger societal issues, applications of machine learning tend to driven by data availability and visions of the next 'new' thing. Thus, Armstrong argues that 'the responsibility of the designer to protect user interest and value has never been so imperative' (2021: 13). To address inequalities, we need to 'cultivate critical design practice that advocate for humans', their environments and their non-human counterparts (Armstrong, 2021: 31). The challenge for designers is to try to understand and design with machine learning algorithms that are both invisible and intangible. To do this, designers do not necessarily need to learn to code, but have to grasp the limits and the capabilities of the technology in the emerging predictive world.

Feminist counter-data and queering AI

Just as there have been an increasing number of researchers, computer scientists and designers questioning the ways that the datafication of society reproduces inequality in recent years, there has also been growth in activists and community groups challenging the status quo through practice. For example, since 2016 María Salguero, who goes by the name of Princesa, has been collecting data about femicide in Mexico. This counter-data initiative logs the gender-related killings of women and girls and places them on an interactive Google map. Despite media attention, human rights rulings and a specially commissioned report in 2019, femicides and 'transfemicides' in Mexico have continued to increase. While the crime of femicide was recognized in law, no specific policies were put in place to ensure adequate data collection. Public bodies repeatedly defer responsibility, fail to investigate and blame victims. For example, when the Mexican student Lesvy Osorio was killed in 2017, the 'Public Prosecutor's Office of Mexico City shared on social media that the victim was an alcoholic and drug user who had been living out of wedlock with her boyfriend' (D'Ignazio and Klein, 2020: 36). Thus, to address misrepresentation such as this, Salguero attaches as much detail as she can to every femicide death added to her map. Using media reports and crowdsourced contributions, she works to draw data together and to put it in the public eye. She aims to make victims visible to highlight the problem, to find patterns and to promote prevention.

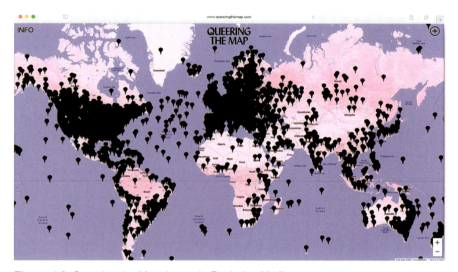

Figure 4.3 Queering the Map. Lucas LaRochelle, 2017.

Similarly, Lucas LaRochelle, created 'Queering the Map' to increase the visibility of diverse queer experiences of space beyond the typical bars, bookstores and bathhouses (fig. 4.3). The map is community generated allowing people to pin their experiences of queer life, ranging from 'collective action to stories of coming out, encounters with violence, to moments of rapturous love' (LaRochelle, 2019).

Posts by contributors are not curated, although they are moderated for hate, spam and unsafe content. LaRochelle states that the resulting map is 'fundamentally messy, contradictory and confusing' and that is part of its aim in terms of highlighting queer space making as ever changing and rooted in action. 'Queering the Map' highlights that 'we cannot *be* queer in a fixed sense, but rather that we are *doing* queer through acts of resistance' (LaRochelle, 2019). Thus, the project disrupts normative representations and the labelling of specific people and places as queer.

KEY CONCEPT: QUEERING

'To undertake "queering" is to deploy queer as a verb' which means 'to challenge and resist expectations or norms' (McCann and Monaghan, 2020: 3). As Sara Ahmed (2006) has argued, heterosexuality as a 'compulsory orientation' produces more than just sexuality. It reproduces gender norms, whiteness, and notions of family, among other normative discourses. Due to this intersectionality, to queer something 'disturbs the order of things' (Ahmed, 2006: 565). 'Sexual disorientation slides quickly in social disorientation, as a disorientation in how things are arranged' (Ahmed, 2006: 565). Thus, queering is 'an ongoing application of disruption' that 'may involve mischief and clowning as much as serious critique' (Light, 2011: 432). To queer design practice then, as Ann Light argues, is not an 'analysis to inform design', but a 'hands-on method' that challenges what passes as 'normal' and opens up space for other values and lifestyles emerge.

In counter-data projects public visibility is not always desirable, however. For example, the Sovereign Bodies Institute (SBI) is committed to building on 'indigenous traditions of data gathering and knowledge transfer to create, disseminate, and put into action research on gender and sexual violence against Indigenous people' (SBI website, 2022). One manifestation of this is the MMIWG2 database which 'cares for' cases of missing and murdered indigenous women, girls and two spirit people from 1900 to the present. The database is held by the SBI and is accessible to community groups, activists and researchers by request. It is not publicly available because the SBI is deeply committed to 'upholding the sacredness of the data' and want to ensure that anyone with access works with the data in a way that is consistent with indigenous values (SBI website, 2022). In addition to their commitment to data gathering and analysis, the SBI aims to 'transform data to action to protect and heal their peoples' (SBI website, 2022).

Decentralized technologies such as blockchain and distributed database protocols are making it easier for community groups to collect, preserve, share and control data without involving big Tech companies. For example, Āhau.io in Aotearoa is an indigenous community data platform that allows whānau, hapū and iwi (families, subtribes and tribes) to manage important ancestral information in secure whānau managed databases and servers. Community initiatives to build data are part of Sarah Williams's (2020) approach to using data for public good. She writes 'building data together strengthens communities around shared interests' (Williams, 2020: xv). Building data is not always necessary, however, and in many cases data may readily exist. Williams's calls on us to hack and share data through data visualization, a topic we return to below.

Feminist Internet, a collective made up of designers, artists, journalists, poets, performers and researchers, also explore the potential of new technologies to challenge heteropatriarchy. Dedicated to making the internet a more feminist space, they argue that 'there is no feminism, only possible feminisms', and 'there is no internet, only possible internets' (Feminist Internet, 2022). The aims of the collective are further defined in their eight-point manifesto. The first point states that if *Feminist Internet* are successful in making the internet a space that causes no harm, the group believe 'they will have erased the need for feminism' (Wikipedia, 2022). Other points include focusing on the eradication of violence; working to cooperate rather than compete; exploring alternatives to consumer culture; striving to educate and give equal access to information; and recoding gender by bringing a variety of experiences to the surface (Wikipedia, 2022a).

Since its inception in 2017, Feminist Internet have produced a number of projects that objectify these values. For example, F'XA is an AI-powered chatbot that teaches people about AI bias and makes sure that chatbots do not knowingly or unknowingly reproduce gender inequality (fig. 4.4). Interactions with the chatbot begin with it offering definitions of AI. The chatbot tells the user that it is not storing any data from the conversation and the reasons why this is important. It goes on to describe the 'Personal Intelligence Standards' created by Feminist Internet. For example, these standards informed design decisions such as 'never using "I" so that people are aware that they are not talking to a person; using definitions and understandings of AI from people of different races and genders; and using a range of skin tones in emojis 'to acknowledge its voice as something multiplicitous' (Comuzi, 2022).

Figure 4.4 F'XA: Feminist Guide to AI Bias. Feminist Internet, 2019.

Would you like me to remember
your name and pronouns?

Figure 4.5 Queering Voice AI:SYB. Feminist Internet, 2021.

More recently, Feminist Internet created SYB, a voice interface that promotes queer joy and connects users to queer and trans media (fig. 4.5). The project emerged from a one-week course at the University of the Art London's Creative Computing Institute called Queering Voice AI. Run by Andrew Mallinson and Cami Rincon, the course brought together a team of mainly trans and non-binary people to prototype a voice interface designed with their community in mind. During initial discussions the team decided to focus on centring and creating 'queer joy' to disrupt dominant media discourse which often highlights the trauma of trans and non-binary experience. Based on their preferences, SYB recommends queer and trans media to its users.

The prototype was designed using Trans Competent Requirements for Voice AI (Rincon, Keyes and Cath, 2021). These requirements include trans specific privacy requirements; trans specific purpose; representative and gender affirming personas created by trans and non-binary people. For example, users can personalize SYB choosing a range of voices and set a gender. SYB doesn't need a gender, however, and setting one will not change the personality of the interface. The project team were keen to include a multitude of possibilities in order to move beyond problematic associations of women and their voices with personal assistants (Hester, 2016). Rather than dehumanizing AI and trying to make the interface more obviously a machine, the team decided to humanize SYB. Trans and non-binary people are often dehumanized in the media – so queering entails more humanizing (Mallinson, 2021). Users also have autonomy over their data, so they can ask for their data to be deleted or for SYB to remember their preferences. As Mallison states, SYB is queered at every level. Thus, rather than

QUESTIONS FOR DESIGNERS: QUEERING EMERGING TECHNOLOGY

Emerging technologies are often prototyped and created at a rapid pace. Designers involved in these processes should consider:

- Who is the typical imagined user of the technology? How does this influence design decisions?

- How can those people often excluded from the development of new technologies (such as non-binary people, lesbians and older women) be centred in your design?

- What are the typical design strategies and aesthetics used to address these users? Can you open up a space for other values and experiences through your design?

- Can you build multiple voices and experiences among these groups into the experience?

- Can you ensure that people have autonomy over their own data and their responses are built into UX/UI?

assimilating and fixing the problems that big tech has created, Feminist Internet take them into their own hands and build and purpose them differently.

F'XA and SYB are examples of good practice that can be used as inspiration by designers interested in gender justice. F'XA educates and communicates the limitations of machine learning. SYB includes diverse users in the development and deployment of AI. Both projects are examples of designers and computer programmers giving people agency as users in the design process. As Armstrong argues, 'designers need to help hand control of data back to people' (2021: 122). 'We can let machine learning prey on those our society already victimises, or we can use the technology as a mechanism for equity and justice' (Armstrong, 2021: 126).

Visualizing inequality

The responsibility that we have as designers does not just apply to data practices and new technologies such as artificial intelligence and machine learning. The visualization of data also comes with its own ethics. Andy Kirk defines data

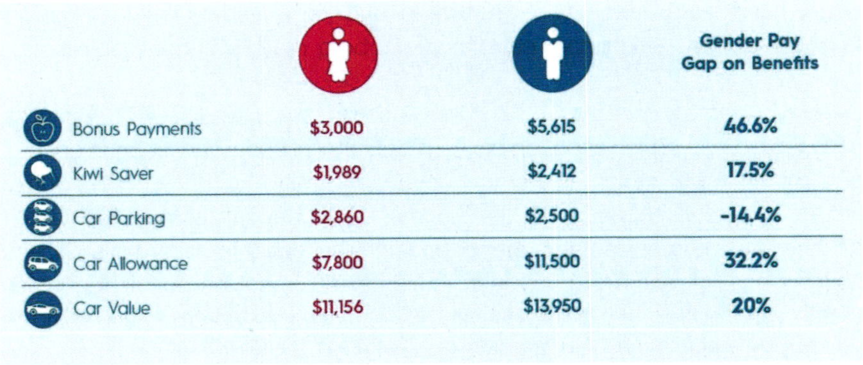

			Gender Pay Gap on Benefits
Bonus Payments	$3,000	$5,615	46.6%
Kiwi Saver	$1,989	$2,412	17.5%
Car Parking	$2,860	$2,500	-14.4%
Car Allowance	$7,800	$11,500	32.2%
Car Value	$11,156	$13,950	20%

Figure 4.6 Disparities in Bonuses and Benefits' (2021) Stuff, Pay Equity Analysis: Strategic Pay.

visualization as 'the representation and presentation of data to facilitate understanding' (2019: 19). This definition emphasizes the key role of designers in selecting the form and aesthetics of visualization.

Kirk advises adhering to 'three principles of good visualization' informed by Dieter Rams's general principles of good design, which are 'good data visualization is trustworthy'; accessible, and elegant (Kirk, 2019: 19). Accessibility is clearly an essential part of data visualization. The strength of information design is that compared to text, it offers the ability to visualize complex data so that the user can grasp a message at first glance.

At the same time, however, accessibility can mean that familiar tropes are reproduced. In terms of gender, this means that data visualizations often include using pink for women and blue for men; isotypes with women in dresses and men in trousers; and reproduction of the gender binary. While some data visualizations using pink for women and blue for men continue to surface (e.g. fig. 4.6), this seems to be changing. For example, most press in the UK and US have their own colour systems. *The Telegraph* newspaper in the UK chose purple and green to represent men and women when visualizing the gender pay gap, referencing the colours of the suffrage movement.

However, the selection of two colours continues to reproduce gender binaries. In 2020, Alison Booth analysed forty articles published by *The New York Times* and *The Wall Street Journal* that included data analysis or visualizations of gender-based data. '[O]nly five – or 12.5% – included terms or specific data that accounted for people who identify as neither female nor male' (Booth, 2021). Booth notes that stories that acknowledged nonbinary identities were typically focused on the LGBTQI+ community, profile pieces or those found in the lifestyle sections. Thus, the majority of data visualizations

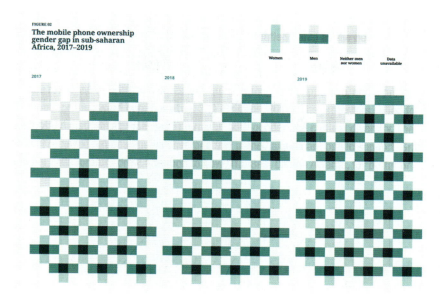

Figure 4.7 Gender Equality Creativity Platform. Gates Foundation/Pentagram, 2021. Courtesy of the Gates Foundation.

reflect and reinforce the lack of data regarding those who fall outside gender binaries.

The representation of 'missing data' was central to the data visualization system created by Pentagram to communicate gender inequality for the Bill and Melinda Gates foundation. The Gender Equality Creative Platform designed by a team led by Giorgia Lupi uses + and = motifs to 'explicitly call out missing data as a type of data point itself' (Pentagram, 2022). The graphic system using symbols to account for those who are 'neither men nor women' and those for whom there is 'no data available' (fig. 4.7). Guidelines were produced for partners worldwide to be able to use the system. While the classification of 'neither men nor women' is not ideal because it marks non-binary people as 'other', the colour palette and graphics demonstrate that other types of visualizations are possible when representing and presenting gender data. As the description of the project suggests, like much of Lupi's work 'the project utilises the principles of "data humanism" – using data to uncover the human stories behind the numbers and statistics, and to challenge the idea that data as a visual language must be impersonal and intimidating' (Pentagram, 2022).

Lupi first defined data humanism in her manifesto in 2017. She observed how big data had become an 'intrinsic and iconic feature of our present' and recognized the boom in graphic visualization that had taken place. Lupi observes, however, how 'cool infographics' were unable to deal with the complexities of big data, and 'we were left with gigabytes of unreadable 3D pie charts and cheap translucent user interfaces' (Lupi, 2017: para 4). She names this 'peak infographics' and argues for a 'second wave of more thoughtful and meaningful visualisation' (Lupi, 2017: para 8). Data humanism, for Lupi, is this second wave. She writes '[t]he more ubiquitous data becomes, the more we need to experiment with how to make it unique, contextual, intimate' (Lupi, 2017: para 12). This involves connecting numbers to knowledge, behaviour and people by changing graphic visualization practices. The first point in Lupi's manifesto calls upon designers to embrace complexity. She suggests that whenever the goal of data visualization is to 'open people's eyes to new knowledge' then complexity is inevitable (Lupi, 2017: para 17). For example, in data visualizations produced for the Italian newspaper, *Corriere della Sera*, Lupi drew from multiple data sources (quantitative and qualitative) and combined them in one single elaborate visual narrative. This allowed the viewer to 'jump-in', follow their interest, and get 'lost exploring individual elements, minor tales and large trends' (Lupi, 2017: para 18). Complex data visualizations, Lupi writes, encourage slowness and reflections on data that are often missing from contemporary media.

The second point in Lupi's data humanism manifesto is to 'move beyond standards'. This means avoiding digital data tools that offer pre-packaged universal solutions. She writes, blindly throwing technology at the problem often leads to results that are 'not only practically useless but also deeply wrong' (Lupi, 2017: para 21). Lupi's solution is to draw data visualizations first to understand what is contained in the numbers and their structure. Drawing is not limited to an existing set of visual representations of data and by moving away from the computer, designers can draw on hundreds of years of 'visual information encoding' (Lupi, 2017: para 26). Drawing also is more personal and indicative of its maker. This relates to the third point in Lupi's manifesto which is to always 'sneak context in'. She argues that we need to 'reclaim a personal approach to how data is captured, analysed and displayed' emphasizing that subjectivity and context play a big part in its creation and interpretation (Lupi, 2017: para 29).

To exemplify this approach, Lupi and Stephanie Posavec undertook a project to express meaningful and intimate data narratives. In *Dear Data*, they produced hand-drawn visualizations of their everyday lives and sent them to each other across the Atlantic every Sunday for one year (fig. 4.8). Over time, they gained a complex understanding of each other's experiences through the data but also through the visualizations that added a 'human touch to the world of computing and algorithms, using drawing instead of coding as our form of expression' (Lupi, 2017: para 31). The project also exemplifies the final point in Lupi's manifesto that 'data is not perfect'. Data are created by humans, and thus should embrace imperfection and approximation to connect with ourselves and others at a

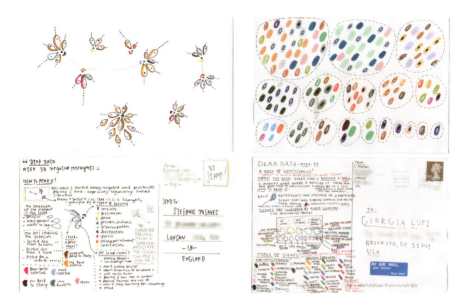

Figure 4.8 *Dear Data*. Giorgia Lupi and Stefanie Posavec, 2016.

deeper level. It is for this reason that data humanism allows for and communicates emotion and multi-sensory experience.

While Lupi does not publicly define her work as feminist, her practice aligns with feminist data visualization principles outlined by D'Ignazio and Klein (2017). Rather than claim to reflect the objectivity and neutrality of data, data humanism emphasizes how data is always a product of the situated knowledge of the designer, as well as from specific people and contexts. The focus on complexity compliments a non-binary approach to data visualization that is premised on multiplicity. The emphasis on the human emotional experience that comes across in *Dear Data*, also reflects the recognition of embodied and affective experiences in feminist theory. This is not only communicated by the aesthetics of the visualization, but the narrative about the data and instructions on how to read it. As Miriam Kienle argues the 'importance of incomplete, imperfect and non-neutral data' holds regardless of its mode of collection and style of representation (2019: 152). Thus, despite their aesthetic preferences, the majority of designers could adopt a feminist approach to data visualization if they wanted to.

Indeed, as D'Ignazio and Klein suggest, if feminist approaches to data visualization recognize that emotion and sensory experience are equal to more rational ways of experiencing the world, then perhaps we should think about 'tactile, experiential and social ways of accessing data visualisation' (D'Ignazio and Klein, 2017: 3). This could result in a variety of expressions including data

Figure 4.9 'Air Transformed: Better with Data Society Commission'. Stefanie Posavec and Miriam Quick, 2019.

murals, sculptures, walks, quilts and installations. For example, Stephanie Posavec has created visualizations that are wearable (fig. 4.9), danceable and playable (fig. 4.10). 'Touching Air', for instance, comprises necklaces created using open air quality data to inspire discussion about the effect of pollution on the body; and 'Open Data Playground' gives people the opportunity to physically play with open data sets and interpret the data as they see fit.

Participatory data visualization can also involve users in collecting and visualizing their own data. For example, the Moodbank (2014), a pop-up bank and collaborative art and design project, invited the public to name, draw and deposit their mood. The project began at a time when corporations, such as banks, were starting to implement digital tools to track mood. Thus, as a counter-data project, the Moodbank enabled visitors to take ownership of their own data. Over 1,000 mood deposits were made resulting in a rich and complex representation of collective emotions over time. Visitors remarked on the cathartic effect of depositing their mood, having it recognized as equal with other emotions and of observing similar feelings in others (Amery, 2022).

As D'Ignazio and Klein argue, feminist approaches to data visualization should 'acknowledge the user as a source of knowledge in the design as well as the reception of any visual interface' (2017: 3). Thus, designers wanting to empower

Figure 4.10 'Open Data Playground'. Web We Want Festival. Stefanie Posavec, 2015.

communities should consider whether people can be included in the visualization of data as well as its collection and analysis.

QUESTIONS FOR DESIGNERS: FEMINIST DATA VISUALIZATION

When embarking on a data visualization project designers should consider:

- Can you include more gender categories in your visualization?
- Is it possible to highlight missing data in your design?
- What colours and graphics have you used? Do they reproduce gender norms?
- Can communicate your own situated knowledge, either through visualization or text?
- Can you highlight the emotional or sensory experience of the data?
- Can you include communities in data collection, visualization and analysis?

CASE STUDY: VISUALIZING GENDER-BASED VIOLENCE IN NEPAL, BARBARA GROSSMAN-THOMPSON, USA, AND CHARLOTTA SALMI, UK

Dr Barbara Grossman-Thompson is an Associate Professor of International Studies at California State University. Grossman-Thompson is originally from San Diego and works in the field of comparative sociology. Her research focuses on gendered organization of labour in South Asia with an emphasis on Nepal. It asks how Nepali women articulate and understand their identities as female wage-labourers in the context of globalization.

Dr Charlotta Salmi is a Senior Lecturer in Postcolonial and Global Literature at Queen Mary, University of London. Salmi comes from Finland and grew up in a bilingual Swedish and Finnish speaking family. She moved to the UK to study. Salmi's work focuses on how different forms of graphic storytelling – comics, graphic novels, and street art – are used by and represent social movements.

Gender based violence is a global problem. In Nepal '25% of women reportedly experience intimate partner violence or sexual violence', thus addressing 'violence against women and girls is a sustainable development priority' (Salmi, n.d.). In recent years, street art in Nepal has become a popular platform to promote women's rights and raise awareness about gender equality. During fieldwork in the cities of Kathmandu and Pokara, Barbara Grossman-Thompson and Charlotta Salmi studied how four types of violence (domestic abuse, trafficking, street harassment, menstruation-based discrimination) were portrayed in comics, zines, murals, graffiti and street art. They found that that it was mostly developmental and humanitarian organizations that were using street art to disseminate messages to the public. Indeed, a number of well-known public murals have been commissioned by international organizations and produced by foreign artists. For example, a mural designed and created by the Minneapolis-based street artist, Pink Riches, features a woman in chains.

To explore the use of street art as an awareness-raising tool further, Grossman-Thompson and Salmi conducted interviews and focus groups with NGOs, activists and artists. They found that a troubling aspect of how street-art was being used was that the very people most at risk from gender-based violence had limited involvement in the making process including messaging, planning, design and creation. Grossman-Thompson and Salmi asked, how, if at all, the street art that had been produced spoke to the different women and girls who were being called upon to condemn violence and recognize their rights. They set about trying to create more culturally sensitive and inclusive practices.

Grossman-Thompson and Salmi tackled this by implementing two creative initiatives: an open-access digital archive of graphic representations of gender-based violence; and a series of graphic art workshops for 600 girls (aged between twelve and seventeen). The project aimed to empower women and girls and to reduce gender-based violence by improving understanding of how street art challenges or reproduces assumptions about violence; facilitating knowledge exchange between academics, government agencies, arts collectives and NGOs about representational practice; building capacity among local NGOs working on gender-based violence; and encouraging girls to participate in the creative production of anti-gender-based violence materials (Salmi, n.d.).

Pokara student workshops

As part of this project, Grossman-Thompson and Salmi ran workshops in two schools in Pokara, a city in the centre of Nepal. Working with Sattya Media Arts Collective and Empowering Women Nepal, they ran workshops over eight days at two schools working with girls aged between fourteen and seventeen years old. The workshops began by engaging the girls in discussions of existing street art. Drawing on their experience running the Girls Leadership Program in Pokara, Empowering Women Nepal ran sessions focused on gender-based violence that were culturally appropriate and sensitive to local issues. The students then learnt about graphic design and street art techniques from Sattya Media Arts Collective. They went on to plan, design and create their own murals (fig. 4.11). The student workshops illustrated a 'bottom-up' approach to public messaging rather than a 'top-down' model that excludes local communities. They enabled knowledge exchange between all involved, empowered the girls and, hopefully, will go some way to reducing incidents of gender-based violence.

Figure 4.11 Graphic Mural. Visualising Gender-Based Violence in Nepal, 2019. Courtesy of Barbara Grossman-Thompson and Charlotta Salmi.

QUEERING ALGORITHMS

Experiment with ways in which you might be able to challenge, resist and disrupt algorithms. Write notes below. Use these experiments to reflect on how machine learning algorithms code bias.

One example of disrupting algorithms is the way in which the makeup, accessories and other props used in drag can resist facial recognition technologies designed to predict age, gender, mood, and identity (#DRAGVSAI, 2022).

SURVEILLANCE

SOCIAL MEDIA

REAL-TIME CHAT BOTS

© Dr Sarah Elsie Baker

CHAPTER FOUR ACTIVITY

GENDERED LIFE DATA DRAWING

1. CHOOSE ONE OF THE FOLLOWING MAIN QUESTIONS:

   a. How much of the housework do I do compared to people I live with?

   b. How often do I feel restricted by gender norms?

   c. How often do I apologise?

   d. How many gendered products have I seen?

2. THINK OF ADDITIONAL QUESTIONS TO HELP GIVE DETAIL AND CONTEXT TO YOUR MAIN QUESTION. E.g. in respect to 'c. How often do I apologise?' you could consider why you are apologizing, whether it is necessary and who it is to.

   a.

   b. _____

   c. _____

3. GATHER THE DATA OVER A PERIOD OF TIME: record using paper or a phone in real time. Try to include details

4. SPEND TIME WITH THE DATA: organize and categorise. Look for patterns, categories and anomalies.

6. GET VISUALLY INSPIRED: research different ways of representing data. Think about variety of colour, symbol and shape. Explore visual references from nature, science and art.

5. DECIDE WHAT IS THE MAIN STORY AND HOW YOU WILL REPRESENT THE DATA: do you want to represent the data chronologically, geographically or per importance of categories, for example.

7. SKETCH AND DRAFT IDEAS: experiment with different ways of representing the data.

8. DRAW THE FINAL PICTURE AND LEGEND.

Inspired by the approach to data collection in Observe, Collect, Draw (Posavec and Lupi, 2018)

5
FEMINIST DESIGN FUTURES

Introduction: design and the future

Design practice is frequently concerned with the future, whether it involves a person making a temporary clothesline to be used two minutes from now, or a professional designer creating an interface for the next cutting-edge technological innovation. An imagined future in the first case might involve a strong gust of wind, or in the second case a competing technology about to be launched onto the market. Uniting all cases, however, is the fact that design involves taking inspiration from the past and the present, while pre-empting what is yet to come. As Anne Balsamo summarizes, '[d]esigners work the scene of technological emergence: they hack the present to create the conditions of the future' (2010:7). Designers and design scholars have always understood there was a strong connection between design, newness, and futurity (Yelavich and Adams, 2014: 12). In the history of professional practice, design has often been seen as a synonym for innovation, used to make products stand out in the marketplace and to drive sales revenue. Of course, nothing is unique, and while the future offers the possibility of the different world, it is far from free from constraint.

Corporations and governments are heavily invested in foreseeing and creating the future. At present, it is frequently new technological developments that are said to be influencing our current experience and the future that is yet to come. For example, references to the 'fourth industrial revolution' saturate the language of industry experts, government officials, and academics. The first industrial revolution in the late eighteenth century is said to be characterized by steam power and the mechanization of craft and agricultural practices; the second at the end of the nineteenth century by the invention of the automobile and the use of electricity, gas and oil; the third industrial revolution in the 1980s is marked by the digital revolution and rise of the internet; and the fourth in the twenty-first century associated with the development of artificial intelligence, virtual reality, genetic editing and the internet of things. It is debated whether we are truly experiencing a 'fourth' industrial revolution, and whether a turn to the 'fifth' revolution is around the corner, characterized by a drive to connect frontier technologies to purpose and inclusivity (Van Erden, 2020). Apart from this recent turn to consider inclusion, however, the history of successive industrial revolutions frequently privileges technology over social and cultural factors and perpetuates Western-centric narratives that exclude the role of women.

While the validity of the rhetoric of industrial revolutions that leaders are so keen on can be challenged, corporate visions influence both the design of worlds and our perceptions of future possibility. For example, since 2009 Microsoft has produced 'Productivity Future Visions' that use video to represent what life will look like in the near future. Microsoft's software and hardware, screens, and interfaces, are projected into a future that is supposedly 'neutral' and shared by all. Yet, until recently, people in these visions have tended to white, Western, young and middle-class. Environments are full of glass touch screens, completed to-do lists and clean surfaces. Technologies are depicted as enabling, as increasing our ability to seamlessly communicate with one another, to work efficiently, and to control nature.

The telling of this story of a clinical future is not innocent. As forms of promotion, the videos work to embed potential technologies in the minds of consumers. They also disassociate new technologies from inequality and negative environmental consequences, as well as highlighting their emancipatory potential. As has been documented throughout the book, and will be explored further in the next chapter, the realities of how new technologies impact our everyday lives tends to very different from envisioned futures. Most future worlds reinforce the binary divisions that uphold systems of privilege and oppression, and their design is complicit in 'defuturing' (Fry, 2020). Tony Fry (2020) uses the term 'defuturing' to describe how design has been, and still is, complicit in the environmental crisis which makes the future for human beings uncertain. Even 'green' or 'sustainable' design practices tend to assume that technology can simply be developed or modified to address sustainability, rather than reconsidering the destructive nature of current systems. Future visions, such as those produced by Microsoft, reproduce dominant narratives of progress and productivity, and these ideas have changed little since the 1950s.

Speculative design, the focus of this chapter, uses design approaches to ask if another future is possible. It is a design practice that produces visions of alternative presents and possible futures. Informed by critical theory, speculative projects often ask questions about the role of new technologies in our everyday lives and the conditions of contemporary consumer culture. Yet, until recently, there has been little engagement with gender in this body of work. This chapter begins by defining speculative design and exploring its history. It outlines some of the key techniques used in speculative design practice. This introduction to the field is important because it considers why there has been an absence of references to social inequality by speculative designers, and because it outlines techniques that could be adopted by those wanting to redesign gender.

Feminism has 'always addressed the question of the future, of how to ensure the future differs from the past' (Grosz, 2005: 155), and the chapter documents alternative futures imagined by science fiction writers. These examples work as potential inspiration both in terms of their subject matter and their approach to futuring. The chapter draws on feminist theory to interrogate the understandings of time used in speculative design. By analysing examples of speculative design projects that explore gender, the chapter highlights the importance of public participation, contextual relevance and anachronic methods (taking things out of time).

Speculative futures and design fictions

Speculative design emerged as a distinct design practice in the late 1990s in the UK and is most notably associated with Anthony Dunne and Fiona Raby. Sitting under the umbrella of critical design, speculative design proposals challenge 'narrow assumptions, preconceptions, and givens about the role products play in everyday life' (Dunne and Raby, 2013: 34). Since the late 1990s, speculative design has grown in scope and popularity, and Dunne and Raby have continued to define its characteristics. In their book, *Speculative Everything*, Dunne and Raby begin by returning to the A/B Manifesto, devised in 2009, distinguishing between critical design (concerned with citizens, design for debate, and provocation) and affirmative design (focused on consumers, design for production, and innovation). Critical design, Dunne and Raby write, is 'critical thought translated into materiality' (2013: 35) and is particularly useful in the current climate because it 'can shift the discussion from one of the abstract generalities separated from our lives to tangible examples grounded in our experiences as members of a consumer society' (2013: 51).

Dunne and Raby aim to decouple design from the marketplace and use the language of design to pose questions, entertain and provoke. For example, in *Is This Your Future?* they created a range of hypothetical products to explore the 'ethical, cultural and social impact of different energy futures' (Dunne and Raby, 2004) (fig. 5.1 and 5.2). Aimed at children aged between seven and fourteen, Dunne and Raby produced a range of scenarios in an attempt to get the audience to consider 'a set of values driven by social and technological changes – value fictions rather than science fictions' (Dunne and Raby, 2004). The scenarios included a domestic hydrogen production programme using child labour represented by family uniforms featuring corporate logos, biofuel created from human excrement objectified by poo party bags and a lunch box enabling children to take their poo home with them, and meat-based microbial fuel cells exemplified by a radio powered by a teddy bear blood bag. The scenarios are based on emergent technologies and ask the audience to consider what would happen if these forms of energy production became a reality in the near future.

While almost fifteen years old, *Is This Your Future?* is a pertinent illustration of the defining features of speculative design. It brings new technological and scientific themes into the everyday and asks us to consider how we might deal with social, cultural and environmental challenges. Through the creation of prototypes, it explores the possibilities of new technologies and how the design decisions we make influence societies of the future. By bringing alternative scenarios into existence, speculative designers draw our attention to the politics of design and the possibilities of alternative ways of living. As Matt Malpas suggests, '[r]ather than presenting utopic or dystopic visions, speculative design poses challenging statements that attempt to explore the ethical and societal implications of new science and the role product and industrial design plays in delivering this new science' (2012: 187). Speculative projects tend to have a different aesthetic from the techno-utopias of Silicon Valley for example, preferring to situate material objects in ordinary and domestic contexts and/or situating new technologies alongside those that already exist. Despite this, speculative design has tended to draw on the language of contemporary industrial design and has been criticized for reproducing the tropes of techno-scientific consumer culture that it attempts to critique.

In the case of *Is This Your Future?* the audience sees fictional products placed within contexts espousing traditional gender norms and family forms. For example, in the biofuel created from human waste scenario the audience sees a small girl receiving a poo party bag at a pink themed party. In the domestic hydrogen production scenario, a heterosexual couple wave goodbye to their daughter wearing a dress adorned with a corporate logo. While it is likely that these symbols were used to anchor the scenarios in the everyday experiences of children, they also reproduce gender stereotypes and limit the possibilities of what alternative futures might look like. Below we return to consider both the way that speculative design reproduces inequality, and the untapped potential for speculative projects to propose feminist futures.

While speculative scenarios sometimes have reproduced problematic norms, the approach to the future that speculative designers take tends to differ from that of technology companies. As Dunne and Raby note, technology companies are usually 'concerned with predicting or forecasting the future, sometimes it is about new trends and identifying weak signals that can be extrapolated to into the near future, but it is always about trying to pin the future down' (2013: 2). They go on to state that they are not interested in prediction but aim to open up debate about what the future could be. They explain their approach using the futures cone.

KEY CONCEPT: THE FUTURES CONE

The futures cone (fig. 5.1) is a diagram that represents a taxonomy of temporality, a way of classifying thinking about the future. It was originally used in future studies and was based on the categorizations of possible, probable and preferable futures. The diagram itself was first found in the work of Charles Taylor (1988) and was proposed as a method for US government agencies to strategically plan for future scenarios. Since then, it has been increasingly used by those involved in scenario planning and strategic foresight. In 2009, Stuart Candy presented the cone to Dunne and Raby at the Royal College of Art in London. Since that time, it has become part of speculative design and futures thinking and is frequently used to identify the possibilities of multiple futures.

The diagram depicts the future as a series of widening cones extending out from the present. The inside cone is the probable future. This is where the majority of designers operate. It analyses the current context and emerging trends to think about likely future scenarios. The majority of design approaches, methods, tools, established good practice, and even design education, are oriented towards this space. The next is the plausible future. This is the space of scenario planning and foresight, where experts model and plan for plausible futures such as economic crisis and environmental disasters. Modelling plausible futures tends to be used for making sure governments and organizations are prepared and thrive in changing contexts.

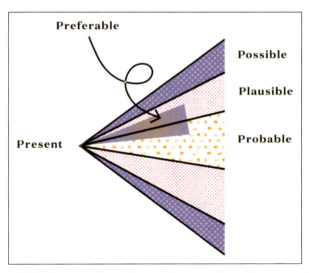

Figure 5.1 The Futures Cone, Speculative Everything, Dunne and Raby, 2013. Drawn by Sarah Parkinson-Howe.

> The widest cone is the possible future and this is where most speculative
> designers situate their work. While fictional, speculative design should be
> scientifically plausible and a believable set of events should have led to the
> fictional scenario.
> This allows people to relate to, and critically reflect upon, the imagined
> future. The preferable future, sits somewhere between the plausible and the
> possible. Of course, the concept of the preferable is complex and depends on
> the perspective of those involved. Speculative designers are usually interested
> in opening up the debates beyond those who typically get to decide what is
> preferable such as governments and corporations.

Within the futures cone, Dunne and Raby position themselves as interested in
the space of possible futures. They aim to broaden who can be involved in
determining futures to include ordinary citizens and argue that designers should
not be trying to define the possible for everyone else. Designers, they suggest,
should work with experts such as ethicists, political scientists, economists and
so on, to generate futures that act as catalysts for public debate (Dunne and
Raby, 2013: 6). Dunne and Raby go on to state that they are not interested in
the realm of fantasy that lies outside of the cone because it is too removed
from reality (2013: 4). Their speculative designs are intentionally provocative,
simplified and fictional. However, the extent to which projects like *Is This Your
Future?* engage the general public is questionable. We return to consider this
point below.

Like most speculative design projects, the scenarios created in *Is This Your
Future?* use techniques that fit within design fiction. Design fiction is a practice
that uses prototyping and storytelling to encourage people to forget the
immediate demands of the contemporary life and think about alternative
presents and futures. It is a 'conflation of design, science fact and science fiction'
(Malpass, 2017: 54). As Bruce Sterling suggests, design fiction involves the
'deliberate use of diegetic prototypes to suspend disbelief about change' (Bosch,
2012). Design fictions are usually 'assemblages of various sorts, part story, part
material, part idea-articulating prop, part functional software' conveying
information, story, place and voice (Bleecker, 2009: 7). They work as conversation
pieces sparking discussions about the 'experiences and social rituals that might
surround the designed object' (2009: 7). By materializing alternative worlds
through diegetic prototypes, design fictions allow audiences to reflect upon the
possibilities of alternative futures. By enabling audiences to temporarily believe
something that is not true, design fictions hold the potential for allowing the
possibilities of futures with more or less progressive gender relations to come
to life.

KEY CONCEPT: DIEGETIC PROTOTYPES

The term diegetic prototype means a prototype existing in a fictional world. It was coined by David Kirby in 2010 to describe the way that props in popular films influenced the development of real-world technologies. For example, in Stanley Kubrick's *2001: A Space Odyssey* released in 1968, viewers see one of the astronauts using what looks like an iPad. Kirby makes the argument that the technological objects shown in the media are performative, in the sense that their portrayal influences our perception of what the future could be. Diegetic prototypes are contextualized by the film's narrative structure and are powerful because they inserted into everyday life. As audiences we are shown their potential use.

One of the techniques that speculative designers use when creating design fictions is the development of counterfactuals. A counterfactional design project creates a narrative whereby an event in the past has been changed and subsequently alters the present. We could consider, for example, what would life and its associated technologies look like today if a matriarchal culture had established itself as culturally dominant in the past? By materializing counterfactuals, speculative designers ask the public to explore how things could be different. Counterfactuals also highlight how future technological development is very much dependent on the decisions we make in the present. The use of this technique also means that speculative artefacts can seem as though they have been brought back from alternative presents or futures. There is a familiarity to speculative objects, often derived from references to current design aesthetics and the conventions of consumer culture, but there is a strangeness too. This makes many speculative artefacts intentionally ambiguous, hoping to draw the user into the conversation. Speculative designers will also often employ the techniques of satire, humour and play, to spark the imagination and engage the public.

Speculative design and inequality

As speculative design has reached its maturity, it has not been without critique. As is evident in the *Is This Your Future?* scenarios, there are a lack of noticeable social inequalities in the future visions that speculative design creates. For example, Luiza Prado de O. Martins and Pedro J. S. Vieira de Oliveira write:

Couples depicted in these near-future scenarios seem to be consistently heterosexual; there is no poverty, there are no noticeable power structures that divide the wealthy and the poor, or the colonialist and the colonised; gender seems to be an immutable, black-and-white truth, clearly defined between men and women, with virtually no space for trans and queer identities (let alone queer and trans voices speaking for themselves).

PRADO de O. MARTINS and VIEIRA de OLIVEIRA, 2014

In the expanded version of text, they continue '[p]overty still happens somewhere else, while the bourgeois speculative design subject copes with catastrophe through consuming sleek, elegant, futuristic, white-cubed and white-boxed gizmos' (Prado de O. Martins and Vieira de Oliveira, 2015: 63). Prado de O. Martins and Vieira de Oliveira suggest that speculative design is 'made by, for, and through the eyes of the Western – and typically Northern-European and-America, intellectual middle classes' (2015: 63).

For example, the Republic of Salivation, produced in 2011 by Michael Burton and Michiko Nitta, is one of the projects that came under such criticism (Thackara, 2013). BurtonNitta envisioned a society where governments were forced to implement food shortages, and food rations were determined by employment. An industrial worker's diet comprised modified starch blocks sent out by the government every two weeks. In search of pleasure in this strict regime, the worker was imagined to make alcohol using the starch blocks and an enzyme in their saliva. They would use food porn to encourage salivation.

One of the major critiques of this project was that this imagined future, meant to draw attention to future food shortages, is an existing reality for many people in the world. As Prado de O. Martins and Vieira de Oliveira suggest, speculative dystopias often reflect the anxiety of the West losing their privileges (2015: 63). For example, the futures cone makes an assumption 'we' are all at similar places and points in time and fails to account for cultural difference (Tonkinwise, 2014: 170). From an intersectional feminist perspective, many speculative projects omit or perpetuate the oppressions found in capitalist, heteronormative, sexist, racist and classist societies (Prado, 2014).

QUESTIONS FOR DESIGNERS: SPECULATIVE DESIGN AND SOCIAL JUSTICE

To avoid reproducing inequality, speculative designers should consider the following:

- Does the dystopian world already exist somewhere? Does the project contain any of the following 'a) Slaves or any depiction of middle-class *(white)* people suddenly turned into slaves; b) People of Color in the role of Robots, Subaltern or *others* in general'? (Prado de O. Martins and Vieira de Oliveira, 2014: a)

- Does the imagined utopian world come at a cost to humans and non-humans elsewhere? Is this cost made explicit?

- Is the design located somewhere specific and contextually appropriate? Does the designer have experience and knowledge of that culture and context?

- Does the story or text used to describe the work generalize contextually specific problems as universal (applying to everyone)?

Early discussions of critical speculative design, particularly the writing of Anthony Dunne, are heavily influenced by Frankfurt School-style critical theory (Bardzell and Bardzell, 2013). Jeffrey Bardzell and Shaowen Bardzell demonstrate how Dunne and Raby use language very similar to that of the Frankfurt school when discussing their approach. For example, they talk of an 'illusion of choice', 'passivity' and 'easy pleasure and conformist values' (Bardzell and Bardzell, 2013: 3298). The views of the Frankfurt School, particularly Theodore Adorno, have been criticized for being elitist, in the sense that they suggest that popular culture accessible to mass audiences is, by its very nature, devoid of criticality. Thus, as Prado de O. Martins suggests, by adopting the critical approach of the Frankfurt School, speculative design risks reproducing elitist views of the world unintelligible to people unfamiliar with the languages of art and design.

Therefore, to demonstrate its capacity to create debate, speculative projects need to make an impact beyond art galleries and academic institutions. To enable wider participation, speculative design also requires more contextually-inspired design languages compared to the ones that most projects currently employ. For it to truly fulfil its potential, a different sort of practice is needed: one that draws on a variety of cultural theories, that questions power relations and that engages designers and users in a range of contexts. One such approach is a speculative design informed by feminism.

INTERVIEW: LUIZA PRADO DE O. MARTINS, ARTIST AND RESEARCHER, BRAZIL/GERMANY

Dr Luiza Prado de O. Martins (she/her) is a Berlin-based Brazilian artist, writer, and researcher whose work examines themes around fertility, reproduction, coloniality, gender and race.

SB: Can you tell me a bit about your current practice?

LP: For the past few years, I've been working mostly as an artist, researcher and writer. I don't really see myself as a designer anymore. I'm very interested in questions related to gender equality, although I have shifted my research a bit to explore ideas of population, climate change and eco-fascism (blaming the environmental crisis on overpopulation and immigration etc). My PhD research in design was about technologies related to birth control, that has evolved since I finished to explore eco-fascism too. Arguments regarding using population control to tackle environmental crisis are even found in feminist texts, so I think it's really important to offer a counter argument.

In my artistic work, I am very interested in working with plants and herbalist knowledge, and reclaiming and recovering the histories of this knowledge. In my most recent work, 'Sermon of the Weeds' (2022) I explore complex and contradictory territory at the intersection of patriarchal structures, Christian belief systems and ongoing struggles for reproductive rights. These reflections are developed through an examination of the relationships between humans and plants used for abortion and contraception at various points in history and are performed as mass. The congregation is invited to reflect on the relationships amongst human and more-than-human actors in the struggle for the right to abortion, and the spiritual connections that emerge through these acts of solidarity; these alliances are materialized through an invitation to share communion crisps flavoured with small amounts of herbs used in contraceptive preparations.

SB: My first encounter with your work was by reading your important contribution to the field of critical speculative design. How did you become interested in this area of design?

LP: When I finished my bachelor's in Brazil, I had already been working as a designer for four years, and I didn't see a way out. I didn't enjoy it and the pay was not good. So, I started looking for free study abroad programmes and ended up in Germany. It was a way of postponing the decision originally because I always wanted to study art, but it was not a feasible career path in Brazil. So, I studied design instead. I think the 'frustrated artist' vibes got me interested in speculative design, because I thought, maybe this is something I could do. It was back in Germany, in 2009, so it was a relatively new field and to me, very new. I felt it could be an interesting direction to go in, because it felt closer to art than to the commercial design work I was used to.

SB: What did you see as the problems with the field?

LP: I noticed that the worlds that many speculative designers were imagining were not dissimilar from where I came from, where my family comes from – these dystopian scenarios were not an imaginary thing. It all came to a head in 2013/2014, when I wrote a piece in *Medium* with my partner at the time, Pedro Oliveira. We were both very dissatisfied with what we were seeing in speculative design and were triggered by a very specific conversation about design and violence and a specific project – the Republic of Salvation. What bothered me about that project and made me want to write that text, was the way they talked about lack of access to food. The early 2000s were a key moment for Brazil, and there were a lot of changes happening, and one of them was that in 2013 Brazil was removed from the world hunger map for the first time. This took a lot of effort from the government at the time, the Workers' Party. So, I think there was something very personal in my problem with that specific project. My parents were hungry growing up, and my mum had scurvy because of malnutrition. It's not something that's abstract. I never went hungry, thankfully, but they always shared those experiences. So, it's not a speculative thing, this is a very real thing that traumatizes people. The text Pedro and I wrote was written in 2014. Just two years later there was a coup in Brazil that removed the Workers' Party from power and almost immediately Brazil went back on the world hunger map. At the time, I don't even think I could explain it in these words, why I was so angry. You know, it's been eight years since, so I've reflected a lot about how my own history affects my intellectual life and my work, because obviously, these things are all connected, and they shape what we see. I think, this is an issue too, with speculative design. When the work is coming from such a select group, in such restrictive environments, the conversation is bound to be very limited.

The other day, I was walking around my neighbourhood in Berlin, and I saw a design studio offering services, and one of the services they offered was speculative and critical design. It's interesting to see that now, in 2022, being offered as a service alongside illustration and graphic design. I guess that says a lot about how the field has been commodified, when in theory, it was supposed to provoke a fundamental shift in how we think about design. Ultimately, it's failed at that, quite spectacularly. It's an issue that's already been pointed out, but when 'critical design' is positioned as the only space where we talk about politics – what happens to the rest? Is the rest apolitical? Clearly not.

SB: Do you see a future for critical and speculative design?
LP: Ultimately, I don't think we need to call something speculative or critical design to allow for criticality or speculation. I think it's imperative to understand that design is something that is key in shaping the world. Every human society designs. Everyone designs. It's fundamental to understand design as a cultural and political practice, inherently. It is an inherently political practice because, from the moment that we choose to act and modify the world in some way, we are creating repercussions. It's like throwing a stone in the water, there are going to be waves.

Next week, I'm going to be teaching in a social design and sustainability master's programme here in Berlin, and I've been thinking so much about Octavia Butler and 'The Parable of the Sower'. The refrain that goes through the book is 'all that you touch, you change. All that you change, changes you. The only lasting truth is change, God is change'. If we use that to think about design, that is so powerful. We make the reality that we live in.

SB: So, you are still interested in exploring alternative worlds with communities?
LP: Yes, very much so. One of the requirements of my PhD was to have some kind of practical outcome . . . but I absolutely did not want to design a solution or a product or anything like that. Instead, I focused on thinking about methodologies and doing a series of workshops. So, doing those workshops I think, was very illuminating because it also took me towards a path that wasn't really expected of my research, and it also allowed me to engage with theories and ways of thinking from the Global South. The workshops were very much based on the work of Paulo Freire, a Brazilian educator and Augusto Boal, a playwright, whose work is very connected to Freire's, and he created this methodology called the 'Theatre of the Oppressed', so it was inspired by that. It was very interesting, because it was an attempt to still access, or play around with, ideas that are present in speculative and critical design, but through a different, more collaborative framing – that wouldn't be just, you know, the designer imagining the dystopia.

SB: Having worked at the intersection between design and art, what do you see as the similarities/differences between these disciplines/practices?
LP: I still find design theory interesting, but I find it more exciting to explore design from outside, and not to look out to different fields from within design. As I was finishing my PhD, at that point, because of the themes of my research, I had been looking at forms of violence enacted through design and by design for four years. Gender violence, racial violence, violence was at the intersection of all of those categories. It was emotionally very heavy and when I finished, after so many years of looking into sexual exploitation enacted with intent, it was a lot, and honestly, I was very depressed. So, art was a way of continuing my research, but not in a way that stops at critique and identifies the problem, but also allows me to think about what is possible and what else we can do. That was one of the biggest lessons and one of the most important things that I personally took from this shift from doing work in the field of design to doing work in art. Perhaps that was also the issue with speculative design and critical design. Imagine disaster? Disaster is happening! Let's imagine what else is possible. I need to have hope. I need to think about care, I need to think about joy, I need to think about anti-colonial futures and multiple possibilities.

SB: And for you, that's not possible within the field of design?
LP: It certainly is, I guess. But I think that maybe I'm done with it and I'm more interested in experimenting through other lenses.

SB: What sorts of feminist futures would you like to see materialize?
LP: The fall of racial-hetero-patriarchy! Seriously, I would like to see struggles for gender equality, for racial equality, for climate justice and for prison abolition acknowledged as deeply connected. But, there's no hierarchy in the urgency of these, you know, we need people acting in these different struggles and understanding their interconnections.

Feminist visions of the future

Feminists have often imagined different sorts of futures. These have been expressed through architectural plans, artworks, films, music and literature, and provide rich inspiration as narratives for speculative designs today. Some of the most compelling future visions have come from feminist science fiction.

Science fiction has explored the use of technologies such as assisted reproduction to imagine dystopian worlds whereby compulsory gender and sexual identity are enforced, as well as to dream of utopian visions where citizens are free from gender and sexuality. For example, *The Left Hand of Darkness* by Ursula le Guin published in 1969 is set on the fictional planet of Gethen whose inhabitants are humans with no fixed gender identity. Gethenains adopt female or male sexual characteristics for short periods for sex and procreation. Choice of sex in these periods depends on context and relationships. The narrative of *The Left Hand of Darkness* follows a human, Genly Ai, who is sent to Gethen to try to convince Gethenians to join his confederation of planets. Genly Ai's lack of cultural understanding, particularly about gender, hinders his progress. The story draws attention to the complexities of colonization, as well as how sex and gender affect social life, politics and nation. Le Guin's work does not just explore alien worlds, but also causes us to reflect upon earthly pasts and presents. For example, her short story *Sur,* written in 1982, is an account of South American women discovering the South Pole in the time between Scott's initial 1902–4 expedition and his 1911–12 failed polar attempt. This counterfactual narrative causes us to consider how things might have changed today had this event occurred and been recorded. In addition, by writing women into official histories, Le Guin presents the 'possibility of non-European women's prior claim to historical knowledge' (Glasberg, 2012: 20).

Octavia Butler also mixes past, present and future to explore alternative worlds. Butler is recognized as central to the Afrofuturism movement and her novels frequently combine African-American history, culture and spiritualism with science fiction. Moving in a non-linear fashion from past to present to future, Butler's work highlights inequality and questions Western discourses of progress. For example, drawing upon the history of plantation slavery in the USA, her novel *Wild Seed,* written in 1980, prompts the reader to consider the abuses of power made possible by genetic engineering. The novel has two central characters, Doro, a spirit made immortal by killing people who becomes fixated on breeding superhumans, and Anyanwu, a female shapeshifter with healing powers. Doro's exploitation of people as genetic experiments echoes the methods of New World slave owners and draws attention to the histories of racial slavery. Doro's destruction is ultimately tamed by Anyanwu's shapeshifting abilities. A number of academics have suggested that Anyanwu embodies Donna Haraway's 'cyborg' whereby people are 'not afraid of their joint kinship with animals and machines, not afraid of permanently partial identities and contradictory standpoints' (Haraway, 1991: 154).

Donna Haraway has spoken very candidly about the influence of feminist science fiction on her academic work. In *Staying with the Trouble*, Haraway tries her hand at feminist science fiction in the *Camille Stories: Children of Compost*. The stories, originally written collaboratively, invite the reader to consider

KEY CONCEPT: AFROFUTURISM

Afrofuturism is an aesthetic and philosophy that was first coined by Mark Dery in 1994. It describes music, art and literature that address the interplay of technoscience with the culture and histories of the African diaspora. Afrofuturist works place Black experience at the centre of science fiction and speculative futures, and often explore the concepts of 'otherness' and the 'alien'. The term has been used to describe a range of artists including Sun Ra, a musician who combined African sounds with the space-age in the 1950s; writers such as Samuel R. Delany and Octavia Butler; and visual artists including Jean-Michel Basquiat and Renee Cox. Afrofuturists have frequently been interested in gender and sexuality and 'examinations of inter-racial and inter-species "mixing," alternative family and community structure, and disruptions of gender binaries have been central to Afrofuturist thought' (Reid-Pharr, 2020). Afrofuturism frequently challenges Western notions 'progress' and, as Ytasha L. Womack states, 'is where the past and future meet' (Pezanoski-Browne, 2013).

Influenced by Afrofuturism, cultural critics and artists have begun to identify and create speculative futures drawing on unique cultural experiences from their own places in the world. For example, Aotearoa Futurism fuses indigenous Māori culture with science fiction.

alternative ways of relating to humans and non-humans, or in Haraway's terms 'making kin'. In Camille 1, we read of a small community of compost established in West Virginia in 2020 formed with the common goal of addressing 'accelerating mass extinctions, violent climate change, social disintegration, widening wars, [and] ongoing human population increase' (Haraway, 2016: 145). By 2025, the community felt ready to have their first babies that were to be bonded with endangered animal symbionts with the view to protecting non-human species and their habitats. Camille is one of five children born with at least three parents. Before she was born, she was given some of the genes of the Monarch butterfly and was raised to be attuned to her interdependence upon the environment around her. The *Camille Stories* go on to recount the lives of five generations living symbiotically with Monarch butterflies, tracing their migrations from Mexico to the USA to Canada, and exploring their experiences along the way.

For Haraway, and for the reader of *Staying with the Trouble*, the *Camille Stories* work as an experimental illustration of the philosophy laid out in the rest of the book. Haraway argues that:

> It matters what matters we use to think other matters with; it matters what stories we tell to tell other stories with; it matters what knots knot knots, what thoughts think thoughts, what ties tie ties. It matters what stories make worlds, what worlds make stories.'
>
> 2016: 12

It is through speculative fabulation, Haraway suggests, that alternative ways of worlding happen.

In *Staying with the Trouble*, Haraway argues that speculative fabulation, science fact, and speculative feminism, need each other if we are to imagine futures beyond inequality and environmental degradation. She talks of 'sf' as:

KEY CONCEPT: FABULATION

To 'fabulate' is defined as 'to relate as fable or myth' or 'to invent, concoct or fabricate'. Feminist philosophers including Vinciane Despret, Saidiya Hartman and Donna Haraway have argued that to fabulate, or create stories, is to open up potential for new ways of living. Critical fabulation offers alternative narratives critical of dominant discourses, and speculative fabulation generates stories about the possibilities of pasts, presents and futures.

a method of tracing, of following a thread in the dark, in a dangerous true tale of adventure, where who lives and who dies and how might become clearer for the cultivating of multispecies justice.

HARAWAY, 2016: 3

Tracing is simultaneously making and unmaking, and in the process, we are 'becoming-with'. In this sense 'sf' is material, it connects plants, people, animals and their environments. Stories influence the types of artefacts created and artefacts embody narrative, they affect us, change our bodies and influence our ideas. Daniela K. Rosner (2018) has adopted the concept of fabulation, specifically critical fabulation, and developed it as a design approach. For Rosner, critical fabulation involves designers seeking out different inheritances from which to act and different concepts with which to imagine. She argues that designers should analyse the design tradition for its holes and learn collectively how to remake alternative futures.

In the next chapter we explore what ideas regarding 'sf' and entanglement might offer design more widely, and I lay out some alternative inheritances that may offer potential for imagining design otherwise.

Futuring tools and approaches to time

Dominant notions of the future are themselves very much tied to Western linear understandings of time. In linear temporality, the past is thought of as fixed behind us as objective truth and the future ahead as full of progress and possibility. This notion of time erases histories and drives the narratives of progression and growth that are central to capitalism. The universalization of a Western concept of time was fundamental to colonialization and continues to legitimate ongoing violence. As Daniel R. Wildcat argues:

Once history-as-time is universalized and human beings are, so to speak, all put on the same clock, it is inevitable that in the big picture of human history some peoples will be viewed as 'on time,' 'ahead of time,' or 'running late.' It makes little difference that the clock hands rotate in circles, for they are thought of and acted on as if they were wheels moving down a single road called progress.

2005: 433

Linear time, as feminist theorists have reminded us, closes down the possibility of radical change. For example, as Fanny Soderback (2012) writes, the insistence upon a singular version of the past risks 'forgetfulness' about alternatives, while simultaneously trapping us into a singular narrative and foreclosing the possibility of a radical break.

The futures cone reproduces notions of linear time and thus its potential as a model for generating alternative futures is limited. For example, in some versions of the cone, such as the one reproduced by Dunne and Raby above, the past is absent. By avoiding the past altogether, this representation prevents any discussion of the politics of the design canon (in that it has tended to value European and American design movements and male designers). In other versions of the cone, history is depicted as a single line, as if the future has many possibilities, but the past does not. A linear version of history would imply that anyone designing and creating artefacts outside of 'official' design histories is not a designer at all.

The limitations of the futures cone mean that when used as a tool to imagine speculative futures, the outputs are in danger of reproducing the very same problems they attempt to critique. In the case of the cone that ignores the past, objects can emerge that employ many of the aesthetic traditions of the design canon, with little reflection on where or how these are brought about. In the case of the cone that represents the past as a singular progressive entity, alternative pasts (frequently those of groups that have been repressed and colonized) are overlooked in favour of a dominant narrative. In both cases, the outputs tend to reproduce modernist visions of the future.

Of course, there are many different ways of understanding time that could be used as inspiration for speculative design methods. As Rita Felski suggests, history is 'not one broad river, but a number of distinct and separate streams each moving with its own pace and tempo' (2000: 3). Even in Western cultures, there are many experiences of time from the micro to the macro, from the everyday to 'clock time'. Felski suggests that we should consider the 'messy variety of human lives, activities, and experiences as they affect the full compass and breadth of historical time' (2000: 3). This would mean taking alternative and ordinary histories seriously, as well as turning our attention to memory and 'modes of thought that stay close to the lived relations of the everyday' (Samuel 2012: ix).

As Afrofuturists and indigenous designers have taught us, understandings of time vary across cultures. For example, Prado de O. Martins and Vieira de Oliveira argue that learning from magical realism and 'Chicanafuturism' might produce more critical speculative projects in Latin American contexts. They suggest that speculative design should not be a solitary exercise, but an 'open space of collective action and debate' that allows for multiple non-linear narratives where 'both the future and the past are collectively articulated from the present' (Prado de O. Martins and Vieira de Oliveira, 2016: 31). For example, in Prado de O. Martins's PhD research she uses improvised theatre and role-play to explore the future of contraceptive and abortive medications. The workshops she held mixed fact and fiction, current events and imagined futures to avoid linear and hegemonic understandings of fertility (Prado, 2016). Prado de O. Martins and Vieira de Oliveira's approach acknowledges that ideas of the past and of the future are speculations that can only be redesigned from the present.

In terms of speculative projects that are focused on gender, feminist approaches to time also offer methodological inspiration. Feminists have been critical of linear time because it has perpetuated a history where women's experiences have been excluded, as was explored in Chapter 2. At the same time, linear time, and its associated narratives of progress, lend itself to claims that feminism is not needed because a state of gender equality has been reached i.e. trans women and non-binary people should be satisfied because their experience is 'better' than it would have been in the past. As highlighted in Chapter 1, a linear history of feminism itself also problematically puts arguments neatly in 'waves' with caricatures of each wave negating the richness of the work.

Discussion of temporality (approaches to time) and genealogy (lines of descent) in feminist theory could, and should, inform the creation of new speculative methods for design. For example, much of the work of Karen Barad (2016), feminist philosopher and physicist, has engaged with temporality. Barad turns to quantum physics to understand the material realities of time. Drawing on the work of Niels Bohr, she develops the concept of the 'thick present'. In several experiments, Bohr's work demonstrates how time, like space and matter, is tied to particular phenomena rather than an external parameter. The past was never simply there to begin with, and the future is not simply what will unfold. At each point in time there is an entire world in a very specific configuration, a thick now simultaneously made up of pasts and futures. These pasts and futures are alive in present not only as personal experience and as social reality, but materially in bodies and environments. Barad suggests that quantum physics joins forces with indigenous knowledges and Afrofuturism and blows away any homogenous notion of progress and time.

Donna Haraway has also used the concept of the 'thick present'. For Haraway, the thick present works to move us away from the idea of Edenic pasts and apocalyptic or salvific futures (2016a: 1). It calls us to be truly present and explore our entanglements in a myriad of places, times, matter and meanings. Taking the 'thick present' seriously as designers means exploring the lived relations of everything around us. It involves an ethics of care that recognizes the responsibility we have to people, animals, plants, places and things for generations past and for those yet to come. We return to consider how these ideas might influence design practice more broadly in the next chapter.

Speculative design inspired by the thick present would avoid both nostalgically looking back to a pristine 'natural' past, as well as the progress narratives of a technologically advanced future. 'Old' technologies would be seen as having as much potential as new, and by examining alternative histories, a variety of pasts could be opened up. New futures could be created by exploring past materialities, alternative experiences, 'failures' or what might have been. For example, the domestic tasks, technologies, and spaces that feminists imagined in the 1920s, that were documented in Chapter 2, could prove rich source material for imagining feminist futures today. To challenge the dominant visions and aesthetics of the future, methods and tools should encourage the anachronic (taking things out of time) and the eclectic. While dominant depictions of the future may be pervasive, beneath the surface people's experiences of pasts, presents and futures are very different. So, too, is the access that people have to the material and/or ideological resources to make their future visions a possibility. By interrogating the very conception of the future, designers may be more equipped to generate alternative visions.

QUESTIONS FOR DESIGNERS: SPECULATIVE DESIGN AND TEMPORALITY

To explore conceptions of time and create new futuring methods, designers should consider the following:

- What concept of time is informing the project? Could a more contextual understanding of time generate a different approach or vision? I.e. If working in Oaxaca, Mexico, would indigenous understandings be more appropriate or generative?

- What reference points are being used as inspiration for the look and feel of the future? Where do these come from?

- What technologies are being explored? How do these exist in the present and the past? What implications do they have for humans, non-humans and the environment? Would the understanding of these implications be improved through greater primary research?

- Is the project reproducing dystopian or utopian narratives? Is this intentional? Would the project benefit from added complexity?

CASE STUDY: FREAK SCIENCE, MARY MAGGIC, VIENNA, AUSTRIA

Mary Maggic is a non-binary Chinese American artist currently based in Vienna, Austria. Their work spans speculative design, amateur science, performance, installation and film. Maggic's work has been exhibited internationally including at the Philadelphia Museum of Art (US), Migros Museum of Contemporary Art (Switzerland), and Institute of Contemporary Arts London (UK).

Freak Science is a design fiction that explores the possibility of hacking hormones. The project draws attention to the ways that synthetic hormones such as contraception and hormone therapy are used as technologies of control in industrial capitalism. For example, queer and transgender people are subject to a range of tests and criteria before they can access hormones and thus institutions, corporations and governments are able to discipline and manage the sexual differentiation of bodies. By highlighting how institutions and scientific fields produce fictions about normative gender and reproduction, *Freak Science* asks us to consider the radical possibilities of appropriating science for our own means by making hormones accessible through DIY practices.

   To explore the prospect of hormones beyond institutions, the first thing we have to accept, according to Maggic, is that 'all bodies are queer, so there is no such thing as a stable body' (Maggic, 2020). Bodies are always becoming, they are evolving over time and contingent on others (human and non-human life) to exist. In addition, in the context of industrial capitalism, 'hormone mimicking molecules [are] leaching out into the environment and mutating our bodies and bodies of non-human species' (Maggic, 2020). In the face of this 'invisible yet pervasive and inescapable phenomenon', *Freak Science* wants us to contemplate how might we give up our '(eco)heteronormative limits and conjure empathy for our collective alien becoming' (Maggic, 2020). Rather than seeking technological solutions, the project embraces design for debate, and through scientific experimentation, visualization, installation, intervention and video, calls on us to reflect upon the ethics of the production and consumption of synthetic hormones.

Open Source Estrogen

Open-Source Estrogen, one of the first design fictions created by Maggic and part of the *Freak Science* project, develops a system of DIY protocols for 'the emancipation of the estrogen biomolecule' (2020). It uses lay-scientific terms to make the processes of hormone creation accessible to regular people. The aims of the project are communicated via a short video, *Housewives Making Drugs,* which shows the viewer a world where a DIY kitchen laboratory could be a reality (fig. 5.2). The kitchen, having

Figure 5.2 *Open Source Estrogen: Housewives Making Drugs*. Maggic, 2015. Courtesy of the artist, Mary Maggic.

always been a site for 'domestic science', is a highly appropriate context for the design fiction. The possibilities of open source production are emphasized because, as the project website suggests, 'the kitchen is a politically charged space prescribed to women as their proper dwelling, therefore making it the precise context to perform an estrogen synthesis recipe' (Maggic, 2020). The kitchen, alongside the idea of the housewife, are historically, culturally and politically loaded with meaning and this is accentuated by a 1950s soundtrack and excerpts from vintage advertising and artwork. Everyday practices of kitchen alchemy (cooking) are appropriated to convey potentially baffling scientific concepts.

Video and website graphics are bright, kitsch, and pop-inspired. The kitsch and humorous elements of *Open Source Estrogen* are emphasized further in a longer, more recent, fictional cooking show, *Housewives Making Drugs*, made in collaboration with Orgasmic Creative. Using parody and witty banter, trans-femme stars, Maria and Maria, introduce the viewer to the limited access to hormones and go on to teach the audience how to cook their own hormones.

The design fiction draws upon recent technological developments to make the self-creation and administering of hormones a convincing possibility. Maggic identifies a number of methods, or scientific protocols, the first being *#00 Chicken Egg Extraction*. They ask could 'chickens raised in estrogen-polluted environments deposit hormones in their eggs yolks, thereby serving as the open source estrogen?' (Maggic, 2020). Chickens, Maggic suggests, are similar to woman, in that both have been, and continue to be, commodified for the biotech industry. Chickens have been 'genetically modified to lay eggs containing pharmaceutical drugs', and woman have had their eggs and foetal material harvested for profit.

The second protocol, *#01 Yeast Estrogen Factories*, highlights the ways that yeast can potentially be genetically engineered to produce oestrogen from a cholesterol precursor (fig. 5.3). The third, *#02 Agrobacterium Mediated Transformation (Hormonal Plants),* explores whether tobacco plants can be modified to produce oestrogen, and the forth, *#03 (Xeno) Estrogen Recycling,* identifies the purification, recycling and extraction of estrogen from urine as having radical potential.

Through *Estrofem Lab*, a set of mobile tools, protocols and workshops, Maggic aims to provide the contextual framework for citizen science and oestrogen hacking. Collaborating with others in hands-on experimentation, workshops generate mishaps and accidents that feed into future practice.

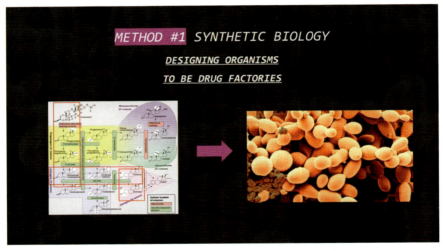

Figure 5.3 *Open Source Estrogen: #01 Yeast Estrogen Factories.* Maggic, 2015. Courtesy of the artist, Mary Maggic.

Estrofem Lab asks its participants to consider the ethics of biochemistry when oestrogen creation is made into an open source recipe. What are its physiological and environmental dangers, for example? Could we use bio-technoscientific capabilities to eradicate the gender binary? And what would this mean for ecosystems already affected by environmental impact of synthetic oestrogen? Ultimately, through design fiction *Freak Science* provides us with a way into scientific exploration usually reserved for big pharma and points us to the possibilities of a radically differently gendered future.

Speculative design and gender

While speculative design has been criticized for reproducing inequality, there are a number of designers who have explored gender relations using speculative methods, some more successfully than others.

'Gender Tools' (2016) by Mia Cinelli uses product design to question the role of sex and anatomy in defining gender norms and tasks (fig.5.4). Cinelli borrows the design languages of hardware, kitchenware and sex toys and makes them 'fleshy'. This results in tools that are both disturbing and comical. The ambiguity of the tools provokes users to think about the gendering of technologies and bodies.

While the project may draw attention to the bodies involved in labour, it uses the slick aesthetics typical in much speculative design and critiqued by designers such as Prado de O. Martins and Vieira de Oliveira. The images have a stark modernist quality and the models used in the images are white, so too is the skin of the tools. In addition, the meaning of the ambiguous prototypes may only be accessible to those familiar with speculative design or those who read the companying text about the project.

Menstruation Machine: Takashi's Take (2010) produced by Sputniko (Hiromi Ozaki) also draws the languages of product design. A student of Anthony Dunn and

Figure 5.4 *Gender Tools*, Mia Cinelli, 2016. © Mia Cinelli, 2016.

Fiona Raby at the Royal College of Art in London, Sputniko designed her final project around the fictional character of Takashi, a young transgender Japanese woman who, being unsatisfied with just 'appearing female', wanted to experience menstruation. Sputniko created a metal menstruation machine that looks like a chastity belt fitted with a blood dispensing mechanism and electrodes that stimulate the lower abdomen (fig. 5.5). The machine simulates the pain and bleeding of a five-day menstruation process. She also produced a pop song and video that depicts Takashi dressing up and wearing the machine when out with her female friends.

Sputniko created the menstruation machine to explore what menstruation meant biologically, culturally and politically. She wanted to consider why women were still menstruating when technologies could have been developed that stop the process (see Sputniko, 2010). One of Sputniko's motivations was to draw attention to gender inequalities, government policy and the pharmaceutical industry in Japan, including the fact it took the Japanese government nine years to approve the contraceptive pill and only three months to approve Viagra. To encourage

Figure 5.5 *Menstruation Machine: Takashi's Take*, 2010. © Sputniko!

critical reflection on consumer technologies among young people, Sputniko posted the video on Youtube and it was picked up by a number of popular blogs.

Despite this relative success, this project has its limitations. For example, *Menstruation Machine* has been criticized for its naive understanding of gender and queer theory, including the use of the term 'transvestite' and the concept of 'biologically dressing up' in its project description (Sputniko, 2010). In addition, as Prado de O. Martins notes, the 'very portrayal of a gender-nonconforming person (by a cissexual woman, nonetheless) for shock value highlight[s] the project's problematic approach to gender identity' (2014: 4). At the same time, however, the *Menstruation Machine* manages to create a world that is neither dystopian or utopian. It uses kitsch, pop aesthetics different from the typical masculine 'white boxed gismos' found in much speculative design. Drawing on popular resources, such as teen fashion and the music video, it successfully captures the imagination.

Queer Technologies (2007–12) by Zac Blas, is more critically engaged with gender and queer theory. Conceptualized as an organization, *Queer Technologies* produces 'critical applications, tools, and situations for queer technological agency, interventions, and sociality' (Blas, 2008). Although not defined as 'speculative design', the tools produced as part of the project have similar qualities. For example, *ENgenderingGenderChangers*, produced in 2008, are a variety of serial adapters produced to critique the male/female gender binary. This includes adapters that are shown on their packaging as converting 'Male

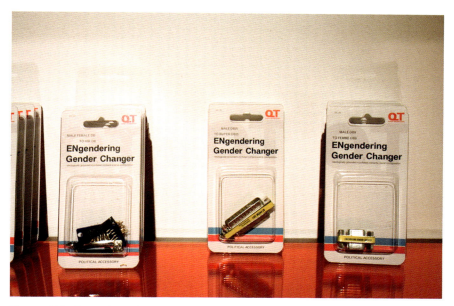

Figure 5.6 *EngenderingGenderchangers, Queer Technologies*, Zach Blas. 2007–12. Courtesy of Zach Blas.

D86 to Femme D86', 'Male/Female D8 to HIR D8' and 'Male D825 to Butch D825' (fig.5.6). The *ENgenderingGenderChangers* were placed on the shelves in electronic stores as 'product, artwork and political tool' to draw attention to the 'heteronormative, capitalist, militarized underpinnings' of technology (Blas, 2008). The adapters were also displayed at the 'Disingenuous Bar' (a play on Apple's Genius Bar), a heterotopic space where people could come for political support for their 'technical' problems.

This product uses consumer experiences to draw attention to gender norms and heteronormativity, as well as their influence upon technology. Much like other speculative projects, it is 'critical thought translated into materiality' (Dunne and Raby, 2013: 35). While the project does not imagine an alternative future, it does inform people about queer politics in all its complexity.

(Im)possible Baby (2014–17) designed by Ai Hasegawa et al. also considers the possibilities of queer futures (fig. 5.7). The project draws inspiration from scientific developments in genetic technology and considers the implications of reproduction beyond heterosexual relationships. Using the DNA data, 'what if' family photos were created visualizing a lesbian couple's future children. A photo album was created and given to the couple as a gift. A thirty-minute documentary followed the process and aired on Japanese national television.

Figure 5.7 *(Im)possible Baby*, Ai Hasegawa et al. 2014–17. Courtesy of Ai Hasegawa.

Figure 5.8 *In Posse*, Thesmophoria, Kapelica Gallery. Charlotte Jarvis. 2020. Project by Charlotte Jarvis, photo by Jana Purtle.

(Im)possible Baby asks audiences to consider the social, cultural and ethical implications of bioethics. The project was able to reach a wide audience through the documentary that included interviews with scientists and the couple themselves. Nevertheless, by reproducing the image of the nuclear family (albeit with two parents who identify as female) the project is limited in terms of offering radical alternatives to current family forms.

A more recent project, *In Posse*, by the artist Charlotte Jarvis is more radical in exploring reproductive futures (fig. 5.8). *In Posse* aims to 'disrupt the patriarchy by making semen from female cells' and by doing so examine the meaning of sex and gender now and in the future (Jarvis, 2020: 3). The project has been realized in three parts: firstly, Jarvis has been working with scientists to grow spermatozoa (sperm cells) using her body; a female form of seminal plasma (the fluid part of semen) has also been developed using 'material donated by multiple women, trans and gender non-binary people' (Jarvis, 2020: 22). The artist then organized a reimagining and re-enactment of the ancient Greek women-only festival Thesmophoria to stage and use the semen. The festivals are codesigned with participants and collaborative rites and rituals are developed around protocols for semen stimulant. The events aim to take participants on a journey away from normal life into the 'wilderness', and as such, work as critical fabulations opening up possibilities for new ways of living.

QUESTIONS FOR DESIGNERS: GENDER FUTURES

Speculative designers that are keen to focus on gendered futures should consider the following:

- Does the project question or reify gender inequality? Does it offer alternative ways of living in terms of gender i.e. non-binary experience, alternative family forms, the burdens of social reproduction?

- Does the project unintentionally reproduce any oppressive structures in terms of gender and/or intersectionality?

- Does the design reinforce dominant narratives and aesthetics of the future? If it does, why has this design decision been made? Could alternative visions be created by drawing on alternative aesthetic traditions such as pop, queer, kitsch or craft aesthetics?

- Could the portrayal of gender be considered insensitive? How you tested this with users with a range of gender identities?

- Does/could the project highlight the audience's own role in perpetuating social injustice?

Feminist Futures (2019–), a collaborative worldbuilding project by Paisley Smith and Caitlin Conlen, also attempts to include a broad range of people to imagine feminist futures. Adopting participatory methods drawn from design-thinking, those in Smith and Conlen's workshops create their own fictional futures. Using prototyping tools such as felt and plasticine, artefacts from these futures are brought to life by participants. As Stuart Candy notes, however, mediation, in terms of translating ideas into legible experiences and staging these experiences, is vital so that projects exist beyond the ideation stage.

In each of these examples, users encounter feminist speculative artefacts that encourage them to envisage different worlds through experience. The advantages of experiential learning are well documented (Oxley and Ilea, 2015), and through design, users can inhabit and imagine different ways of being. By adopting the tropes of consumer culture, entertainment and technology that people are so familiar with, and reappropriating them for feminist ends, designers can make feminism more accessible. Whether this is through popular media in the case of the *Menstruation Machine* and *(Im)possible Baby*; by appropriating commercial contexts like *Queer Technologies*; or through active workshop participation in the case of *Feminist Futures* and *In Posse*; feminist speculative design should aim to create conversations about desirable gender futures with diverse audiences.

QUESTIONS FOR DESIGNERS: SPECULATIVE PARTICIPATION

For speculative design to engage the public in debates about the future, designers should think about the following:

- How is the speculative artefact going to generate debate?

- What methods and media will connect the world and artefact with the public?

- Does the artefact use language that is accessible to the audience?

- How will the visions and/or thoughts of the user be incorporated back into the design?

- Can participatory design methods be used to create a collaborative vision? If participatory methods are used, how will the ideas generated be bought to life?

While the projects documented here clearly address gender inequality through speculative methods, feminist speculative design has much wider potential. Media discourse surrounding gender and feminism is often polarizing, and feminist speculative design can offer a refreshingly nuanced perspective, while at the same time being relatively easy to understand. Speculative methods could bring to life many of the debates discussed in the chapters in this book. By highlighting the discriminatory nature of technologies and imagining futures through diegetic prototypes, the implications of technologies can be experienced and debated without real cost to humans, non-humans and/or the environment. By designing feminist futures, the advantages of gender equity could be communicated, and the freedoms and pleasures of a world where a proliferation of gendered experiences are accepted and celebrated can be emphasized.

PARTICIPATORY FUTURES TOOL

1. Ask 3 people what they expect gender relations to be like in 2040.
Summarise their ideas here.

Reflection: Based on these visions how do the people you spoke to understand time
(e.g. did they find it hard to think about the future, did they employ a linear version of
progress, and/or articulate a more cyclical or historical vision)? Why do you think this is?

_____

_____

_____

_____

_____

_____

2. Start to imagine one of these worlds. What would home life, work or public space
look and feel like?

_____

_____

_____

_____

_____

_____

© **Dr Sarah Elsie Baker**

PARTICIPATORY FUTURES TOOL

3. Choose one artefact from this world. Draw and describe it here.

Reflection: Would an encounter with this artefact create a discussion about the future of gender? How might you increase public debate using this artefact?

_____

_____

_____

_____

_____

_____

CHAPTER FIVE ACTIVITY

SPECULATING WITH THE PAST

1. Choose and complete one of the following activities focused on the past:

- Research a local invention created by a woman.
- Document a memory of gendered labour.
- Collect visual material of local design or craft practice typically associated with femininity.

2. Taking inspiration from one of these pasts, design one of the following speculative objects to challenge or reify gender inequality:

- A Toy
- A Digital Experience
- An Appliance
- A Medical Treatment

3. Draw and describe the artefact here.

6
SUSTAINABLE PRACTICE AND DESIGN BEYOND BINARIES

Introduction: feminism and ecological crisis

The impacts of climate change, deforestation and pollution across the world disproportionally affect some more than others. For example, as observed in Chapter 4, the current Sustainable Development Goal data suggests that those who identify as women are more likely to encounter food insecurity and more acutely experience the effects of disasters caused by climate change (UN Women, 2022). Climate change is a 'threat multipler'. For example, as climate change drives conflict, the risks of gender-based violence such as human trafficking, child marriage and sexual violence increase (UN Women, 2022a). Extreme heat caused by global warming has been linked to stillbirth and the greater prevalence of diseases that worsen maternal and neonatal outcomes (UN Women, 2022a). The inequalities exacerbated by climate change are more acute for 'indigenous and Afro-descendent women and girls, older women, LGBTIQ+ people, women and girls with disabilities, migrant women, and those living in rural, remote, conflict and disaster-prone areas' (UN Women, 2022a). This is not helped by the agendas of most humanitarian organizations. As Matcha Phorn-In, an activist working with indigenous girls, women, and LGBTIQ+ people in Thailand suggests, 'humanitarian programmes tend to be heteronormative and can reinforce the patriarchal structure of society if they do not take into account sexual and gender diversity' (UN Women, 2018).

Recognition of the connections between gender inequalities and ecological crisis is by no means new. Feminists have long pointed to patriarchal culture as being one of the causes of both environmental degradation and the exploitation of women. As Rosie Braidotti observes, feminists have been acutely 'aware of the dangers involved in being assigned to nature. Nature is a cover for a hierarchical naturalization of inequalities, which circulates within the socio-cultural system of patriarchy as a pretext for discrimination' (Braidotti, 2022: 70). In ecofeminism, a term said to be coined by Françoise d'Eaubonne in 1974, the relationship between women and nature became subject to greater scrutiny. Ecofeminists argued that social norms about gender and the natural environment produce an uncomplete view of the world. They observed that both women and nature were frequently represented as chaotic, irrational and in need of control, whereas men were characterized as rational and ordered. Thus, men were deemed 'naturally' capable of directing the use and development of both women and nature leading to oppression and exploitation. In *Feminism or Death*, for example, d'Eaubonne documents how 'ancient man's control of agricultural technologies resulted in an androcentric society, where the appropriation of women's bodies, labor and power was paired with exploitative agricultural methods and industrialization' (Gorecki, 2022: para 3). Thus, in contrast to perspectives that see the earth as a resource to capitalize upon, ecofeminists posit that the earth is 'sacred', recognize 'humanity's dependency on the natural world', and embrace 'all life as valuable' (Miles, 2022).

To suggest one originator of the term ecofeminism is problematic because the connection between the subordination of women and nature was being discussed by other feminists during the 1970s (Gorecki, 2022: para 8). Ecofeminism, like feminism, encompasses many different perspectives, and much of the early work, such as that by d'Eaubonne, seems essentialist and racist by today's standards (Gorecki, 2022: para 12). However, early works such as *Feminism or Death* established ecofeminism as a movement and enable critique 'that can move us toward the ecofeminism we want to see in the world today' (Gorecki, 2022: para 13).

As the ecofeminist movement continued to develop in the 1980s, a number of distinct schools of thought emerged that have been characterized as 'radical ecofeminism' and 'cultural ecofeminism' (Miles, 2022). 'Radical ecofeminism' continued the arguments of earlier theorists, challenging the associations of women with nature, and attempting to dismantle the negative associations of both women and nature as needing to be controlled. 'Cultural ecofeminists, on the other hand, tactically embraced the association between women and nature and argued that this relationship was more intimate because of women's gender roles (as a nurturer) and biology (menstruation, pregnancy and lactation) (Miles, 2022: para 6). 'Cultural ecofeminists' suggest that women have a more enate connection to the natural world and this relationship should be prized by society. 'Cultural ecofeminism also has roots in nature-based religions and goddess and nature worship as a way of redeeming both the spirituality of nature and women's instrumental role in that spirituality' (Miles, 2022: para 6). In reality, of course, ecofeminist arguments were more complex than these categorizations. Nevertheless, the legacies of these schools of thought continue to influence approaches to gender and nature today, including some of the design approaches explored below.

In the 1990s, the early days of the ecofeminist movement were criticized as privileging the experiences of white women, and works by theorists and activists from the Global South emerged (e.g. Mies and Shiva, 1993). These discussions highlighted both the central role that indigenous women and women of colour have in caring for, connecting with, and building a relationship with the natural world; and the importance of indigenous worldviews in informing contemporary practice.

In this chapter we draw together ecofeminist discussions, pluriversal design approaches, queer theory and indigenous perspectives to explore design beyond binaries. We consider how sustainable design approaches can often reproduce essentialist perspectives of both gender and nature. We turn to queer ecology and indigenous worldviews to explore alternative approaches. I focus specifically on mātauranga Māori (Māori knowledge) because that is the indigenous world view that I have most experience of. The chapter concludes by considering ways to unmake design practice.

Towards non-binary design

As introduced in Chapter 1, feminist and decolonial thinkers have identified 'othering' (in addition to extermination and structural exploitation), as one of the ways in which the matrix of domination is maintained. In the previous chapters we have observed how design practices deemed as 'feminine' have been assigned lower status; how 'traditional' practices have often been excluded from the definition of 'design'; how women are judged when they show emotion in the workplace; how 'objective' data and data visualization has been privileged; and how the concept of 'progress' works to exclude alternative histories and narratives.

These observations, among many others in the book, are all illustrative of the ways in which design, as the materialization of Enlightenment, reflects and reproduces power relations maintained through binaries. As Tony Fry and Adam Nocek argue, 'what threatens us as a species' has as much to do with 'world-historical events' such as a warming planet, as it does with how humanity has been framed and imagined historically (2021: 1). This framing, with its binary logic, 'determines how we care and protect the vulnerable, what resources are available and for whom, and ultimately who gets to count as human and who does not' (Fry and Nocek, 2021: 1). They continue, '[t]hus, the historical production of Enlightened Man, which many of us now hold responsible for the ecological devastation, colonial violence, and geopolitical unrest, cannot be seen outside of the frame of design' (Fry and Nocek, 2021: 2).

As introduced above, 'ecofeminist philosophy often starts with a discussion of the [. . .] dualisms that have structured Western thought' particularly nature/

culture and woman/man (Adams and Gruen, 2014: 202) and how this has led to a logic of domination. In terms of design, this logic has perpetuated 'a separation of human life from other forms of life, vegetal and animal' (Meyer quoted in Napawan, Burke and Yui, 2017). This conceptualizes people as outside of the ecosystems of which they are part, and environments become entities to be controlled, managed and owned. Although designers are now trained to be socially responsible and ecologically aware, sustainable design practice can often reinforce this discourse of separation. As Claire Napawan, Ellen Burke and Sahoko Yui note:

> by locating ourselves 'outside' of our ecosystem, we no longer perceive that we rely on it for our daily domestic needs but rather imagine that we satisfy those needs through our own invention and technological mastery.
>
> 2017: 4

Solar technologies and electric cars, for example, while having some positive effects, continue to involve environmental and social justice issues associated with the extraction of natural resources, manufacturing, energy, transportation and waste. For instance, it has been documented how many cheap solar panels rely upon Uyghur forced labour in Xinjiang in China (Braw, 2021), and that women in these labour camps have endured sexual abuse, torture and forced sterilization (Ochab, 2021). As Rebecca Solnit puts it, 'free-range chickens and Priuses are great, but they alone aren't adequate tools for creating a truly different society and ecology' (Solnit, 2014: 81). What passes for 'environmentally responsible design' is not enough to deal with ecological crisis. 'Design can't limit itself to changing the patterns of human consumption, to altering supply chains, or to sourcing biodegradable materials. It must envision the possibility of designing new conditions for being human' (Fry and Nocek, 2021).

Tony Fry and Adam Nocek argue that the challenge for design 'is to undermine its own ontological ground' (2021: 3). Design must strive for a mode of designing that works against the separation and juxtaposition of 'ideal, active subjects' and 'passive and inert objects' (Fry and Nocek, 2021: 3–4). It must look to approaches, processes and methods that address the entanglement of people, animals, plants and minerals, and the mutual relationships that exist between all actors. Thus, as Fry and Nocek go on to argue, to imagine a solution, design practice needs to become unrecognizable to itself. It needs to move away from 'rational subjectivity that knows what is preferable and how to bring it into being' which is still present in design methods such as 'wicked problems', 'speculative futures' and 'knowing in action' (Fry and Nocek, 2021: 14). As Alfredo Gutiérrez Borrero writes in the same volume, '[d]esign must un-design its own designing, but in so doing, it cannot make this a design project' (Fry and Nocek, 2021: 14). This is easier in theory than in practice and is uncharted territory at least in terms of

Anglo-European professional design frameworks. This transformation would 'require designers to entertain crisis in a way that does not regard it as a problem to be solved' (Fry and Nocek, 2021: 15). This proposition is particularly challenging when the inclination and training of the majority of designers is to work towards a solution.

However, practicing designers increasingly encounter the limits of current design methods in dealing with issues pertaining to ecological crisis and social justice. As Arturo Escobar observes, design theorists and practitioners have already begun to explore design for transitions, a movement that challenges binaries such as mind/body, subject/object and nature/culture. Nobody, he writes, 'really performs as a pure wound-up Cartesian toy' (Escobar, 2018: 131). In our everyday lives, it is impossible to partition life entirely according to fixed divides and the 'impetus to reconnect (socially, ecologically and spiritually) is always there' (Escobar, 2018: 131). Escobar gives the example of gardening, which while an 'otherwise-objectifying relation[. . .] with the natural world', is also a way of relating to the non-human (2018: 131).

Despite increasingly encountering these limits, in terms of practical design processes and methods we are still stuck with many of the old solutionist tendencies. As Fry and Nocek write, universal design approaches that call for social, ecological and political change using 'pre-packaged innovation toolkits' are largely 'window-dressing when it comes to a deep and sustained engagement with design's implication in and possible transformation of planetary crisis' (2021: 2). This is exemplified by the story that Madina Tlostanova tells of overhearing a colleague who was trying to include 'environmentally informed optics' when teaching students. The teacher asked students to imagine their clients not as people, but 'the Sun and Moon' (Tlostanova, 2021: 163). This, she writes is illustrative of how design methods in their current state 'comically attempt [. . .] to draw the whole universe into a presumably incontestable commercialised vision' (Tlostanova, 2021: 163).

While there is no doubt about the limits of an approach that tries to repurpose human-centred methodologies, in some cases there can be advantages to treating non-human actors as users. For example, in 'Pollinator Pathmaker', Alexandra Daisy Ginsburg asks us to consider what a garden would look like if it were designed from a pollinator's perspective in response to the decline in pollinator populations around the world. Ginsburg created an algorithmic tool that allows gardeners to see their garden as other pollinators would, and then produce a planting plan (fig. 6.1).

Nevertheless, when design theorists and practitioners look towards transitional approaches and methods they have tended to focus on sustainability and the environment over related social justice issues such as gender. For example, a number of academics have called for an increased focus on power and politics in transition design, as well as wider methodological engagement with other

Figure 6.1 The Pollinator Pathmaker online tool, 2021 © Alexandra Daisy Ginsberg.

disciplines including feminism (Boehnert, Lockton and Mulder, 2018; Gaziulusoy and Öztekin, 2019).

When gender and feminist perspectives are considered in discussions of transition design, as they are in *Designs for the Pluriverse* by Escobar (2018), they can reproduce gender binaries. In Escobar's discussion of the wide range of work that critiques life-stifling dualisms, he spends significant time discussing feminist approaches, specifically those from the Global South. He argues that '[f]eminists from the Global South are particularly attuned to the manifold relational politics and ways of being that correspond to multiple axes of power and oppression' (Escobar, 2018: 90). Feminists, he suggests, have a strong genealogy of thought that emerged from the exploration of situated knowledge, the corporeal and intersectionality which is reflected in a contemporary feminist commitment to other ways of worlding.

Notable for its absence in *Designs for the Pluriverse*, however, is any mention of queer theory or activism that has been instrumental in challenging the binaries of sex and gender and imagining different sorts of futures. Escobar does refer in passing to the idea that gender maybe something 'life-stifling'. He writes:

Whether the concept of gender is even applicable to preconquest societies, or even to contemporary non-Western and nonmodern societies, remains a matter of debate, given the relational fabric that, to a greater or lesser extent, continues to characterize such societies, which admits of no strictly separate and preconstituted categories of masculine and feminine.

2018: 90

When outlining his philosophy of 'strong relationality' without subjects, objects and processes that exist by themselves, he also writes of 'the bisexual spider god/goddess Anansi' in the Fanti-Ashanti tradition from the Gulf of Benin (Escobar, 2018: 250). However, the bisexuality of Anansi is not highlighted as significant.

Drawing on the work of ecofeminist Claudia von Welholf, Escobar argues that it is patriarchy that is the 'source of the contemporary civilizational model that is wreaking havoc on humans and nature' (2018: 32). Patriarchy, based on hierarchies and domination, has prevailed over matriarchal cultures respectful of relational and place-based forms of living. He suggests that '[m]atristic cultures were characterised by conversations highlighting inclusion, participation, collaboration, understanding, respect, sacredness and the always-recurrent cyclic renovation of life' (Escobar, 2018: 32). He emphasizes that matriarchy does not mean the dominance of women over men, rather that being and doing is defined by a different conception of life for everyone.

Escobar writes that, 'in the beginning, there was the mother (in the last instance, Mother Earth)' (2018: 32) and this is a relationship that continues to be the case for many indigenous people today. For example, he writes of indigenous people in the Americas who are engaged in the 'Liberación de la Madre Tierra (the Liberation of Mother Earth)' who argue that it is time to abandon the 'superstitious belief in progress and the modern epoch as the best of all worlds' (Escobar, 2018: 36). He points to the arguments of von Welhof regarding the need to create 'new matriarchies' that are 'inspired by matriarchal principles of the past' adapted to the contemporary moment (2018: 37). At the end of the book, Escobar returns to consider 'The liberation of Mother Earth as Design Principle' (Escobar, 2018: 240). He argues that 'a plural sense of civilizational transitions that contemplates – each vision in its own way – the Liberation of Mother Earth as a fundamental transition design principle is the most viable historical project that humanity can undertake at present" (Escobar, 2018: 241). In this last sentence, Escobar adds 'each vision in its own way', yet one is left with the lasting impression that tackling environmental crisis would involve new matriarchies liberating Mother Earth.

The analysis of patriarchy in *Designs for the Pluriverse* is astute, and fostering the values of inclusion, participation, collaboration and understanding is paramount. However, when adopted outside of Indigenous relational cultures,

I consider the concepts of Mother Earth and working towards 'new matriarchies' to be problematic. The conflation of conditions of inclusion, participation and collaboration with a more 'natural' maternal figure essentializes biology and gender when translated into Western frameworks. While the mother figure may only be used as a metaphor, as Catriona Sandilands argues, the constructed 'woman-nature' (1997: 19) relies on a stable notion of identity that is easily assimilated into patriarchal hierarchies of domination.

Gender identity has never been a stable category and it would be a dreadful mistake to require it to be so in the name of a sustainable future. The ecofeminism on which Escobar draws, slips too easily into 'a glorified celebration of the eternal feminine and in so doing reinforce[s] the very dichotomies it purported to unmake' including man/woman, nature/culture, and spirituality/ science (Braidotti, 2022: 87). Feminist and queer theorists have criticized the heteronormative and maternalist assumptions of ecofeminist discussions of spirituality, care and nurturing (Gaard, 1997) and a similar critique could be made of the way heterosexuality and heterosexism are unchallenged in *Designs for the Pluriverse*. Thus, I would argue that to imagine relational futures, transition design should draw on concepts that are not so easily gendered or natured.

Ecofeminist positions regarding women's innate connections to nature have also led to some problematic positions in terms of technology. For example, Helen Hester notes how through the mobilization of nature and the natural in the ecofeminist Maria Mies' work she becomes 'perilously close to romanticising physical endangerment' that can be experienced through pregnancy and childbirth (Hester, 2018: 16). While Mies dismisses technologically assisted reproduction as a bad thing on the basis it 'alienates both men and women from their bodies', she celebrates the unpredictable and spontaneously wild (also alienating) forces of natural childbirth without technological intervention (Hester, 2018: 16). As Hester observes 'Mies' love letter to disempowerment seems to bear little relation to the way in which many people experience the vulnerabilities and anxieties attendant on biological reproduction' (Hester, 2018: 16). The value placed on 'natural' processes evident in Mies' argument is representative of a general tendency in ecofeminism to value the 'home-spun' over the mass produced.

In Escobar's analysis of 'post-human' futures, he outlines two competing discourses: 'return to earth' and the 'human beyond biology'. By 'return to the earth' he means 'developing a genuine capacity to live with the profound implications entailed by the seemingly simple principle of radical interdependence' (Escobar, 2018: 258); and he argues the 'human beyond biology' is the 'the overcoming and total transcendence of the organic bias of life dreamed up by the technopatriarchs of the moment' (2018: 258). Escobar asks whether designers will 'be able to contribute to dissuading unreflective publics from succumbing to the virtual realities offered by the patriarchal and capitalistic technological imaginations of the day?' (2018: 258).

By framing the dilemma for designers in this way, Escobar implies a distinction between technologies seen as 'new', such as virtual reality, and those outside the scope of the 'technopatriarchs'. While perhaps unintentional, this reproduces the 'traditional/modern' binary that is part of the 'othering' outlined as problematic above. In a similar way to Mies, this understanding of life bears little resemblance to the everyday experiences of most people. Emerging technologies including synthetic biology, nanotech, geoengineering, space exploration and virtual reality are not only in patriarchal hands: we are all entangled, albeit in different ways and with significantly different amounts of power. Thus, while it would be foolish to unequivocally embrace the liberatory powers of technoscience, I believe that we should not dismiss them wholesale either. Could 'the virtual realities offered by the patriarchal and capitalistic technological imaginations' generate ways of 'returning to earth', for example?

One recent example of the way that digital technologies can offer alternative ways of thinking about the relationship between gender and the environment is the project *Space Witches* by Rosa Nussbaum. An interactive digital installation inspired by the writing of Silvia Federici, *Space Witches* 're-examines the concept of the commons, our attitude to shared resources and localized embodied knowledge through a feminist lens' (Nussbaum, 2021). Through the stories shared by three characters, Space Witch, Zombie Mouse and Cockroach Nadezhda, we learn about the intertwined histories of witchcraft, gender, and landownership. For example, we hear how a cockroach got to space causing us to ponder on inter-species relationships and what space travel would be like if based on the logics of magic and care (fig. 6.2).

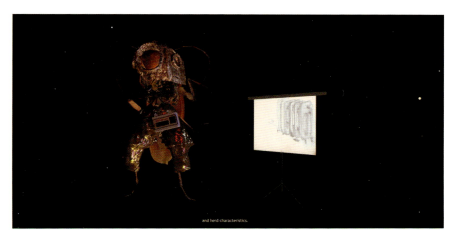

and herd characteristics.

Figure 6.2 *Space Witches*, Nadezhda the Space Cockroach Tells her Story. Rosa Nussbaum. 2021.

QUESTIONS FOR DESIGNERS: NATURE/CULTURE BINARIES IN DESIGN PRACTICE

The ways that we have been trained (informally and formally) as designers often mean that we reproduce binaries. Consider these questions in relation to your practice:

- In your practice, and in your field more generally, are there common associations made between particular technologies, gendered aesthetics, and the natural/artificial?

- How is 'nature' (this may take the form of resources, materials, actors) conceptualized in your practice? Do you control, use, draw from, or work with 'nature'?

- Do the design methods you use privilege the human? What other actors are involved in your practice, and do you respond to their needs?

- Are there design methods that you consider more appropriate for exploring the needs of the more-than-human?

Thus, rather than distinguish between types of technologies as inherently 'good' or 'bad', or between 'return to earth' and the 'human beyond biology', we need to cultivate a queer feminist design ethic that seeks to imagine 'the material and social world otherwise, not bifurcated, and hierarchal structures, but in organic and fluid configurations' (Canli, 2018: 663). While ecofeminism theorizations begin to do this work, celebration of matriarchy and the eternal feminine can limit the radical possibilities of de-gendering and undesigning design. Therefore, we consider queer approaches to nature and ecology in this next section.

More-than-human entanglement, post-nature and queer ecology

As Laura Forlano documents, ideas of the 'posthuman' (and related concepts such as the non-human, multispecies and more-than-human) have become central to resisting binary categories and 'exploring the multiple agencies, dependencies, entanglements, and relations that make up our world' (1997: 17). Donna Haraway is one of the pioneers who advocated for 'multiple ways of being that go beyond the human, with her two well-known manifestos on cyborgs and companion species' (Forlano, 1997: 23). As introduced in Chapter 2, Donna Haraway's concept of the cyborg is representative of a politics that challenges the binaries of mind/body, nature/culture and human/non-human. By arguing that there is 'nothing about being female that naturally binds women' (Haraway, 1991: 149), Haraway challenges 'back-to-nature' mysticism and notions of the eternal feminine. By emphasizing how people have always been entangled with animals, organisms and technological artefacts, Haraway explores partial connections rather than the binaries of universals/particulars.

For example, in *Staying with the Trouble*, Haraway documents how oestrogen links 'an aging California dog, pregnant mares on the western Canadian prairies, human women who came to be known as des daughters, lots of menopausal US women, and assorted other players' (2016a: 105). She writes that it is no longer news that corporations, labs, technologies and multispecies lives are entangled but the details matter. The details, she suggests, require us to be responsible for multi-species flourishing. Having taken Premarin (hormone replacement therapy containing oestrogen) makes Haraway 'more accountable to the well-being of ranchers, northern prairie ecologies, horses, activists, scientists, and women with breast cancer than [she] would otherwise be' (2016: 116). She concludes, we are all responsible, but not in the same ways. 'The differences matter—in ecologies, economies, species, lives' (Haraway, 2016: 116). Thus, Haraway's approach to entanglement and technological possibility is a theory of ecological relationality inspired by a feminist ethic of 'response-ability', rather than legitimation of technofixes and market growth (see Boehnert, 2018).

Feminist designers have begun to explore these entanglements, often conceptualized as 'more-than-human' design. For example, Nadia Campo Woytuk and Marie Louise Juul Søndergaard have produced 'Biomenstrual', a multispecies approach to menstrual care. Woytuk and Søndergaard observe how menstrual hygiene or management involves absorbing, collecting and disposing of menstrual blood. In 'Biomenstrual' they consider how we can design a menstrual management technology that opens up possibilities for cohabitation and collaboration with other species. They produced a spellbook in which they share their own practices, knowledges, recipes, spells and summonings. The book includes recipes for biomaterials and tools for crafting biomenstrual pads that enable menstrual blood to be used for composting (fig. 6.3). 'Biomenstrual' causes us to consider the mutualism involved in our existence – that without other critters our bodies would not be alive and that we can give back by changing our everyday practices.

More-than-human design seeks to benefit nonhuman as well as human stakeholders. As Stanislav Roudavski argues, as with 'other forms of design, more-than-human design can achieve better outcomes by designing "with" nonhuman users and not only "for" them' (2020: 738). He argues this can be achieved by providing novel means to include nonhumans stakeholders in the design process as well as in decision making and management. Roudavski

Figure 6.3 'Biomenstrual': More-than-human Design of Menstrual Care Practices. Nadia Campo Woytuk and Marie Louise Juul Søndergaard, 2021. Courtesy of Nadia Campo Woytuk and Marie Louise Juul Søndergaard.

writes, the challenge for designing with nonhumans is to acknowledge and cultivate skills emanating from nonhuman as well as human practices and cultures. The need to 'design with' rather than 'for', 'highlights the existence and importance of overlapping human/nonhuman worlds: spaces, structures, behaviours, memories, stories' (Roudavski, 2020: 738). Indeed, while more-than-human design may serve as an important counter-methodology in the face of the dominance of human centred design, all design involves impact upon animals, organisms and environments (even if indirectly). Haraway's story about taking hormone replacement therapy exemplifies these entanglements.

Explorations of the relationship between the body and technology from queer theorists have further challenged the distinction mind/body, nature/culture and human/non-human. In their introduction to *Somatechnics*, Nikki Sullivan and Samantha Murray document how in discussions of technology the body has often been conceived as existing 'as a fleshly substrate that simply is prior to, or in excess of its regulation' (2009: 1). This surfaces in second-wave feminist work when technology is either seen as a way to transcend and/or transform female embodiment, or as a tool of patriarchy. Sullivan and Murray argue that technology should not be conceived as separate from the self, rather as always already mutually interdependent.

Thus, Somatechnics, like Xenofeminism discussed in Chapter 2, is part of the 'post-natural' turn in queer feminist theory. As many queer writers and theorists have observed, acts against nature have often been used as a secular means of disciplining queer bodies and as a refuge for injustice. For example, Oscar Wilde recognized that the natural was often a short cut for the normal, the

KEY CONCEPT: SOMATECHNICS

The term somatechnics highlights that soma (the body) and technics (technology) are inseparable. The concept emerged following discussions at 'body modification' conferences held at Macquarie University in Australia and is associated with a 'technological turn in and of queer studies' (Sullivan and Murray, 2009:xi). Participants at the conference including Joseph Pugliese, Nikki Sullivan, Samantha Murray and Susan Stryker were discussing the limitations of the phrase 'body modification' because this supposes that body is something that can be separated from the rest of the world. 'Body modification', they argued, cannot be separated from other ways of 'doing' the body. For example, wearing contact lens, taking hormones, makeup and hip replacements are examples of everyday modifications. Less visible technologies of power such as gender norms also (in)form the making of bodies.

marriageable and the domestic (Halberstam in Young, 2019: para 36). As Karen Barad (2011) writes, the logic that maintains the nature/culture binary is perverse. On the one hand, humans are understood as having agency over nature whereby nature is the victim. At the same time, humans who commit 'acts against nature' are said to be more akin to nature, like animals for instance. 'In other words, the "perpetrator" is seen as damaging nature from the outside, yet at the same time is reviled for becoming part of Nature' (Barad, 2011: 121).

As Jack Halberstam (2020) observes in *Wild Things: The Disorder of Desire,* 'acts against nature' or accusations of 'wildness' have historically been used to justify settler colonialism and other forms of violence. For instance, wildness is frequently opposed to the modern, the civilized, the cultivated and the real. In the eighteenth and nineteenth centuries, wildness 'could be relied on as shorthand for the supposed savagery of Indigenous peoples and specifically their "savage sexualities"' (Halberstam, 2020: 8). These 'savage sexualities' were 'actually alternative forms of desire and kinship but were cast by missionaries as "backsliding" into heathendom' (Kuanui, quoted in Halberstam, 2020: 8). As we will explore more below, despite this history, Halberstam argues that wildness offers potential for opening 'up the possibility of unmaking and unbuilding worlds' (2020: 4).

The natural, however, neither 'holds sway over human understandings of good and evil, normal and perverse, bodies and life', nor offers potential for a queer feminist politics (Halberstam, 2020: 6). As Laboria Cubuniks argues, 'anyone who's been deemed "unnatural" in the face of reigning biological norms, anyone who's experienced injustice wrought in the name of natural order, will realise that the glorification of "nature" has nothing to offer us' (2015). Recognition of the injustices carried out under the pretence of the natural, coupled with the new condition of the body aided by new technologies, mean that alternative genders and self-designed sexes are a possibility (Braidotti, 2022). As Laboria Cubuniks insists, 'if nature is unjust, change nature!' (2015).

This does not mean diminishing people's feelings about their closeness to 'nature'. As Alyssa Battistoni puts it, there is no problem with people feeling that having a womb makes them close to the earth, as long as 'anyone who wanted to, could have a womb, and people with wombs could do things other than making babies, and if we recognized that there are a lot of ways to be close to the earth through use of our bodies, whatever parts we might have (and however technologically mediated they might be)' (2018: para 23).

In addition, the post-natural does not represent a move away from addressing environmental collapse or ecology, nor does it argue that everything is 'artificial'. On the contrary, it means focusing our attention on the interconnected and entangled conditions of life on earth for all, human, plant, animal and mineral. One example of such an approach is queer ecology.

Queer ecology emerged in the 1990s and, building on ecofeminism and work such as that of Haraway, strives to develop connections between sexual and ecological politics. As Rachel Stein writes:

> by analysing how discourses of nature have been used to enforce heteronormativity, to police sexuality, and to punish and exclude those persons who have been deemed sexually transgressive, we can begin to understand the deep, underlying commonalities between struggles against sexual oppression and other struggles for environmental justice.
>
> 2004: 7

Queer ecological scholarship and practice highlights the interconnectedness of humans and other species, and the sheer diversity of nonhuman sex and gender. As Lee Pivnik writes, 'our simplified collective understanding of human gender and sexuality collapses on itself when we are confronted by a fungus with 28,000 sexes' (2017: para 9). Pivnik founded The Institute for Queer Ecology (IQECO) in 2017, a community that brings together artists and designers 'unified and grounded by the theoretical framework of queer ecology, an adaptive practice concerned with interconnectivity, intimacy and multispecies relationality' (IQECO, 2022: para 1). IQECO is 'an ever-evolving collaborative organism that seeks to bring peripheral solutions to environmental degradation to the forefront of public consciousness' (IQECO, 2022: para 1). The institute produces artworks themselves and aims to 'share transformation and cooperation as strategies for environmental adaptation and ecological survival' (IQECO, 2022: para 4). For example, in 2021 IQECO produced H.O.R.I.Z.O.N (Habitat One: Regenerative

Figure 6.4 H.O.R.I.Z.O.N (Habitat One: Regenerative Interactive Zone of Nurture). The Institute for Queer Ecology. 2021. Courtesy of Institute of Queer Ecology.

Figure 6.5 H.O.R.I.Z.O.N (Habitat One: Regenerative Interactive Zone of Nurture). The Institute for Queer Ecology. 2021. Courtesy of Institute of Queer Ecology.

Interactive Zone of Nurture), a downloadable, participatory artwork taking the form of a simulation game (fig. 6.4). Inspired by utopian communities such as Lavender Hill, a queer commune established in Ithaca, New York, in 1973, users become inhabitants of a remote wilderness island and participate in the creation of a 'digital commune'. Each location in the island houses a unique sector of content that users can enjoy and contribute to. In the forest, for instance, you can leave or pick up information about wildlife or scavenging.

Among the artists and designers involved in IQECO are Beth Stephens and Annie Sprinkle. Stevens and Sprinkle are pioneers of queer ecology and are famous for coining the term 'eco-sexual'. They argue that nature should be considered a 'lover' not a 'mother' and by doing so challenge the idea that nature should always be there to serve us unconditionally. Through film, performance art and writing, the couple provocatively express the pleasure involved in making love to the earth. For example, in 2011 Stevens and Sprinkle co-produced an ecosex wedding to coal as a form of psycho-magic healing in which dancers, ecologists, healers, artists, writers, psycho-magicians and sex workers expressed their desires. Ecosex is not just manifested through creative practice, but Stevens and Sprinkle also define it as a new gender identity and an environmental activist strategy. Other queer ecofeminist projects combine environmental activism with sex-positive practices. For example, in the project, 'Beauty Kit', by Isabel Burr Raty, the body is harvested for 'eco-erogenous para-

Figure 6.6 'Beauty Kit' bio-autonomous farming workshop at ČIPke, Kersnikova Institute Ljubljana, Slovenia, October 2020. Photograph by Hana Marn.

pharmaceutics' (fig. 6.6). The first chapter of this ongoing project is centred on empowering the female* body by harvesting erotic juices and manufacturing them into gender neutral cosmetics. Through participatory playful art practice the project draws attention to ecology, exploitation, sexuality and agency.

Rather than creating alternative expressions of human/non-human relationships, other artists and designers choose to emphasize the diverse sex life of non-human organisms. For example, in the six films entitled *Green Porno*, Isabella Rossellini enacts the mating rituals of various insects and other animals. In an episode about shrimp, she demonstrates how the crustaceans change from male to female with age, while also telling the audience about the consequences of over-fishing. The artist, Niya B, also draws attention to the gender of non-humans. In the work 'Trans:plant' she produced a non-hierarchical and gender-neutral family of approximately 400 Aloe Vera plants grown with asexual reproduction. The plants were then adopted by people who were asked to give them gender-ambiguous names.

Therefore, as Rosi Braidotti observes, in queer ecofeminist theory and creative practice 'the boundaries between the environmental and technological dissolve and become porous' (2022: 87). As the IQECO suggest, 'queerness and ecology together make visible the interconnected, entangled conditions of life on earth' (IQECO, 2022a: para 1). At the level of the individual – the organism – queerness is transformation, fluidity and constant becoming (mutability). At the level of the collective – ecology – queerness is symbiosis and cooperation (mutualism). These insights are not new. As we will explore in the next section, the acknowledgement of mutability and mutualism has a long history in indigenous thought.

INTERVIEW: SIXTO-JUAN ZAVALA, DESIGNER AND ILLUSTRATOR, TEXAS/LONDON

Sixto-Juan Zavala (he/him) is a designer and illustrator from Texas and is currently based in London. He has worked in the creative field for over ten years and is interested in culture, marginalized groups, and the environment, particularly how visual communication and spatial design can facilitate cultural change.

SB: Could you tell us a little bit about your background and what inspired your interest in queer ecology?
SJZ: My background is in graphic design, illustration, and exhibition design. I did my BFA in Communication Design at Texas State University, worked in the field for about nine years, and then did an MA in Narrative Environments at UAL: Central Saint Martins. When I was in the second year of doing my MA we were able to pick our own topic to research and

create a narrative environment for. I was interested in LGBTQ+ communities and queer spaces but also interested in the environment and ecology. In my desk research I learned about queer ecology, which is a theory that intersects queer theory and eco-criticism. It resonated with me and sounded like something I could explore through my work.

SB: What are the main ideas or theories that form the basis of your approach? Is/how is this different from mainstream approaches towards sustainable design?
SJZ: Some theory that informs my work includes eco-criticism and what I am calling 'plant thinking', which looks at ecological issues critically and thinks about how anthropocentric and speciesist ideas can be challenged, attempts to empathize with plants and the non-human, and emphasizes the importance of indigenous perspectives. A couple writers include Robin Wall Kimmerer and Michael Marder.

Queer theory was an important influence on the project through its investment in non-hierarchical approaches (such as Deleuze and Guattari's ideas on the rhizome), interest in 'otherness', and preference for multiplicity and gradients as opposed to binaries. Some important theorists in that field are Doreen Massey and Jack Halberstam.

Queer ecology is a queering of ecological thinking and a greening of queer thinking that challenges heteronormative perspectives projected onto nature. I see queerness as always having been a part of nature. Catriona Sandilands and Nicole Seymour have made major contributions to the field.

My MA in Narrative Environments helped me to think about how stories can be told through space over time so narrative theory was also important. This included questioning where our stories come from, what kinds of past stories can be revisited, what are some new stories to be told, and asking how we can challenge how stories have been told so far. Donna J. Haraway's writing and Ursula K. Le Guin's essay 'The Carrier Bag Theory of Fiction' was helpful for that.

I suppose these ideas and theorists may not be traditional staples in teaching about sustainable design. Other resources particular to sustainable design might be Victor Papanek's *Design for the Real World* and Andrew Shea's *Designing for Social Change*.

SB: Could you talk about your recent work Queer Botany?
SJZ: Queer Botany is a project that started in 2020 from my MA major project. Inspired by queer ecology, I wanted to try focusing in on the botanical aspect of ecosystems, especially since I found a lot of correlations between queerness and plants. There are many cultural associations between flowers and LGBTQ+ culture, such as in the slur 'pansy' (for effeminate men) or in the work of Sappho, the ancient Greek lesbian poet, who is known for often referencing violet flowers in her love poems. There are tons more though if you look into it. Plants also have a broad and fluid sexual diversity with many of them being able to reproduce asexually and sexually. Most flowering plants have perfect flowers (a.k.a.

Figure 6.7 Section of Queer Ecology Map. Walthamstow Marshes, 2021. Design and photography by Sixto-Juan Zavala.

bisexual, androgynous, or hermaphrodite flowers) with both seed-producing and pollen-producing organs in the same flower (fig. 6.7). There's a lot that could also be said about the scientific categorization of plants, predominantly influenced by western European and heteronormative perspectives, and how plants often defy being placed in boxes.

I started with hosting online botanical drawing sessions where we could share some early content and stories from a queer botanical perspective. Participants could connect with plants through the meditative act of looking, sensing and observing, while generating some drawings at the end. Along with collaborators we did a site-specific project at Walthamstow Marshes in May 2021 in northeast London where we designed and installed four interpretive displays about plants growing in the area, we also printed a map, and gave guided walks sharing stories about the plants (fig. 6.2). In February 2022, Chelsea Physic Garden asked for help with a trail, interpretative design and programming throughout the month of February for LGBTQ+ History Month called 'A Dash of Lavender'. In the summer of 2022, the artist Daniel Baker asked if I could help with interpretive displays for the Platinum Garden, a project he was working on at Sutton House and Breaker's Yard, a National Trust property in Hackney, London. It is an LGBTQ+-led garden, inspired by Derek Jarman's garden at Prospect Cottage in Kent, that integrated queer stories about the plants grown there. I've also given talks and

Figure 6.8 Queer Botany Map. Walthamstow Marshes, 2021. Design and photography by Sixto-Juan Zavala.

collaborated with producers, facilitators and artists on programming like guided walks, in-person drawing sessions and workshops. These have all been great opportunities to continue research in queer botany.

SB: Many of the people involved in queer ecology describe themselves as artists. Do you think your training as a designer gives you a slightly different perspective? Can the ideas be just as useful for designers?

SJZ: I like to think of myself primarily as a designer, but I also have worked in events and art, while more recently I've been writing and facilitating workshops. I love collaborating with artists and have worked with a broad variety of media. I do think having a design background has given me a slightly different perspective. Much of what I think about is communication and particularly the visual aspects of communication. I do believe the ideas I've been researching in regard to queer theory, queer ecology, eco-criticism and narrative can all be applied to design. Of course, the environmental aspect of my research impacts what kinds of materials are used, where they are sourced, and what happens to them after a project. I think a way to queer design can be through intentionally obscuring, as opposed to defaulting to international-style legible sans-serif typography. Earlier in my career as a designer I didn't see myself as a storyteller but now I do. As designers we are facilitating the communication of content from our client or the intention of a project and all of this can be seen through a narrative with a beginning, middle and end. For my work, queer ecological ideas influence the perspective and the content that is being shared, as well as a focus on LGBTQ+ audiences. Even when I work on projects that are not necessarily related to Queer Botany, I still can't help but think about environmental impact, plant metaphors, and ways to uplift marginalized perspectives.

SB: What sort of design futures would you like to see materialize?
SJZ: I would like to see a design future that does not innately connect design to capitalism. A lot of people think of graphic design as advertising or branding for companies but obviously it is so much more. Designed things often sound like a luxury. Good design can be applied to social movements and can help to facilitate cultural change. My utopian ideal would be a society where people aren't struggling to make ends meet, can get free education and can actually follow a career doing something they believe in without having to worry about going broke doing it.

I believe humans are a part of nature and we should design in a way that thinks about nature, not as a resource to exploit but, as a complex entangled system that includes other humans, other living things and abiotic systems. How will our messages, actions and materials interact with them? This might materialize in designs that help humans but also are mutualistic with multi species benefits.

Perhaps we design too many things? Humans have made so many things that quickly end up as waste that lasts for a long time and does not benefit humans, other creatures or the environment. Maybe we should try to materialize less and responsibly dismantle things to allow room for the non-human to grow?

SB: If you could give one piece of advice to designers interested in gender justice what would it be?
SJZ: I'd say not to be afraid.

Indigenous worldviews, design and 'becoming-with'

As Rosi Bradoitti summarizes, indigenous thought and ecofeminism find common ground in their 'refusal to separate humanity as an exceptional category from the living environment' (2022: 91). Indigenous worldviews understand 'the human as a complex and heterogenous multi-species collectivity', and enforcing the binary between humans and non-humans would 'reiterate the violent mark of colonialism upon the lands and the people it dispossessed' (Bradotti, 2022: 92). As we will read about below, this view of the cosmos also means that indigenous approaches to gender and sexuality are often radically different from Euro-American understandings.

Acknowledgment of the interconnectedness of life is the foundation for traditional ecological knowledge that is shared by diverse indigenous communities (Ito, 2017) and has supported sustainable existence 'for 7,000 indigenous nations around the world over 40,000 years' (Hughes quoted in Boehnert, 2018: 51). Most indigenous ways of knowing recognize other species not only as persons but as 'teachers who can [. . .] inspire how we might live' (Kimmener, 2015: para 13). 'We can learn a new solar economy from plants, medicines from mycelia, and architecture from the ants' (Kimmener, 2015: para 13). As Joanna Boehnert summarizes, indigenous cultures have created forms of 'jurisprudence wherein 'law and nature were bound together' and where 'social organisation and cultural values are based on learning the lessons of nature' (Lauderdale quoted in Boehnert, 2018: 52).

For example, a core tenet of mātauranga Māori (Māori knowledge) is that humans are not at the centre of creation. As Kevin Shedlock and Petera Hudson summarize, 'mātauranga Māori provides a holistic perspective of celestial and terrestrial interconnectedness developed over thousands of years dating back to pre-Māori trans-Pacific journeys' (2022: 8). One recent example of a move to reinstate this perspective is Te Awa Tupua (the Whanganui River) in Aotearoa which was granted legal status as a person in 2017. Granting of legal personhood is based on Māori understandings of the river as an 'indivisible and living whole and as the spiritual ancestor of the Whanganui Iwi (a Māori tribe)' (Kramm, 2020: para 9). Māori who live along the river have long fought to uphold the mana (extraordinary power, essence or presence) and mauri (life force) of the river. In light of increased pollution and higher water temperatures, granting legal personhood is one way of fighting against the degradation of the river.

In mātauranga Māori (Māori knowledge systems) all subjects/objects, human and non-human, have mauri (life force) and can be considered taonga (highly prized) if Māori people view them as such. This includes the new as well as the customary, and contradicts typical representations of indigenous peoples as only interested in traditional practices. Māori, like many other indigenous groups, 'have a long, mostly unrecognised, history of ingenious innovation and adaption of new technologies' (Keegan and Sciasia, 2018: 359). This history, coupled with a perspective of interconnectedness, provides Māori with a preparedness and an ethical framework to relate to non-human actors.

For instance, Shedlock and Hudson (2022) argue that a Kaupapa Māori (Māori principles) model for the development of machine learning can address inequality in AI systems and sustainable practice. As visualized in figure 6.9, this approach would include an alternative attitude towards framing which explores

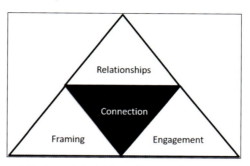

Figure 6.9 Kaupapa Māori modelled IT artefact model. Kevin Shedlock and Petera Hudson, 2022. Courtesy of Kevin Shedlock and Petera Hudson.

the IT artefact's purpose and reason for existing from a Māori perspective; 'maintaining relationships of rapport and accountability during the IT artefact construction'; and 'engaging with the IT artefacts beneficiaries during its creation' (Shedlock and Hudson, 2022: 4).

The Te Aranga Māori Design Principles also apply a Kaupapa Māori framework to design. The principles, as well as the network of Māori design professionals, Ngā Aho, emerged from a hui (meeting) involving the Ministry for the Environment and Māori designers and architects in 2007. The hui was arranged to address the lack of a clear vision and meaningful involvement of Māori in the development of the New Zealand Urban Design Protocol. The idea of 'urban design' did not resonate with a connected and holistic Māori worldview, and thus design principles were developed to foster engagement with the Māori cultural landscape. The principles provide guidelines for culturally appropriate design

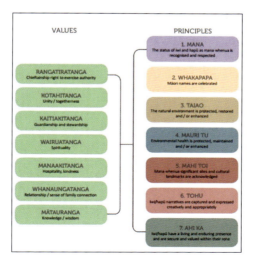

Figure 6.10 Te Aranga Design Principles. Tāmaki Regeneration Company. 2016.

processes and responses. They are outcome-based, founded on intrinsic Māori cultural values and responsive to place. (fig. 6.10). Thus, while the principles are specific to Māori and are currently being applied to the design of urban space, the values could also be used to design other artifacts in Aotearoa. The Te Aranga Design Principles, and the collaborative approach to their creation, could also be useful as a model for other indigenous groups. Much like the Buen Vivir-Centric Design approach outlined in Chapter 2, the principles can be used as an example to inspire other context-based expressions.

The cultural and environmental knowledge that indigenous groups hold has become increasingly recognized as valuable by corporations and governments, particularly in light of recent environmental crisis and social inequality. As Native American scholar and activist Vine Deloria argues, this is because the tradition, beliefs and customs of indigenous people, in this case Native American people, 'are guidelines for preserving life and the future of all nature' (quoted in Lauderdale 2007: 739). As Albarrán González (2020a) documented in her research, it is not only cultural and environmental knowledge that is valuable but also aesthetics and crafts practices.

While recognition of indigenous rights, knowledge and aesthetics is positive, unless wider issues of colonialism are addressed, inequity and environmental degradation will continue. As Tina Ngata argues, 'some of the most difficult and harmful spaces to navigate have been with organisations, agencies and projects that assume Māori names and offer Māori karakia [blessings] right before engaging in very colonial practices' (2022: para 10). Ngata continues:

> Our relationship cannot rest on your desire to draw from mātauranga Maori. Our ability to relate to each other must come with an honest reckoning, and a Tiriti [Treaty of Waitangi] partnership of integrity must start with an understanding of our perspectives.
>
> 2022: para 12

Thus, while many non-indigenous designers may have the desire to engage with indigenous perspectives, the design community must be careful not to appropriate indigenous ideas simply to add to the perceived value of individual designers and corporations. As Albarrán González has argued, we must acknowledge design (process, patterns and techniques) as part of the rights of indigenous communities' (2020a: 222–3). Thus, as designers we must ask ourselves how we can humbly engage in life-long learning about indigenous worldviews and from indigenous designers, how we can challenge colonialism, and design with (not for) indigenous communities. Co-design practices centred on developing long-term relationships can be one way forward, although as Penny Hagen observes, there is 'a tension between dominant euro-centric models' and 'culturally grounded, indigenous based practices' (2021: para 2). Thus, fostering authentic participation and elevating lived experience can

QUESTIONS FOR DESIGNERS: INDIGENOUS WORLDVIEWS AND DESIGN

This is a very broad topic, however some introductory questions are included here:

- Are you aware of the histories of colonialization in the place where you come from, work or study?

- Are there indigenous design approaches or frameworks that have been developed in your geographic location?

- If you are non-indigenous and you want to draw upon indigenous knowledge and design, what is your motivation, insight, and process?

- Why do you want to work with indigenous knowledge? Does this motivation go beyond your individual desires? Are you prepared to authentically engage and sometimes feel uncomfortable?

- Have you consulted with indigenous groups or advisors? Have you developed reciprocal long-term relationships? Can you partner with other indigenous design professionals or researchers?

- Have you considered indigenous intellectual property and copyright law?

- Are you going to use indigenous design methods specific to your location?

- What are you giving back? How will indigenous communities be able to engage with the work you produce?

sometimes involve 'sitting with, and reckoning with, deep, necessary discomfort' (Ngata, 2022: 28). As designers that care about collaboration with humans and non-humans we must also 'care for awkward spaces' (Tham, 2020).

While there can be tension between indigenous approaches and euro-centric design models, many indigenous understandings of gender and sexuality resonate with queer theory and queer ecology. As Elizabeth Kerekere suggests, due to the emphasis on relational ways of being in indigenous communities '[t]akatāpui [Māori who identify with diverse sexes, genders and sexualities] were part of the whanau [family], we were not separate, we were not put down, we were not vilified for just being who we are' (quoted in Harris, 2017: para 6). Much like the ideas of queer ecology introduced above, many indigenous communities recognize the mutability of organisms, artefacts and identities. People, like the worlds around them, change and transform over time, in a state of constant becoming; and our bodies, being interconnected with other organisms, plants, and minerals that help keep us alive, are always 'becoming-with'.

In their discussion of indigenous transgender and transcultural practices, Maddee Clarke draws parallels between 'trans* as a mode of seeing and relating' and indigenous worldviews (2017: para 5). They write 'trans* is not a thing or being, it is rather the processes through which thingness and beingness are constituted. As a prefix, trans* marks the "with", "through", "of", "in" and "across" that make life possible' (Clarke, 2017: para 5). Clarke continues, the transgender body is produced in a context of 'shared vulnerability . . . open to the planet', reliant on the 'becoming of others in order to become' (2017: para 6). Clarke uses the concept of becoming-with to consider how 'geopolitical trauma can open up a space for relationality and mutual dialogue among indigenous trans people' (2017: para 6). Trans* illuminates the contingent and non-binary nature of identity and our interdependence on all forms of life. In its radical contingency it offers potential to unite women, trans, queer, and first nations communities while holding difference within these markers (Allen cited in Clarke, 2017: para. 9).

Indigenous communities have many ways of expressing 'becoming-with'. For example, as Elizabeth Kerekere suggests, in Maori culture '[t]ipua were supernatural creatures who could change form or gender. Tipua can be seen today in takatāpui who embody both female and male in remarkable ways' (2015: 12). Kerekere tells the story of 'the ancestor Tāwhaki who was on a journey when he encountered Tongameha, a tipua (spiritual force who had the ability to change form and gender)' (2017: 65). Tongameha changed their male form into a beautiful female in an attempt to seduce Tāwhaki. Other tipua include Hine-ngutu, a knot of totara wood, and Pururau, a fish that was easily recognizable because a small tree grew from its' head (Gudgeon, 1906: 28.). Tipua are non-binary entities traversing the human and non-human, the male and the female, the supernatural and the real, the past, present and future. Stories of tipua tell us how to become-with, and how to understand our relationship with ancestors past, present and future, human and non-human.

Academics and designers working outside of indigenous cultures have also started to create interactive stories to help us to acknowledge our entanglements in ecological transformation. For example, 'Feral Atlas', a multimedia atlas created by Anna Tsing and others, collates 'feral' ecologies created by scientists, humanists and artists for the user to explore the 'ecological worlds created when nonhuman entities become tangled up with human infrastructure projects' (Tsing et al., 2020). Using interactive maps, illustration, video, poetry and more, the user can traverse the impacts and entanglements of the 'anthropocene' (fig 6.11).

For example, if the user clicks on an illustration of Lantana Camara, they learn how colonialization spread the seeds of the plant from British botanical gardens

Figure 6.11 'Feral Atlas: The More-Than-Human Anthropocene', 2020. Edited by Anna L. Tsing, Jennifer Deger, Alder Saxena Keleman and Feifei Zhou.

all over the globe. One of the most invasive species on the planet, Lantana is now invading monocrop teak plantations and causing aggression in elephants. Users can then look more deeply into how the 'ecological simplifications of the plantation, the industrial nursery, the factory, and the hospital have each given rise to a host of feral effects, including the cultivation of pests and pathogens' (Tsing et al., 2020). Instead of jumping into imagining better futures, 'Feral Atlas' encourages the practice of staying present and asks users to hold their 'ground and not turn away from the horror. . . [they] confront' (Tsing et al., 2020). I would argue that it is this approach to design that we should try to foster, one that goes beyond binaries and does not leap to designing solutions, nor attempt to appropriate indigenous concepts and apply them in isolation. Thus, while queer ecology and indigenous worldviews offer inspirational ways of seeing the world, how does design become unrecognizable to itself outside of these spheres? What sort of design methods might help us to stay present and unbuild conventional design practice?

CASE STUDY: KANAKA MAOLI (NATIVE HAWAIIAN) CRAFT-BASED MEDIA, LEHUAUAKEA, US, HAWAII

Lehuauakea is a māhū (non-binary/queer) mixed-Native Hawaiian interdisciplinary artist and kapa maker. Lehua's Kānaka Maoli family descends from several lineages connected to Maui, Kaua'i, Kohala and Hāmākua where their family resides. They have participated in solo and group shows around the Pacific Ocean, was the School for Advanced Research 2021 Ronald and Susan Dubin Native Artist Fellow (US), and opened their first curatorial research project DISplace at Five Oaks Museum in 2020/21 (US).

> I am being – a consciousness with living flesh, blood, and bone.
> I am body – striving for equilibrium in my environment.
> I am human – and walk with ancestors who gave me lungs to breathe and hands to create.
>
> YEHAW, 2020

Lehuauakea's creative practice spans across Kanaka Maoli (Native Hawaiian) craft-based media resulting in textile works, installation and painting. Their main area of focus is creating kapa (bark cloth) that are hand-stamped using ohe kāpala (bamboo stamps). Lehuauakea makes the kapa out of wauke bark, carves the bamboo i'e kuku used to beat the bark, and uses natural earth pigments and plant dyes to create patterns that traverse both the customary and contemporary. They explain that the practice is a form of intergenerational storytelling, and the creative works are 'microscopic representations of mythologies, origin stories, and environmental relationships since time immemorial' (Lehuauakea, 2021). Kapa 'are typically used for clothing, bedding, ceremony, birthing babies and burying the deceased' and Lehuauakea would like to inspire a resurgence in the use of kapa in everyday life (Henshaw, 2022).

The stories represented in their recent works address the subjects of 'cultural and biological ecologies, spectrums of indigeneity, and what it means to live within the context of contemporary environmental degradation' (Lehuauakea, 2022). Lehuauakea speaks of the ways in which Hawaii as an island nation is feeling the effects of climate change and how important it is to centre indigenous voices. The practice of making and printing kapa is a sustainable practice tied to the land through the planting and harvesting of materials. Kapa may also return to the land if buried with the deceased. It is these cycles of human and non-human life 'beyond the Gregorian clock or the 9-to-5 schedule' that Lehuauakea also wants to highlight as a more sustainable way of living (Henshaw, 2022).

Kapa making is much more than 'studio practice' for the interdisciplinary artist, they state ultimately kapa-making is 'a way of being, a way of relation, and a way of life that works towards a communal goal of renewed sustainability and resilience' as Kānaka Maoli (Lehuauakea, 2022). Intimately tied to Lehuauakea's identity, kapa-making unites their connection to the land, their understanding of their ancestry, and their queer identity.

'Mana Māhū' (2020) and 'No Mākou Ke Ānuenue' (2022)

The kapa 'Mana Māhū' (2020) (fig. 6.12) and 'No Mākou Ke Ānuenue' (2022) (fig. 6.13) more directly refer to Lehuauakea's identification as māhū. Māhū are non-binary and/or queer Kanaka Maoli. Being māhū, Lehuauakea suggests, is 'not as much of an identity label as it is a designation of the responsibility that one assumes within their given community' (Soto, 2022). Pre-colonization, for example, māhū were respected elders, knowledge keepers and spiritual practitioners that embodied both masculine and feminine energies. While beating kapa was typically reserved for women and the painting of the cloth for men, individuals who were māhū could be involved in both activities. After the impact of colonization, and under the influence of religious missionaries, both kapa-making and the respect given to māhū diminished (Soto, 2022). Thus, Lehuauakea looks to reclaim indigenous practices and identities through their work.

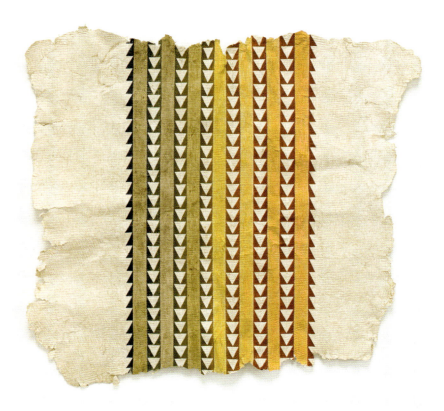

Figure 6.12 'Mana Māhū', Lehuauakea. Photo: Mario Galucci, 2020.

Figure 6.13 'No Mākou Ke Ānuenue'. Lehuauakea, 2022.

'Mana Māhū' (2020) uses earth pigments from Chinook, Klamath, Modoc, Siletz and Tillamook lands and handmade plant dyes painted on kapa paper. Lehuauakea created the piece to honour 'the spectrum of the earth's colours and the spectrums of gender identity within our Native communities' (Yehaw, 2020). The work is a celebration of the mana (spiritual energy of power and strength) of māhū people.

'No Mākou Ke ānuenue' (2022), which translates as 'The Rainbow For Us All' also refers to the diversity of gender expressions and experiences. The range of earth pigments and plant dyes represent diversity and the pattern references sharks' teeth, which are symbolic of fierceness but also protection and spiritual power. The wave and movement in the piece speaks to the idea that there is 'not just one way to be Hawaiian, not just one way to be queer' (Human Rights Campaign, 2022).

By producing works such as 'Mana Māhū' and 'No Mākou Ke Ānuenue' Lehuauakea hopes that 'one day we can break from the colonial stigmas that were place upon us and honour the multitude of roles that our ancestors once held (Soto, 2022).

Unmaking design practice

As argued by Fry and Nocek above, in order to engage in truly sustainable practice, design needs to move beyond rational 'solutionist' thinking. Solutionist tendencies, they argue, are even found in design methods that try to move outside of solving problems such as 'wicked problems', 'speculative futures' and 'knowing in action' (2021: 14). For instance, the wicked problem approach was conceived by Horst Rittel in the late 1960s (Buchanan, 1992: 15). Rittel was critical of the linear and rational models of problem solving that were being employed by designers at the time. He observed how solving a problem in one context through design often caused more problems in another. Thus, Rittel argued that a new approach was needed, one that took into consideration the complexity, contradiction and interconnectedness of social issues (Rittel quoted in Buchanan, 1992: 15).

Despite this intention, Ben Sweeting, Sally Sutherland and Tom Ainsworth (2021) have observed that when using a wicked problem approach it is common to hear designers talk of 'taming' problems. While 'taming' is indeed different from solving problems because it emphasizes the tentativeness of design proposals, they question what is meant by 'taming', and ask whether 'taming problems' is what designers should be aiming for. They highlight that taming is most frequently used to describe 'taming animals to make them behave predictably in human social contexts' (2021: para 5). This implies that wickedness is 'something to be controlled, mitigated, or made predictable' (2021: para 5). Sweeting, Sutherland and Ainsworth propose exploring how wickedness, in the form of conflict, difference, play, tension, uncertainty and unmanageability, may be of value rather than something to be tidied away.

Elsewhere, Sutherland and Ainsworth argue for 'post-rational' modes of design that embrace 'plurality, multiple relationalities and multisensoriality as fundamental components of future-focused design practice' (2021: 4460). They emphasize three characteristics of 'post-rational' modes. These are 'complexity and plurality', 'design beyond outcome' and 'design beyond solutionism'. For example, they use the design project *The Breast Milk of the Volcano* (Unknown Fields, 2016) to illustrate a design approach that embraces complexity and entanglement. Multimedia storytelling that traverses times and spaces, histories and futures brings together the interdependent relationalities of 'breastmilk' and 'lithium' in the context of Salar de Uyuni, the largest salt flat in the world. As Sutherland and Ainsworth suggest, after hearing these narratives we start to imagine redesigning artefacts 'not based on how they slide into our pockets, or feel in our hand, but [. . .] for the networks that they set in motion', the new relationships and power dynamics they create (Young, 2018 quoted in Sutherland and Ainsworth, 2021a: 4463). The value of design, they argue, is 'its ability to mediate multi-sensory experiences, materiality and the everyday' which can prioritize sociality and shared togetherness (Sutherland and Ainsworth, 2021a: 4466).

Indeed, as Judy Attfield (2000) suggests in her book *Wild Things: The Material Culture of Everyday Life*, design and materiality always exceed classification. Wild things are the parts of objects that are untamed, what gets left behind after the everyday is scrutinized from a rational perspective with its associated value. It is the 'burps, hisses, whispers, crackles and slurps that sound engineers refer to as "wild" and that get filtered out in the production process of sound recording' (Highmore, 2007: 248). For Attfield, wild things are the 'unwanted, unanticipated, extraneous, excessive meanings that are often left out in accounts of objects' (Highmore, 2007: 2 48). Thus, not only are design problems wild, so too are designed artefacts.

In *Wild Things: The Disorder of Desire*, Halberstam alerts us to how 'wildness has been associated with queerness and queer bodies throughout the twentieth century' (Halberstam, 2020: blurb). As highlighted above, the wild has 'served to name the orders of being that colonial authority comes to tame: the others to a disastrous discourse of civilization, the racialized orientation to order, the reifying operations of racial discourse (wild "things")' (Halberstam, 2020: 4). However, Halberstam argues that wildness challenges the very process of signification as '[i]t cannot mean because it has been cast as that which exceeds meaning' (2020: 39). It has been used to describe bodies and modes of being that fall outside of the definitional systems produced to describe them. This, he suggests, means that wildness questions the hierarchies of being on which Euro-American personhood has been built (subject/object, human/non-human etc) and provides alternative ways to know and be. Thus, Halberstam argues that it is worth reengaging with the problematic history of wildness because the concept opens up the possibility of unmaking and inbuilding worlds.

To engage with wildness is not to romanticize the 'natural', nor should it be confused with 'rewilding', a term that suggests there was some sort of Edenic past that should be reinstated. Wildness for Halberstam is 'the absence of order, the entropic force of a chaos that constantly spins away from biopolitical attempts to manage life and bodies and desires' (2020: 7). Wildness, he writes, 'has no goal, no point of liberation that beckons off in the distance, no shape that must be assumed, no outcome that must be desired. Wildness, instead, disorders desire and desires disorder' (2020: 7). Thus, wildness in a design context would be, as Sutherland and Ainsworth suggest, beyond outcome and solutionism.

Halberstam uses the example of the children's book *Where the Wild Things Are* by Maurice Sendak to illustrate his point. The book begins with Max, 'a young boy dressed in wolf's clothing, creating disorder in the family home' (Halberstam, 2020: 4). After being called a 'wild thing' by his mother and sent to his room, Max imagines another world. That night a forest grows in his room and we follow Max to where the wild things are. 'Rather than a place of wonder and innocence, the wild in Sendak's genius conjuring is a place of ruination, destitution, anarchy and despair' (Halberstam, 2020: 5). Max, as Halberstam proposes, is 'an anticolonial wanderer who refuses to settle the wild places he visits and who rejects the leadership he is offered' (2020: 4). Sendak sets the reader up to follow Max not to know, love or destroy the wild things, but 'to map the shape of the world that depends on their rejection' (Halberstam, 2020: 6). Halberstam suggests that this is illustrative of an aesthetics of bewilderment, a confounding, yet enchanting sense of unknowing the world.

More broadly, Halberstam argues that if we want to address social and environmental injustice then 'world-making, as we currently conceive of it can only proceed by way of unworlding' (2022: para 1). Concepts such as the human/non-human, subject/object, animal/vegetable should be 'tipped out of the hierarchical formations and disordered in meaning and in their relations to one another' (Halberstam, 2022: para 1). Halberstam find examples of such practice in 1970s aesthetic experiments that 'revel in collapse, destruction and ruination' (2022: para 2). One such example is anarchitecture movement, specifically the work of Gordon Matta-Clark, whose work used practices of creative destruction and unbuilding. For example, in his work 'Splitting' Matta-Clark famously split a house by sawing two parallel slices through its timber-frame and removing the material between the cuts. The result is a powerfully disorientating critique of progress and creative destruction, a form of unbuilding. Halberstam (2018) argues that Matta-Clark's inventive site-specific cuts into abandoned buildings are full of queer promise. He likens the cuts in Matta-Clark's works to the cutting and stitching of the trans* body. These acts, Halberstam argues 'confront common assumptions about the coherent and incoherent, material and immaterial, internal and external states of bodies and buildings' (Halberstam, 2018: para 4). Thus, Matta-Clark's art offers inspiration for artists and designers who are interested in tearing down the frames of representation in which they work and unbuilding binary understandings. As designers can we move enough away from ways of knowing, being and doing informed by 'either/or' logic and solutionism to make this possible? How might we become (or perhaps more accurately un-become) wild?

A number of feminist researchers and creative practitioners have been exploring these possibilities, specifically working with feral ways of knowing and being. In 2021, Cristina Ampatzidou et al. organized a workshop that took place at the Uroboros Festival which invited creative practitioners to discuss one tool or resource which they understood as feral. Ampatzidou et al. did not predefine the term for their participants, but used it broadly to 'denote the alternative, experimental, more-than-human, and wild' (2021: 154). Participants presented a variety of different tools including 'card decks, experimental walks, gameplay guides, manuals, typologies, and metaphors' (Ampatzidou et al., 2021: 154). Iryna Zamuruieva presented an approach to sensory walks that engage with a

Figure 6.14 Špela Petrič, *Phytocracy*, 2018. Photo by Miha Godec presented at Drevesni Park.

place through smell, sight, touch and hearting. For example, in Auckland a smell-walk led by Zamuruieva caused fellow walkers to reflect upon the changes to urban smell-scapes, the living cultures around them, and a common understanding of the streets they shared. Špela Petrič presented a card deck asking creative practitioners to 'embody different Anarchetypes – humorous and often absurd characters representing various realworld cultural values and approaches to plants' (Ampatzidou et al., 2021: 155). This is part of *Deep Phytocracy*, a participatory performance project, where people are asked to use tools designed specifically by Petrič to 'grasp plant agency' and politics (fig. 6. 14).

Feral design approaches are clearly emergent and, one would hope by their very nature, beyond classification. Ampatzidou et al., note, however, that the main ways participants used their tools were to:

1 To foreground embodied, situated, and bottom-up ways of working with other-than-human, notably multispecies, entities, and issues that decentre human and human control;

2 To reappropriate creative processes in ways and for purposes different to the original intentions, and;

3 To accept, expect, enable and even encourage thoughts, feelings, and actions to develop in their own ways, beyond the creative practitioner's (or anyone's) control and social norms.' (2021: 155)

Becoming feral or embracing the wild, then, means looking beyond the human and to that which exceeds classification. We need to get lost before we can find our way and to explore what design centred on a loss of control, bewilderment and unworlding might look like, if it is even possible. There are some tentative propositions here, but one thing is certain, moving to designing beyond binaries is an invitation to play, experiment and reimagine, practices designers are certainly well-versed in.

QUESTIONS FOR DESIGNERS: WILD METHODS

It has been argued in this chapter that if we want to address social injustice and ecological crisis then designers have to radically rethink their practice. Consider these questions to start to imagine your practice otherwise:

- Do you automatically jump to solutionist thinking? How can we help designers to stay present and embrace complexity?

- How can you include multisensory experience in your practice?

- Would designing to create new power dynamics and relationships mean we design differently?

- Can thinking about the wildness of people and things inspire alterative design approaches?

- Can you imagine and create a design world based upon fostering bewilderment and unbuilding?

CHAPTER SIX ACTIVITY

MAPPING ENTANGLEMENTS

Choose a material object that contributes to your experience of gender.
- What is it?
- How is it made?
- Who and what are involved in this process (human, animal, plants, minerals etc)?
- How are they connected?

Try to map this here.

CHAPTER SIX ACTIVITY

FERAL EXPERIMENTS

'Feral broadly denotes the alternative, experimental, more-than-human, and wild', challenging dominant designerly ways of thinking, being and doing (Ampatzidou et al., 2021).

Try these experiments and see what happens. Come up with feral experiments of your own.

Give a non-human in your house/garden the status of a human. Redesign their life.

Make a potion and spell to conjure your gender future.

Go on a walk, follow smells rather than a route.

Design something for your ancestors.

Dissect an iconic gendered object.

INSERT YOUR OWN EXPERIMENT HERE

Leave something you have designed in the elements. Document what happens.

INSERT YOUR OWN EXPERIMENT HERE

EPILOGUE

I began this book by telling the story of the birth of my second baby. Writing this epilogue two years later he is definitely not a baby anymore. He's little person who talks a lot and adores monster trucks, an obsession that became even more intense after I slipped on one and broke my ankle. With the help of doctors, nurses, a plate, lots of screws, drugs and some good bacteria, my ankle is healing well. If I wasn't one before, I am most definitely a cyborg now. While I have been returning to health, our planet has seemed less healthy. Aotearoa has had one of its wettest summers on record, as well as devastating cyclones and floods. My kids said to me, 'Tangaroa (the Māori god of the sea) is crying' and it certainly feels that way.

Throughout the book we have touched on the interconnection between gender inequality and climate change, and I think any sort of epilogue in the current context has to consider how design might reimagine itself in order to foster environmental, as well as social, justice. I have argued that gender justice in design will not be achieved by only addressing the tasks of diversifying the workforce or recognizing the needs of women. We have to change design values, processes and tools, and this move must be inclusive of the overarching need for design to address it's role in the worsening ecological crisis. This perspective is reflected in the queer feminist design approaches and practices that I have outlined in the book and should include:

- Exploring how norms are created though design practice and looking to challenge those that limit quality of life.
- Challenging the definition of design that emerged through the industrialization and professionalization of the practice.
- Questioning the hegemonic masculinities at work in design cultures.
- Reflecting upon our own situated knowledge and action when working on design projects.
- Making gender inequality visible and disrupting convention by putting diverse users at the centre.
- Co-creating alternative visions of the future that counter dominant narratives of progress.

- Exploring our interconnections with non-humans and experimenting with ways of (un)becoming-with.

These activities demand an intersectional approach that challenges the binary logic which separates man/woman, mind/body, nature/culture, subjects/objects, spirituality/science etc. As I argued in Chapter 6, design needs to reimagine itself outside of 'rational subjectivity' and solutionism. We should be cognisant of the 'designerly ways' we have been taught and resist our 'natural' tendencies towards 'good' design.

This does not mean that tools are useless, however, rather that we need to rethink what they can be. When we think of design tools, our minds automatically jump towards technologies such as the printing press and the latest software, or toolkits which include universal approaches to follow. Yet this definition is limiting. Simply construed, tools extend 'one's ability to transform features of a particular environment' and can have multiple forms (Ampatzidou et al., 2021: 153). They can be 'tangible or imagined, inanimate or biological, object-based', or performative (Ampatzidou et al., 2021: 153). In the case of this book, the feminist toolkit comprises of concepts, questions and activities. These tools come with their own politics, my version of queer feminism, but, as the theory of inter-action indicates, they will not necessarily be used in the ways I intend. Tools can be overlooked, misunderstood, rebelled against and through their use new ideas and practices emerge. Indeed, I have designed the tools in the book not as something to stick to, or unashamedly follow, but as ways to question current practice and develop new ways of working.

As Tony Fry and Adam Nocek (2021) argue, 'our moment' is increasingly one in which 'resilience' takes precedence over growth, and with recent global weather events it is hard to disagree. It seems our future is one in which disorder, breakdown and redirection will become fundamental to the conditions of designing and where place-based autonomous design becomes key to survival. Yet autonomy or self-direction alone does not mean the inevitability of gender justice. We must create tools that challenge and resist gender inequality in design, while at the same time enabling designers to adapt these tools to their own contexts and experiences. I hope to have achieved this in the preceding chapters. A queer feminist ethic involves taking responsibility for the power relations we create though our designs and cultivating conditions of reciprocity and care. It means striving to think otherwise and the conscious and continual re/making of design values, processes and tools according to where and when we are in the world. In that sense, this book is just a starting point, a toolkit for redesigning gender that is ready for its life beyond me.

REFERENCES

Adam, A. (1998). *Artificial Knowing: Gender and the Thinking Machine*. Routledge.

Adams, C.J. and L. Gruen (eds.) (2014). *Ecofeminism: Feminist Intersections with Other Animals and the Earth*. Bloomsbury Academic.

Agid, S. (2012). 'Worldmaking: Working Through Theory/Practice in Design, Design and Culture'. *Design and Culture*. 4 (1): 27–54.

Ahmed, S. (2006). 'Orientations: Towards a Queer Phenomenology'. *GLQ: A Journal of Lesbian and Gay Studies*. 12 (4): 543–74.

Akrich, M. (1992). 'The De-scription of Technical Objects', in W. Bijker and J. Law (eds.) *Shaping Technology*. The MIT Press.

Aksamija, A., R. Majzoub and M. Philippou (2021). *Design to Live: Everyday Inventions from a Refugee Camp*. The MIT Press.

Albarrán González, D. (2020). 'Buen Vivir-Centric Design: Decolonising Identity and Multiple Worldviews'. Available online: https://vimeo.com/472076038 (accessed 17 May 2022).

Albarrán González, D. (2020a). 'Towards a Buen Vivir-Centric Design: Decolonising Artisanal Design with Mayan Weavers from the Highlands of Chiapas, Mexico'. (Doctoral thesis, Auckland University of Technology.) http://hdl.handle.net/10292/13492.

Alford, C. (2017). 'How Systems Mapping Can Help You Build a Better Theory of Change in Too Deep'. *Kumu*. Available online: https://blog.kumu.io/how-systems-mapping-can-help-you-build-a-better-theory-of-change-4c85ae4301a8 (accessed 17 March 2022).

Amery, M. (ed.) (2022). *Brokered Dreams: 98 Uses for Vacant Space*. Letting Space with Wellington Independent Arts Trust.

Ampatzidou, C. et al. (2021). 'Feral Ways of Knowing and Doing: Tools and Resources for Transformational Creative Practice'. *Pivot 2021*. 22–23 July. Available online: https://pivot2021conference.com/wp-content/uploads/2021/06/0016_AMPATZIDOU.pdf (accessed 18 August 2022).

Anscombe, I. (1985). *A Woman's Touch: Woman in Design from 1860 until the Present Day*. Penguin Books.

Arceneaux-Sutton, T. (2021). 'A Black Renaissance Woman: Louise E. Jefferson', in B. Levit (ed.), *Baseline Shift*: *Untold Stories of Women in Graphic Design*. Princeton Architectural Press.

Archer, L. B. (1965). *Systematic Method for Designers*. Council of Industrial Design.

Armstrong, H. (2021). *Big Data, Big Design: Why Designers Should Care about Artificial Intelligence*. Princeton Architectural Press.

Arnett-Philips, N. (2020). 'Field Guide 2020: Towards Openness'. *Design Assembly*. Available online: https://designassembly.org.nz/2020/09/11/field-guide-2020-towards-openness/ (accessed 2 January 2022).

Attfield, J. (1989). '*FORM*/female FOLLOWS FUNCTION/male: Feminist Critiques of Design', in J.A. Walker (ed.), *Design History and the History of Design*. Pluto Press.

Attfield, J. (2000). *Wild Things: The Material Culture of Everyday Life*. Berg.

Attfield, J. and P. Kirkham (1989). *A View from the Interior: Women, Feminism and Design*. University of Minnesota.

Austin, J. L. (1975). *How to do Things with Words*. Harvard University Press.

Author Unknown (1843). 'The Government School of Design'. *Illustrated London News*. 2: 375–6. https://victorianweb.org/art/institutions/2.html.

Bahous, S. (2022). 'Speech: Our Ability to Fulfil the SDG's Promises Depends on our Decision to Put Women and Girls at the Centre'. Available online: https://www.unwomen.org/en/news-stories/speech/2022/07/speech-our-ability-to-fulfil-the-sdgs-promises-depends-on-our-decision-to-put-women-and-girls-at-the-centre (accessed 2 April 2022).

Bain, A.L. (2009). 'Masculinism', in R. Kitchin and N. Thrift (eds.), *International Encyclopaedia of Human Geography*. Elsevier

Baker, S.E. (2022). 'Beyond Demographic Diversity: Towards Intersectional Gender Justice in Professional Design Practice', in S. Dhakal, R. Cameron and J. Burgess (eds.), *A Field Guide to Managing Diversity, Equality and Inclusion in Organisations*. Edward Elgar Publishing.

Balch, O. (2013). 'Buen Vivir: The Social Philosophy Inspiring Movements in South America'. *The Guardian*. Available online: https://www.theguardian.com/sustainable-business/blog/buen-vivir-philosophy-south-america-eduardo-gudynas (accessed 17 May 2022).

Balsamo, A. (2010). 'Design', *International Journal of Learning and Media*. 1 (4): 1–10.

Balsamo, A. (2011). *Designing Culture: The Technological Imagination at Work*. Duke University Press.

Barad, Karen (2007). *Meeting the Universe Halfway: Quantum Physics and the Entanglement of Matter and Meaning*. Duke University Press.

Barad, K. (2011). 'Nature's Queer Performativity'. *Qui Parle*. 19 (2): 121–58.

Barad, K. (2016). 'Troubling Time/s, Undoing the Future'. The School of Culture and Society. Aarhus University. 2 June. Available online: https://www.youtube.com/watch?v=dBnOJioYNHU&ab_channel=FacultyofArts%2CAarhusUniversitet (assessed 1 November 2020).

Bardzell, J. and S. Bardzell (2013). 'What is Critical About Critical Design?' Proceedings of the SIGCHI Conference on Human Factors in Computing Systems. April. 3297–3306.

Barker, M.J. and A. Iantaffi (2019). *Life Isn't Binary: On Being Both, Beyond and Inbetween.* Jessica Kingsley Publishers.

Barnett, T. (2014). 'Monstrous Agents: Cyberfeminist Media and Activism'. *Ada: a Journal of Gender, New Media and Technology*. 5. Available online: https://adanewmedia.org/2014/07/issue5-barnett/ (accessed 12 December 2022).

Bath, C. (2009). 'Searching for a Methodology: Feminist Technology Design in Computer Science' in W. Ernst and I. Horwath (eds.). *Gender in Science and Technology*. Transcript Verlag. Available online: https://www.jstor.org/stable/pdf/j.ctv1xxsrx.6.pdf (accessed 6 July 2022).

Battistoni, A. (2018). 'Faculty Interview: Alyssa Battistoni on Ecofeminism and Xenofeminism'. Available online: https://mronline.org/2018/11/08/faculty-interview-alyssa-battistoni-on-ecofeminism-and-xenofeminism/ (accessed 12 July 2022).

Benton Zavala, A.M. (2018). 'Shifting the Landscape' in an Indigenous – Intercultural–Bilingual School in Mexico. (Doctoral thesis, Auckland University of Technology, Auckland, New Zealand). Available online: http://hdl.handle.net/2292/50415. (accessed 17 May 2022).

Black, A. and N. Burisch (2011). 'Craft Hard, Die Free: Radical Curatorial Strategies for Craftivism' in M.E. Buszek (ed.), *Extra/Ordinary Craft and Contemporary Art*. Duke University Press.

Blas, Z. (2008). 'Queer Technologies 2007–2012'. Available online: http://www.zachblas.info/works/queer-technologies/ (accessed 19 December 2019).

Blase, C. (2011). 'A Woman Called Toothpaste: An Interview with Lucy Whitman'. *The F Word*. 20 May. Available online: https://thefword.org.uk/2011/05/lucy_whitman/ (accessed 18 September 2022).

Bleecker, J. (2009). *Design Fiction: A Short Essay on Design, Science, Fact and Fiction*. Near Future Laboratory. Available online: http://drbfw5wfjlxon.cloudfront.net/writing/DesignFiction_WebEdition.pdf (accessed 18 December 2021).

Boehnert, J. (2018). *Design, Ecology, Politics: Towards the Ecocene*. Bloomsbury Academic.

Boehnert, J., D. Lockton and I. Mulder (2018). 'Editorial: Design for Transitions', in C. Storni et al., (eds.), *Proceedings of DRS2018*, 3: 892–5.

Boissonault, L. (2018). 'Amelia Bloomer Didn't Mean to Start a Fashion Revolution, But Her Name Became Synonymous With Trousers'. *Smithsonian Magazine*. 24 May. Available online: https://www.smithsonianmag.com/history/amelia-bloomer-didnt-mean-start-fashion-revolution-her-name-became-synonymous-trousers-180969164/ (accessed 18 May 2022).

Booth, A. (2021). 'It's Time for Data Visualizations to be More Inclusive of Gender Information'. *Poynter*. 3 March. Available online: https://www.poynter.org/reporting-editing/2021/its-time-for-data-visualizations-to-be-more-inclusive-of-gender-information/ (accessed 17 May 2022).

Bosch, T. (2012). 'Sci-Fi Writer Bruce Sterling Explains the Intriguing New Concept of Design Fiction'. *Slate*. 2012. Available online: https://slate.com/technology/2012/03/bruce-sterling-on-design-fictions.html (accessed 2 April 2022).

Braidotti, R. (2012). 'The Notion of the Univocity of Being or Single Matter Positions Difference as a Verb or Process of Becoming at the Heart of the matter', in R. Dolphijn and I. van der Tuin (eds.), *New Materialism: Interviews and Cartographies*. Open Humanities Press.

Braidotti, R. (2022). *Posthuman Feminism*. Wiley.

Braw, E. (2021). 'When Clean Energy is Powered by Dirty Labour'. *Foreign Policy*. Available at: https://foreignpolicy.com/2021/04/12/clean-energy-china-xinjiang-uyghur-labor/ (accessed 7 August 2022).

Britannica (2022). 'Feminism. Available at: https://www.britannica.com/topic/feminism (accessed 17 May 2022).

Brooks, R. and P. Hodgkinson (eds.) (2021). *Sharing Care: Equal and Primary Carer Fathers and Early Years Parenting*. Bristol University Press.

Broomhall, S. (2017). 'The Fragility of Women's Rights: How Female Guilds Wielded Power Long Ago'. *The Conversation.* 8 March. Available at: https://theconversation.com/the-fragility-of-womens-rights-how-female-guilds-wielded-power-long-ago-73265 (accessed 15 July 2022).

Buchanan, R. (1992). 'Wicked Problems in Design Thinking'. *Design Issues*. 8 (2): 5–21.

Buckley, C. (2020). 'Made in Patriarchy II: Researching (or Re-Searching) Women and Design'. *Design Issues*. 36 (1): 19–29.

Buolamwini, J. and T. Gebru (2018). 'Gender Shades: Intersectional Accuracy Disparities in Commercial Gender Classification'. *Proceedings of Machine Learning Research Conference*. 81: 1–15. Available at: https://proceedings.mlr.press/v81/buolamwini18a/buolamwini18a.pdf (accessed 18 May 2022).

Burnette, J. (2008). 'Women Workers in the British Industrial Revolution'. EH.Net Encyclopedia, 26 March. Available at: http://eh.net/encyclopedia/women-workers-in-the-british-industrial-revolution/ (accessed 17 May 2021).

Burnham, S. (2019). *Design Hacking: Resourceful Innovation and Sustainable Self-Reliance*. Self-Published.

Butler, J. (1999). *Gender Trouble: Feminism and the Subversion of Identity.* Routledge.

Butler, J. (2004). *Undoing Gender*. Routledge.

Buvinic, M. and R. Levine (2016). 'Closing the Gender Data Gap'. *Significance*. The Royal Statistical Society Magazine. April. 13 (2).

Callen, A. (1985). 'Sexual Division of Labour in the Arts and Crafts Movement'. *Woman's Art Journal*. 5 (2): 1–6.

Canli, E. (2018). 'Binary by Design: Unfolding Corporeal Segregation at the Intersection of Gender, Identity and Materiality'. *The Design Journal*, 21 (5): 651–69.

Castro-Gómez, S., and R. Grosfoguel (2007). 'El giro decolonial', in S. Castro-Gómez and R. Grosfoguel (eds.), *El giro decolonial Reflexiones para una diversidad epistémica más allá del capitalismo global*. Bogotá: Siglo del Hombre Editores.

Clarke, M. (2017). 'Becoming With and Together: Indigenous Transgender and Transcultural Practices'. Available at: https://www.artlink.com.au/articles/4604/becomingE28091with-and-together-indigenous-transgender-/ (accessed 9 December 2019).

Clegg, S. and W. Mayfield (1999). 'Gendered by Design: How Women's Place in Design is Still Defined by Gender'. *Design Issues*. 15 (3): 3–16.

Cobham, A. (2020). *The Uncounted*. Polity Press.

Cochrane, K. (2013). 'The Fourth Wave of Feminism: Meet the Rebel Women'. *The Guardian*. 10 December. Available at: https://www.theguardian.com/world/2013/dec/10/fourth-wave-feminism-rebel-women (accessed 17 May 2022).

Coleman, E.G. (2014). 'Hackers', in M. Ryan, L. Emerson and B.J. Robertson (eds.), *The John Hopkins Encyclopaedia of Digital Textuality*. Available at: https://gabriellacoleman.org/wp-content/uploads/2013/04/Coleman-Hacker-John-Hopkins-2013-Final.pdf (accessed 17 August 2022).

Coleman, R., T. Page and H. Palmer (2019). 'Feminist New Materialist Practice: The Mattering of Methods'. *MAI: Feminism and Visual Culture*. Available at: https://maifeminism.com/feminist-new-materialisms-the-mattering-of-methods-editors-note/ (accessed 8 March 2023).

Comuzi (2022). 'F'XA'. Available at: https://www.comuzi.xyz/fxa (accessed 17 May 2022).

Consalvo, M. (2002). 'Cyberfeminism', in S. Jones (ed.), *Encyclopaedia of New Media*. SAGE.

Corbett, S. (2019). 'How Introverts Can Be Activists Too?' *TED Radio Hour*. NPR. 12 April. Available at: https://www.npr.org/transcripts/711196501 (accessed 17 March 2022).

Costanza-Chock, S. (2020). *Design Justice: Community Led Practices to Build the Worlds We Need*. The MIT Press.

Cowan, R.S. (1983). *More Work for Mother: The Ironies of Household Technology from the Open Hearth to the Microwave*. Basic Books.

Crenshaw, K.W. (1989). 'Demarginalizing the Intersection of Race and Sex: A Black Feminist Critique of Antidiscrimination Doctrine, Feminist Theory and Antiracist Politics'. The University of Chicago Legal Forum. 140: 139–67.

Crenshaw, K.W. (1991). 'Mapping the Margins: Intersectionality, Iidentity Politics, and Violence Against Women of Color'. *Stanford Law Review*. *43* (6): 1241–99.

Criado Perez, C. (2019). *Invisible Women: Exposing Data Bias in a World Designed for Men*. Vintage.

Criado-Perez, C. (2020). 'We Need to Close the Gender Data Gap By Including Women in Our Algorithms'. *Time Magazine*. Available at: https://time.com/collection/davos-2020/5764698/gender-data-gap/ (accessed 11 May 2022).

Cross, N. (1993). 'History of Design Methodology', in M.J. de Vries et al. (eds.), *Design Methodology and Relationships with Science*, pp. 15–27. Kluwer Academic Publishers.

Cross, N. (2007). *Designerly Ways of Knowing*. Springer.

Cubuniks, L. (2015). The Xenofeminist Manifesto. Available at: https://laboriacuboniks.net/manifesto/ (accessed 23 May 2022).

D'Ignazio, C. and L.F. Klein (2017). 'Feminist Data Visualisation'. Available at: https://dspace.ceid.org.tr/xmlui/bitstream/handle/1/955/Feminist_Data_Visualization.pdf (accessed 17 September 2022).

D'Ignazio, C. and L.F. Klein (2020). *Data Feminism*. The MIT Press.

D'Ignazio et al., (2016). 'Towards a Feminist Hackathon: The "Make the Breast Pump Not Suck!" Hackathon'. *Journal of Peer Production*. 8. Available at: http://peerproduction.net/issues/issue-8-feminism-and-unhacking-2/peer-reviewed-papers/towards-a-feminist-hackathon-the-make-the-breast-pump-not-suck/ (accessed 25 May 2022).

DeLanda, M. (2016). *Assemblage Theory*. Edinburgh University Press.

DeLaure, M. and M. Fink (2017). *Culture Jamming: Activism and the Art of Cultural Resistance.* New York University Press.

Derby, F.B. (2019). 'Africa's Feminist Roots: Chronicling Feminist Herstories Since Precolonial Period'. *Medium*. Available at: https://medium.com/@MAKEDA_PR/africas-feminist-roots-chronicling-feminist-herstories-since-precolonial-period-8320c143595d (accessed 17 November 2022).

Derrida, J. (1978). *Writing and Difference*. Routledge and Kegan Paul.

Dery, M. (ed.) (1994). *Flame Wars: The Discourse of Cyberculture*. Duke University Press.

Design Council (2020). 'Does Design Have a Diversity Issue'. Our Work. *Design Council*. Available at: https://www.designcouncil.org.uk/our-work/news-opinion/does-design-have-diversity-issue (accessed 19 March 2022).

Design Council (2020a). 'Design Perspectives: Design Skills'. Report. Available at: https://www.designcouncil.org.uk/fileadmin/uploads/dc/Documents/Design%2520Perspectives-%2520Design%2520Skills.pdf (accessed 17 February 2022).

Designers Speak (Up) (2022). 'Directory of Women* Designers'. *Designers Speak (Up)*. Available at: https://designersspeakup.nz/directory-of-women-designers/ (accessed 12 September 2022).

Dorey, K. (2022). 'Stonewall International: The Sustainable Development Goals and LGBT Inclusion'. Available at: https://www.stonewall.org.uk/system/files/sdg-guide.pdf (accessed 24 May 2022).

DragvsAI (2022). 'Get Ready to Drag the Cistem'. *Algorithmic Justice League.* Available at: https://www.ajl.org/drag-vs-ai (accessed 17 May 2022).

Dunne, A. and F. Raby (2004). *Is This Your Future?* Available at: http://dunneandraby. co.uk/content/projects/68/0 (accessed 8 July 2022).

Dunne, A. and F. Raby (2013). *Speculative Everything: Design, Fiction and Social Dreaming*. The MIT Press.

Ehrnbeger, K., M. Räsänen and S. Ilstedt (2012). 'Visualising Gender Norms in Design: Meet the Mega Hurricane Mixer and the Drill Dolphia'. *International Journal of Design*, 6 (3): 85–98.

Ehrnberger, K., M. Räsänen, E. Börjesson, A.C. Hertz and C. Sundbom (2017). 'The Androchair: Performing Gynaecology Through the Practice of Gender Critical Design'. *The Design Journal*. 20 (2): 181–98.

Escobar, A. (2018). *Designs for the Pluriverse: Radical Interdependence, Autonomy and the Making of Worlds*. Duke University Press.

Fallan, K. (2008). 'De-scribing Design: Appropriating Script Analysis to Design History'. *Design Issues*. 24 (4): 61–75.

Fausto-Sterling, A. (1993). 'The Five Sexes: Why Male and Female Are Not Enough'. *Sciences*. March–April: 20–4.

Fausto-Sterling, A. (2000). 'The Five Sexes, Revisited'. *The Sciences*. July/August. Available at: http://www2.kobe-u.ac.jp/~alexroni/IPD%202016%20readings/IPD%20 2016_3/FAUSTO_STERLING-2000-The_Sciences%205%20sexes%20revisited.pdf (accessed 8 July 2022).

Felski, R. (2000). *Doing Time: Feminist Theory and Postmodern Culture*. New York University Press.

Feminist Hacking (2022). 'Feminist Hacking: Building Circuits as An Artistic Practice'. *Feminist Hacker Spaces*. Available at: https://feministhackerspaces.cargo.site/About (accessed 8 July 2022).

Femme Type Directory (2022). 'About'. Available at: https://femme-type.com/about-femme-type/ (accessed 29 July 2022).

Fessler, L. (2017). 'Siri, Define Patriarchy: We Tested Bots Like Siri and Alexa to See Who Would Stand Up to Sexual Harassment'. *Quartz*. 22 February. Available at: https:// qz.com/911681/we-tested-apples-siri-amazon-echos-alexa-microsofts-cortana-and-googles-google-home-to-see-which-personal-assistant-bots-stand-up-for-themselves-in-the-face-of-sexual-harassment (accessed 15 July 2022).

Filmer-Court, C. (2020). '"I made my own world for people like me": Wednesday Holmes on Their Work Representing the LGBTQI+ Community'. *It's Nice That*. Available at: https://www.itsnicethat.com/articles/wednesday-holmes-illustration-200220 (accessed 8 June 2022).

Firestone, S. (1979). *The Dialectic of Sex: The Case for Feminist Revolution*. Women's Press.

Fischer, M. (2016). 'Think Gender is Performance? You Have Judith Butler to Thank for That'. *The Cut*. 13 June. Available at: https://www.thecut.com/2016/06/judith-butler-c-v-r.html (accessed 2 March 2022).

Fischer, M. (2017). 'Camille Paglia Predicated 2017: What the '90s Provocateur Understand About the Trump Era'. *The Cut*. Available at: https://www.thecut. com/2017/03/what-camille-paglia-understands-about-the-trump-era.html (accessed 8 September 2022).

Forlano, L. (2016). 'Hacking the Feminist Disabled Body'. *Journal of Peer Production*. 8. Available at: http://peerproduction.net/issues/issue-8-feminism-and-unhacking-2/ peer-reviewed-papers/issue-8-feminism-and-unhackingpeer-reviewed-papers-2hacking-the-feminist-disabled-body/ (accessed 22 July 2022).

Forlano, L. (2017). 'Posthumanism and Design'. *She Ji: The Journal of Design, Economics, and Innovation*. 3:1, Spring.

Forty, A. (1992). *Objects of Desire: Design and Society Since 1750*. Thames & Hudson.

Fry, T. (2009). *Design Futuring: Sustainability, Ethics and New Practice*. Berg.

Fry, T. (2020). *Defuturing: A New Design Philosophy*. Bloomsbury Academic.

Fry, T. and Nocek, A. (eds.) (2021). *Design in Crisis: New Worlds, Philosophies and Practices.* Routledge.

Gaard, G. (1997). 'Towards a Queer Ecofeminism'. *Hypatia*. 12(1): 114–37.

Gaziulusoy, I and Öztekin, E. (2019). 'Design for Sustainability Transitions: Origins, Attitudes and Future Directions'. *Sustainability*. 11: 3601.

Glasberg, E. (2012). *Antarctica as Cultural Critique: The Gendered Politics of Scientific Exploration and Climate Change*. Palgrave Macmillan.

Gleeson, J. (2021). 'Interview – Judith Butler: We Need to Rethink the Category Woman'. *The Guardian*. 7 September. Available at: https://www.theguardian.com/lifeandstyle/2021/sep/07/judith-butler-interview-gender (accessed 8 July 2022).

Global Fund for Women (2022). 'FAQs'. Available at: https://www.globalfundforwomen.org/faqs/ (accessed 8 April 2022).

Goodall, P. (1983). 'Design and Gender'. *Block 9*: 50–61.

Gordan, V. (2018). 'You've Been Bro-propriated!: 5 Ways to Combat Idea Hijacking'. *The Storytelling Strategist*. Available at: https://thestorytellingstrategist.com/youve-been-bro-propriated-5-ways-to-combat-idea-hijacking/ (accessed 14 July 2022).

Gorecki, J. (2022). 'What Ecofeminist Françoise d'Eaubonne Can Teach Us in the Face of the Climate Emergency'. Available at: https://www.versobooks.com/blogs/5288-what-ecofeminist-francoise-d-eaubonne-can-teach-us-in-the-face-of-the-climate-emergency (accessed 8 November 2022).

Götz, M. (2021). 'Feminist Dissent: Taking Sid/tes in Making 'Purple Noise' in E. Bippus, A. Ganzert and I Otto (eds.), *Taking Sides: Theories, Practices and Cultures of Participation in Dissent*. Available at: https://www.degruyter.com/document/doi/10.1515/9783839449011-006/pdf (accessed 8 June 2022).

Greer, B. (2011). 'Craftivist History' in M.E. Buszek (ed.), *Extra/Ordinary Craft and Contemporary Art*. Duke University Press.

Gregory, A. (1966). 'Design Science' in S.A. Gregory (ed.), *The Design Method*. Springer.

Griffith, C. (2018). 'Power in the Poster: 1997–2017, 43 Black Pins, 40 men, 3 women'. *Designers Speak (Up)*. Available at: https://designersspeakup.nz/2018/08/08/power-in-the-poster/ (accessed 16 July 2022).

Grosz, E. (2005). *Time Travels: Feminism, Nature, Power*. Duke University Press.

Gudgeon, L.T. (1906). 'The Tipua-kura and Other Manifestations of the Spirit World'. *The Journal of Polynesian Society*. 15: 1.

Guerrilla Girls (2022). 'Our Story'. Available at: https://www.guerrillagirls.com/our-story (accessed 16 July 2022).

Hagen, P. (2021). 'Co-design in Aotearoa: Ways of Being, Knowing and Doing'. *The Auckland Co-Design Lab*. Available at: https://www.aucklandco-lab.nz/the-lab-blog/co-design-in-aotearoa-ways-of-being-knowing-and-doing (accessed 24 July 2022).

Halberstam, J. (1998). *Female Masculinity*. Duke University Press.

Halberstam, J. (2007). 'Gender', in B. Burgett and G. Hendler, *Keywords for American Cultural Studies*. New York Uuniversity Press. Available at: https://keywords.nyupress.org/american-cultural-studies/essay/gender/ (accessed 16 January 2022).

Halberstam, J. (2018). 'Unbuilding Gender: Trans* Anarchitectures In and Beyond the Work of Gordon Matta-Clark'. *Places Journal.* Available at: https://placesjournal.org/article/unbuilding-gender/?cn-reloaded=1 (accessed 16 November 2022).

Halberstam, J. (2020). *Wild Things: The Disorder of Desire*. Duke University Press.

Halberstam, J. (2022). 'Unworlding: An Aesthetics of Collapse'. *The Art of Detours*. 20 May. Available at: https://dansehallerne.dk/static/files/documents/unworlding-an-aesthetics-of-collapse-_jack-halberstam.pdf (accessed 16 January 2022).

Haraway, D. (1986). '*Situated Knowledges: The Science Question in Feminism and the Privilege of Partial Perspective*'. *Feminist Studies*. 14 (3): 575–99.

Haraway, D. (1991). 'A Cyborg Manifesto', in *Simians, Cyborgs and Women: The Reinvention of Nature*. Routledge.

Haraway, D. (2011). 'Speculative Fabulations for Technoculture's Generations: Taking Care of Unexpected Country'. Available at: http://australianhumanitiesreview.org/2011/05/01/speculative-fabulations-for-technocultures-generations-taking-care-of-unexpected-country/ (accessed 16 January 2021).

Haraway, D. (2016). *Manifestly Haraway*. University of Minnesota Press.

Haraway, D. (2016a). *Staying with the Trouble: Making Kin in the Chthulucene*. Duke University Press.

Harris, S. (2017). 'Elizabeth Kerekere speaks on Maori LGBTQ term takatāpui'. *NZ Herald*. 3 October. Available at: https://www.nzherald.co.nz/kahu/elizabeth-kerekere-speaks-on-maori-lgbtq-term-takatapui/OYZLT7NZUNUERWBSABOZQ3LME4/ (accessed 16 December 2021).

Hayden, D. (1981). *The Grand Domestic Revolution: A History of Feminist Designs for American Homes, Neighborhoods and Cities*. The MIT Press.

Hayles, K.N. (1999). *How We Became Posthuman: Virtual Bodies in Cybernetics, Literature, and Informatics*. University of Chicago Press.

Heath, J. and A. Potter (2010). *Rebel Sell: Why Culture Can't Be Jammed*. HarperCollins.

Henshaw, M. (2022). 'Lehuauakea uses art to say Native Hawaiians are still here'. *Streetroots*. Available at: https://www.streetroots.org/news/2022/08/16/lehuauakea (accessed 16 August 2022).

Hester, H. (2016). 'Technically Female: Women, Machines and Hyperemployment'. Salvage. Available at: https://salvage.zone/technically-female-women-machines-and-hyperemployment/ (accessed 16 March 2022).

Hester, H. (2017). 'After the Future: n Hypothesis of Post-Cyberfeminism'. *Res*. Available at: http://beingres.org/2017/06/30/afterthefuture-helenhester/ (accessed 23 January 2022).

Hester, H. (2018). *Xenofeminism*. Polity.

Highmore, B. (2007). 'Review: Wild Things: the Material Culture of Every day Life'. *Journal of Design History*. 14: 3: 248–50.

Hilder, R. (2022). 'Design's Gender Problem and What You Can Do About It'. Creative Bloq. 9 March. Available at: https://www.creativebloq.com/features/join-the-fight-for-gender-equality-in-design (accessed 16 September 2022).

Hill-Collins, P. (1990). *Black Feminist Thought: Knowledge, Consciousness, and the Politics of Empowerment*. Routledge.

hooks, b. (2000). *Feminism is For Everybody: Passionate Politics*. South End Press.

Human Rights Campaign (2022). 'AANHPI: "No Mākou Ke Ānuenue" "The Rainbow For Us All" by Artist Lehuauakea'. Video. Available at: https://www.youtube.com/watch?v=vIV4akiywLQ (accessed 15 October 2022).

IE SOGI (2019). 'Data Collection and Management: An Essential Component in Creating Awareness and Providing Effective Measures to Address Violence and Discrimination Based on SOGI'. Report. Available at: https://www.ohchr.org/sites/default/files/2022-01/Report_on_data_summary.pdf (accessed 15 October 2022).

IKEA (2020). 'Fiftyfifty – The Card Game for Everyday Equality'. Available at: https://www.ikea.com/gb/en/campaigns/fiftyfifty-the-card-game-for-everyday-equality-pub7b826150 (accessed 19 March 2022).

IQECO (2022). 'About'. Available at: https://queerecology.org/About (accessed 3 October 2022).

IQECO (2022a). 'Mutability and Mutualism'. Available at: https://queerecology.org/MUTABILITY-MUTUALISM-Seminar-with-the-Institute-for-Postnatural (accessed 3 October 2022).

Ito, J. (2017). 'Resisting Reduction: A Manifesto'. *Journal of Design and Science*. 14 October. Available at: https://jods. mitpress.mit.edu/pub/resisting-reduction/release/19?fbclid=IwAR13c83xV9F6-6mwcSyeKu_ E2da0_iReqlrVZGSXBTtpkLfW58P30g9dWyo (accessed 9 October 2022).

Jarvis, C. (2020). 'In Posse: Female Semen and Other Acts of Resistance'. Assessed 29 July 2022. Available at: https://drive.google.com/file/d/1-SJ_ir8zqmAM3j1CD6s0aoP8dj3XU-st/view (accessed 5 September 2022).

Jenkins, H. (2017). 'What Do You Mean By "Culture Jamming"? An Interview with Moritz Fink and Marilyn DeLaure (Part One)'. *Henry Jenkins*. Available at: http://henryjenkins.org/blog/2017/9/7/an-interview-with-moritz-fink-and-marilyn-delaurie-part-one (accessed 7 October 2022).

Jones, E. (2019). 'Feminist Technologies and Post-Capitalism: Defining and Reflecting Upon Xenofeminism'. *Feminist Review*. *123* (1): 126–34.

Jones, J. C. and D.G. Thornley (ed.) (1963). *Conference on Design Methods*. Pergamon Press.

Julier, G. (2008). *The Culture of Design*. SAGE.

Kang, M., D. Lessard, L. Heston and S. Nordmarken (2017). *Introduction to Women, Gender and Sexuality*. University of Massachusetts Amhurst Libraries.

Kearney, M.C. (2006). *Bought to You By Girl Power: Riot Grrrl's Networked Media Economy*. Routledge.

Keegan, T.T.A.G., and A.D. Sciascia (2018). 'Hangarau me te Māori: Māori and technology', in M. Reilly, S. Duncan, G. Leoni, L. Paterson, L. Carter, M. Rātima and P. Rewi (eds.), *Te Kōparapara: An Introduction to the Māori World*. Auckland University Press.

Kerekere, E. (2015). *Takatāpui: Part of the Whānau. Auckland*. Tīwhanawhana Trust and Mental Health Foundation.

Kerekere, E. (2017). *Part of The Whānau: The Emergence of Takatāpui Identity – He Whāriki Takatāpui*. PhD Thesis. Victoria University of Wellington. http://hdl.handle.net/10063/6369.

Kessler, S.J. (2002). *Lessons from the Intersexed*. Rutgers University Press.

Kienle, M. (2019). 'Dear Data: Feminist Information Design's Resistance to Self-Quantification. *Feminist Studies*. 45 (1): 129–58.

Kiernan, L. and A. Ledwith (2011). 'The Effect of the Merging of Design Disciplines and its Implication for Product Design Education'. *Design Principles and Practices*. 5(4): 173–86.

Kimmener, R.W. (2015). 'Living Beings as Our Kith and Kin – We Need a New Pronoun for Nature'. *Ecologist: Informed by Nature*. 25 April. Available at: https://theecologist.

org/2015/apr/25/living-beings-our-kith-and-kin-we-need-new-pronoun-nature (accessed 9 November 2022).

Kirby, D. (2010). 'The Future is Now: Diegetic Prototypes the Role of Popular Films in Generating Real-World Technological Development'. *Social Studies of Science*. 40 (1): 41–70.

Kirk, A. (2019). *Data Visualisation: A Handbook for Data Driven Design*. SAGE.

Kirkham, P. and J. Attfield (eds.) (1996). *The Gendered Object*. Manchester University Press.

Kirkham, P. and A. Weller (1996). 'Cosmetics: A Clinique Case Study', in P. Kirkham and J. Attfield (eds.) (1996). *The Gendered Object*. Manchester University Press.

Klein, N. (2017). *No Is Not Enough: Resisting Trump's Shock Politics and Winning the World We Need*. Haymarket Books.

Kowaleski, M. and J.M. Bennett (1989). 'Crafts, Guilds and Women in the Middle Ages: Fifty Years After Marian K. Dale'. *Signs*. Working Together in the Middle Ages: Perspectives on Women's Communities. 14 (2): 474–501.

Kramm, M. (2020). 'When a River Becomes a Person'. *Journal of Human Development and Capabilities*. 21(4): 307–19.

Kunzru, H. (1997). 'You are Cyborg'. *Wired*. 1 February. Available at: https://www.wired.com/1997/02/ffharaway/ (accessed 4 May 2022).

Laboria Cuboniks (2018). *The Xenofeminist Manifesto: A Politics of Alienation*. Verso.

LaRochelle, L. (2019). 'Co-Creating a Map of Queer Experience'. Co-Creation Studio at MIT Open Documentary Lab. Available at: https://immerse.news/co-creating-a-map-of-queer-experience-bece7a743ca7 (accessed 9 October 2022).

Latour, B. (2008). 'A Cautious Prometheus? A Few Steps Towards a Philosophy of Design (with Special Attention to Peter Sloterdijk)'. *Design History Society Conference*. 3 September. Available at: http://www.bruno-latour.fr/sites/default/files/112-DESIGN-CORNWALL-GB.pdf (accessed 2 March 2022).

Lauderdale, P. (2007). 'Indigenous Peoples and Environmentalism' in G. Anderson and K. Herr (eds.), *The Encyclopedia of Activism and Social Justice*. SAGE.

Lawson, B. (1983). *How Designers Think: The Design Process Demystified*. Oxford Architectural Press.

Lees-Maffei, G. and L. Sandino (2004). 'Dangerous Liaisons: Relationships between Design, Craft and Art'. *Journal of Design History*. 17 (3): 207–19.

Lehuauakea (2021). 'Native American Artist Fellows/2021/Lehuauakea'. *The School for Advanced Research*. Available at: https://sarweb.org/iarc/native-american-artist-fellowships/2021-artists/lehuauakea/ (accessed 9 November 2022).

Lehuauakea (2022). 'About'. Lehuauakea. Available at: https://lehuauakea.com/about (accessed 9 October 2022).

Levenson, J. (2022). 'What Does Queer Mean in the Creative Industry?' *It's Nice That*. 22 April. Available at: https://www.itsnicethat.com/features/what-does-queer-mean-in-the-creative-industry-creative-industry-220422 (accessed 23 July 2022).

Levit, B. (ed.) (2021). *Baseline Shift*: *Untold Stories of Women in Graphic Design*. Princeton Architectural Press.

Levy, S. (1984). *Hackers: Heroes of the Computer Revolution*. O'Reilly Media.

Lewis, J. and M. Bruce (1989). 'Divided by Design: Gender and the Labour Process in the Design Industry'. 7th Annual UMIST Conference. Available at: https://digital.hagley.org/08065464_divided_by_design. (accessed 16 January 2022).

Light, A. (2011). 'HCI as heterodoxy: Technologies of identity and the queering of interaction with computers'. *Interacting with Computers*. 23: 430–8.

Lockhart, C.A. (2016). 'Where are the Women? Women Industrial Designers from University to Workplace'. PhD Thesis. Queensland University of Technology.

Lorde, A. (1980). 'Age, Race, Class and Sex: Women Redefining Difference'. Copeland Colloquium, Amerst College, April. Available at: https://www.colorado.edu/odece/sites/default/files/attached-files/rba09-sb4converted_8.pdf (accessed 16 January 2022).

Luck, K. (1996). 'Trousers: Feminism in 19th Century America', in P. Kirkham and J. Attfield (eds.), *The Gendered Object*. Manchester University Press.

Luckman, S. (1999). '(En)gendering the Digital Body: Feminism and the Internet'. *Hecate*. 25: 36–48

Lugones, M. (2007). 'Heterosexualism and the Colonial/Modern Gender System'. Hypatia 22 (1): 186–209.

Lupi, G. (2017). 'Data Humanism: The Revolutionary Potential of Data Visualisation'. Printmag. 30 January. Available at: https://www.printmag.com/article/data-humanism-future-of-data-visualization/ (accessed 23 January 2022).

Lupton, E. (2021). 'Confidence Equity', in E. Lupton and J. Tobias, *Extra Bold: A Feminist Inclusive Anti-Racist Nonbinary Field Guide for Graphic Designers*. Princeton Architectural Press.

Lupton, E., and L. Xia (2021). 'Meet Mythical Norm', in E. Lupton and J. Tobias, *Extra Bold: A Feminist Inclusive Anti-Racist Nonbinary Field Guide for Graphic Designers*. Princeton Architectural Press.

Maggic, M. (2020). 'Mary Maggic Official'. Available at: https://maggic.ooo/ (accessed 1 October 2020).

Maher, N. (2017). 'Women are Studying Design – So Where Are All the Female Creative Directors?' *Design Week*. 21 April. Available at: https://www.designweek.co.uk/issues/17-23-april-2017/women-studying-design-female-creative-directors/ (accessed 16 January 2022).

Mahon, M. and L. Kiernan (2017). 'Sisters are Doing it for Themselves?: Exploring Gender in Irish Product Design Education'. DS 88: Proceedings of the 19th International Conference on Engineering and Product Design Education, Building Community: Design Education for a Sustainable Future, Oslo, Norway, 7 and 8 September.

Mallariaki, E. (2018). 'Making a Feminist Alexa'. *Medium*. Available at: https://eirinimalliaraki.medium.com/making-a-feminist-alexa-295944fda4a6 (accessed 16 January 2022).

Mallinson, A. (2021). 'Queering AI'. Available at: https://www.youtube.com/watch?v=YiJcwFBQgn8&t=521s (accessed 19 July 2022).

Malpass, M. (2012). *Contextualising Critical Design: Towards a Taxonomy of Critical Practice in Product Design* (Doctoral Dissertation). Nottingham Trent University.

Malpass, M. (2017). *Critical Design in Context: History, Theory and Practice*. Bloomsbury Academic.

Marshall, L. (2019). 'Facial Recognition Software has a Gender Problem'. CU Boulder Today. Available at: https://www.colorado.edu/today/2019/10/08/facial-recognition-software-has-gender-problem (accessed 16 January 2022).

Matthews, B. (2019). 'Assemblage Theory: Coping with Complexity in Technology Enhanced Language Learning', in F. Meunier et al. (eds.), EUROCALL: 280–4. Available at: https://files.eric.ed.gov/fulltext/ED600974.pdf (accessed 16 January 2022).

Matrix, S.E. (2001). 'Cyberfeminism and Technoculture: An Annotated Bibliography'. *Women's Studies Quarterly*. 29 (3/4): 231–49.

McBrinn, J. (2021). *Queering the Subversive Stitch: Men and the Culture of Needlework*. Bloomsbury Academic.

McCann, H. and W. Monaghan (2020). *Queer Theory Now: From Foundations to Futures*. Springer Nature Ltd.

McCarter, S. (2017). 'From Penelope to Pussyhats: The Ancient Origins of Feminist Craftivism'. *Literary Hub*. 7 June. Available at: https://lithub.com/from-penelope-to-pussyhats-the-ancient-origins-of-feminist-craftivism/ (accessed 17 January 2022).

McCoy, S. (2021). 'Quick and Correct Compositors at the Case: Early Colonial Women Printers' in B. Levit (ed.). *Baseline Shift: Untold Stories of Women in Graphic Design*. Princeton Architectural Press.

McKenzie, S.K., S. Collings, G. Jenkin and J. River (2018). 'Masculinity, Social Connectedness and Mental Health: Men's Diverse Patterns of Practice'. *American Journal of Men's Health*. September, 12 (5): 1247–61.

McQuiston, L. (1988). *Women in Design: A Contemporary View*. Random House Inc.

McVean, A. (2017). 'The History of Hysteria'. McGill University: Office for Science and Society. Available at: https://www.mcgill.ca/oss/article/history-quackery/history-hysteria (accessed 16 January 2022).

Merriam-Webster (2022). 'Gender'. Available at: https://www.merriam-webster.com/dictionary/gender (accessed 16 January 2022).

Mies, M. and V. Shiva (1993). *Ecofeminism*. Bloomsbury Academic.

Miles, K. (2022). 'Ecofeminism: Sociology and Environmentalism'. *Britannica*. Available at: https://www.britannica.com/topic/ecofeminism (accessed 16 January 2022).

Mitchell, J. (1966). *Women: The Longest Revolution*. Available at: https://platypus1917.org/wp-content/uploads/readings/mitchelljuliet_womenlongestrevolution_nlr40.pdf (accessed 19 January 2022).

Moseley, A.M. and A.D. Campbell (2019). 'Pretty Stuff: Gender Bias and the Future of Design Knowledge in the South African Industrial Design Context'. Designed Futures: DEFSA 8th International Conference Proceedings, Cape Town, 184–95.

Moss, C. (2009). 'Female Extension (1997) – Cornelia Sollfrank'. *Rhizome*. Available at: https://rhizome.org/editorial/2009/mar/24/female-extension-1997-cornelia-sollfrank (accessed 19 November 2022).

Munster, A. (1999). 'Is There Postlife After Postfeminism? Tropes of Technics and Life in Cyberfeminism'. *Australian Feminist Studies*, 14 (29): 119–31.

Murphy, Z.L. (2021). 'Amid the Extremes: Aasawari Kulkarni on Pioneering Feminist Typefaces'. Femme Type. 10 February. Available at: https://femme-type.com/amid-the-extremes-aasawari-kulkarni-on-pioneering-feminist-typefaces/ (accessed 16 January 2022).

Napawan, C., E. Burke and S. Yui (2017). 'Women's Work: An Eco-Feminist Approach to Environmental Design'. *Avery Review*. 27. Available at: http:averyreview.com/issues/27/womens-work (accessed 16 August 2022).

Ngata, T. (2022). 'Tina Ngata: To Tackle Terrorism, Start with Colonialism'. *E-Tangata*. 6 November. Available at: https://e-tangata.co.nz/comment-and-analysis/tina-ngata-to-tackle-terrorism-start-with-colonialism/ (accessed 19 September 2022).

Nguyen, M.T. (2012). 'Riot Grrrl, Race and Revival'. *Women & Performance: A Journal of Feminist Theory*, 22 (2–3): 173–96.

Noel, L.A.M. (2021). 'Here's What we Really Want your Class to be About! A Design Thinking Class Responds to the Pandemic'. *Design and Technology Education: An International Journal*, 26 (4).

Nussbaum, R. (2021). 'Space Witches'. Available at: https://rosanussbaum.com/work/space-witches/ (accessed 19 October 2022).

Ochab, E.U. (2021). 'Behind the Camps' Gates: Rape and Sexual Violence Against Uyghur Women'. *Forbes*. Available at: https://www.forbes.com/sites/ewelinaochab/2021/02/03/behind-the-camps-gates-rape-and-sexual-violence-against-uyghur-women/?sh=4916011768a5 (accessed 10 August 2022).

Old Boys Network (1997). '100 Anti-thesis'. Obn.org. Available at: https://obn.org/obn/reading_room/manifestos/html/anti.html (accessed 19 September 2022).

Online Etymology Dictionary (2021). 'Data'. Available at: https://www.etymonline.com/word/data (accessed 10 September 2022).

Onouha, M. (2018). 'On Missing Datasets'. Available at: https://github.com/MimiOnuoha/missing-datasets (accessed 10 September 2022).

Onouha, M. (2018a). 'The Library of Missing Datasets 2.0'. Available at: https://mimionuoha.com/the-library-of-missing-datasets-v-20 (accessed 10 September 2022).

Onouha, M. (2021). 'Natural or Where We Are Allowed to Be'. Available at: https://mimionuoha.com/natural-where-are-we-allowed-to-be (accessed 10 September 2022).

Osakwe, S., and A. Adeniran (2021). 'Strengthening Data Governance in Africa: Project Inception Report'. CSEA. Available at: https://www.africaportal.org/documents/21530/Strengthening-Regional-Data-Governance-in-Africa-_Inception_Report.pdf (accessed 5 March 2023).

Oxley, J. and R. Ilea (eds) (2015). *Experiential Learning in Philosophy*. Routledge.

Paasonen, S. (2011). 'Revisiting Cyberfeminism'. *Communications*, 36: 335–52.

Paoletti, J.B. (2012). *Pink and Blue: Telling the Girls From the Boys in America*. Indiana University Press.

Park, A. and L.R. Mendes (2019). 'FOR ALL: Sustainable Development Goals and LGBTI People'. Report. Available at: https://www.rfsl.se/wp-content/uploads/2019/04/FINAL_FORALL_RFSL_2019.pdf (accessed 10 July 2022).

Parker, R. (2010). *The Subversive Stitch: Embroidery and the Making of the Feminine*. I.B. Taurus.

Pentagram (2022). 'Gender Equality Creative Platform'. Available at: https://www.pentagram.com/work/gender-equality-creative-platform/story (accessed 14 July 2022).

Pezanoski-Browne, A. (2013). 'Ytasha Womack on Afrofuturism and the World of Black Sci-Fi and Fantasy'. *BitchMedia*. Available at: https://www.bitchmedia.org/post/interview-with-ytasha-womack-on-afrofuturism-and-the-world-of-black-sci-fi-and-fantasy (accessed 14 July 2022).

Pivnik, L. (2017). 'Ecocore'. Institute for Queer Ecology. Available at https://queerecology.org/ECOCORE-The-Queer-Issue (accessed 20 May 2023).

Plant, S. (1997). *Zeros + Ones: Digital Women + the New Technoculture*. Doubleday.

Prado de O. Martins, L. (2014). 'Privilege and Oppression: Towards a Feminist Speculative Design'. *DES2104*. Available at: www.drs2014.org/media/654480/0350-file1.pdf (accessed 14 July 2021).

Prado de O. Martins, L. (2016). 'Yarn Sessions: Speculations on Birth Control'. Available at: http://a-pare.de/2016/yarn-sessions-speculations-on-birthcontrol/(accessed 14 July 2021).

Prado de O. Martins, L. and P. Vieira de Oliveira (2014). 'Cheat Sheet for a Non – (Less) Colonialist Speculative Design'. *Medium*. Available at: https://medium.com/a-parede/

cheat-sheet-for-a-non-or-less-colonialist-speculative-design-9a6b4ae3c465
(accessed 14 July 2021).

Prado de O. Martins, L. and P. Vieira de Oliveira (2016). 'Breaking the Cycle of Macondo: Design and Decolonial Futures'. *XRDS*. Summer, 22 (4): 28–32.

Prado de O. Martins, L. and P. Vieira de Oliveira (2015). 'Futuristic Gizmos, Conservative Ideals: On (Speculative) Anachronistic Design'. *Modes of Criticism*. 27 February. Available at: modesofcriticism.org/futuristic-gizmos-conservative-ideals/(accessed 14 July 2021).

Preciado, P.B. (2013). *Testo Junkie: Sex, Drugs and Biopolitics in the Pharmacopornographic Era*. Feminist Press at CUNY.

Queer Design Club (2022). 'About'. Available at: https://www.queerdesign.club/about (accessed 14 July 2022).

Quijano, A. (2000). 'Coloniality of Power, Eurocentrism, and Latin America'. *Nepantla: Views from the South* 1 (3): 533–80.

Reid-Pharr, R. (2020). *Sex, Gender and Afrofuturism*. Assessed 2 November 2020. Available at: https://wappp.hks.harvard.edu/classes/what-gender-history (accessed 14 July 2021).

Reimer, S. (2015). 'It's Just a Very Male Industry': Gender and Work in UK Design Agencies. *Gender, Place & Culture: A Journal of Feminist Geography*, 23 (7): 1033–46.

Richterich, A. (2022). 'Hackerspaces as Technofeminist Sites for Experiential Learning'. *Learning, Media and Technology*, 47 (1):11–25.

Rincon, C., O. Keyes and C. Cath (2021). 'Speaking from Experience: Trans/Non-Binary Requirements for Voice-Activated AI'. Proc. ACM Hum.-Comput. *Interact* 5: 132.

Rmaanushi, J. (2021). 'Gender-inclusive Design is the Only Way: Language Matters'. *Medium*. Available at: https://uxdesign.cc/gender-inclusive-design-is-the-only-way-968494d5afc2 (accessed 14 August 2022).

Roberts, C. (2007). *Messengers of Sex: Hormones, Biomedicine and Feminism*. Cambridge University Press.

Robinson, D. (2020). *Hungry Listening: Resonant Theory for Indigenous Sound Studies*. University of Minnesota Press.

Rogan, E. (2019). 'Navigating the Default – Patriarchal Culture in Design'. *Designers Speak (Up)*. Available at: https://designersspeakup.nz/2019/10/02/navigating-the-default-patriarchal-culture-in-design/ (accessed 14 November 2022).

Rosner, D.K. (2018). *Critical Fabulations: Reworking the Methods and Margins of Design*. The MIT Press.

Roudavski, S. (2020). 'Multispecies Cohabitation and Future Design'. DRS Conference 2020. Available at: https://dl.designresearchsociety.org/cgi/viewcontent.cgi?article=1233&context=drs-conference-papers (accessed 3 December 2022).

Russell, L. (2020). *Glitch Feminism*. Verso.

Salih, S. and Butler, J. (eds) (2004). *The Judith Butler Reader*. Wiley Blackwell.

Salmi, C. (n.d.). 'Visualizing Gender-Based Violence in Graphic Awareness Campaigns in Nepal'. University of Reading Website. Available at: https://research.reading.ac.uk/research-methods-in-vulnerability/visualizing-gender-based-violence-in-graphic-awareness-campaigns-in-nepal/ (accessed 14 July 2022).

Samuel, R. (2012). *Theatres of Memory: Past and Present in Contemporary Culture*. Verso.

Savoie, A. and F. Ross (2021). 'Dora Pritchett, Dora Laing and Patricia Saunders . . .: The Invisible Women of Monotype's Type Drawing Office', in B. Levit (ed.), *Baseline Shift*: *Untold Stories of Women in Graphic Design*. Princeton Architectural Press.

SBI Website (2022). 'MMIWG2 Database'. Available at: https://www.sovereign-bodies. org/mmiw-database (accessed 14 June 2022).

Schön, D.A. 1984. *The Reflective Practitioner: How Professionals Think in Action*. Basic Books.

Schwartz, H. (1996). 'Hearing Aids: Sweet Nothings or an Ear For an Ear' in P. Kirkham and J. Attfield (eds.), *The Gendered Object*. Manchester University Press.

Scott, I. (2016). 'A Brief History of Cyberfeminism'. *Artsy*. October. Available at: https:// vnsmatrix.net/wordpress/wp-content/uploads/how-the-cyberfeminists-worked-to- liberate-women-through-the-internet-izabella-scott-artsy-oct-13-2016-online-journal. pdf (accessed 14 May 2022).

Scott, L. (2020). 'How Coronavirus is Widening the UK Gender Pay Gap'. *The Guardian*. 7 July. Available at: https://www.theguardian.com/world/2020/jul/07/how- coronavirus-is-widening-the-uk-gender-pay-gap (accessed 15 June 2022).

Seager, Joni (2016). 'Missing Women, Blank Maps, and Data Voids: What Gets Counted Counts'. Talk at the Boston Public Library. 22 March 2016. Available at: https://civic. mit.edu/2016/03/22/missing-women -blank-maps-and-data-voids-what-gets- counted-counts/ (accessed 9 October 2022).

Select Committee (1836). 'Report from the Select Committee on Arts and their Connection with Manufacturers with the minutes of evidence, appendix and index'. House of Commons. 16 August.

Sellers, L. (2018). *Women Design: Pioneers in Architecture, Industrial, Graphic and Digital Design from the Twentieth Century to the Present Day*. Frances Lincoln.

Serano, J. (2013). *Excluded: Making Feminism and Queer Movements More Inclusive*. Seal Press

Serano, J. (2013a). 'What is Gender Artifactualism?' *Whipping Girl*. 4 November. Available at: http://juliaserano.blogspot.com/2013/11/what-is-gender-artifactualism. html (accessed 14 January 2022).

Serano, J. (2015). 'Julia Serano on Judith Butler'. *Whipping Girl*. 11 September. Available at: http://juliaserano.blogspot.com/2015/09/julia-serano-on-judith-butler.html (accessed 14 January 2022).

Sharma, A. (2019). 'Air-ink: Printing with Captured Carbon'. Anirudh Sharma. Personal website. Available at: https://anirudh.me/air-ink-printing-with-captured-carbon/ (accessed 14 September 2022).

Shaw, D.B. (2008). *Technoculture: The Key Concepts*. Routledge.

Shedlock, S. (Ngāpuhi, Ngāti Porou, Te Whakatōhea) and P. Hudson (Te Whakatōhea) (2022). 'Kaupapa Māori Concept Modelling for the Creation of Māori IT Artefacts'. *Journal of the Royal Society of New Zealand*: 18–32.

Silva, M.A., K. Ehrnberger, M. Jahnke and A.W. Nilsson (2016). *Tools and Methods for Norm-Creative Innovation*. Available at: https://www.vinnova.se/globalassets/ mikrosajter/nova/guide-eng.pdf (accessed 8 January 2022).

Simon, H.A. (1969). *The Sciences of the Artificial*. The MIT Press.

Soderback, F. (2012). 'Introduction', in H. Gunkel et al., *Undutiful Daughters: New Directions in Feminist Thought and Practice*. Palgrave MacMillan.

Sollfrank, C. (ed.)(2018). *The Beautiful Warriors: Technofeminist Praxis in the 21st Century*. Minor Compositions. Available at: https://transversal.at/blog/the-beautiful- warriors (accessed 17 October 2022).

Sollfrank, C. (2021). 'The Art of Getting Organized. A Different Approach to Old Boys Network', in D. Richter, D. and H. Reckitt (eds.), *OnCurating, 52, Instituting Feminism*, 120–6. Available at: https://www.on-curating.org/issue-52.html (accessed 14 September 2022).

Sollfrank, C. (2022). 'obn_a – A Situated Archive of the Old Boys Network', in A. Schäffler, F. Schäfer and N. Buurman (eds.), *Networks of Care. Politiken des (Er) haltens und (Ent)sorgens*, Berlin, ngbk.

Sollfrank, C. (2022a). '#PurpleNoise – Feminist Noisification of Social Media'. Eeclectic. Available at: https://eeclectic.de/produkt/purplenoise/ (accessed 17 October 2022).

Sollfrank, C. (2022b). 'My First NFT, and Why It Was Not a Life Changing Experience'. *Makery: Media for Labs*. https://www.makery.info/en/2022/05/31/english-my-first-nft-and-why-it-was-not-a-life-changing-experience/ (accessed 17 October 2022).

Solnit, R. (2014). *The Encyclopedia of Trouble and Spaciousness*. Trinity University Press.

Soto, J. (2022). 'Queering Native Hawaiian Narratives: Artist Lehuauakea Talks About the Māhū Experience in Art and Life'. Human Rights Campaign. Available at: https://www.hrc.org/news/queering-native-hawaiian-narratives-artist-lehuauakea-talks-about-te-m%C4%81h%C5%AB-experience-in-art-and-life (accessed 17 November 2022).

Spark (2022). 'Spark Launches Code to Help Make the Internet More Gender Inclusive'. Available at: https://www.sparknz.co.nz/news/Beyond_Binary_Code/ (accessed 13 September 2022).

Sputniko (2010). 'Menstruation Machine – Takashi's Take (2010)'. Available at: http://sputniko.com/2011/08/menstruation-machine-takashistake-2010/(accessed 17 October 2021).

SSL Nagbot (aka L. Nyugen, S. Toupin and S. Bardzell) (2016). 'Feminist Hacking/ Making: Exploring New Gender Horizons of Possibility'. *Journal of Peer Production*. 8. Available at: http://peerproduction.net/issues/issue-8-feminism-and-unhacking-2/ feminist-hackingmaking-exploring-new-gender-horizons-of-possibility/ (accessed 23 October 2022).

Stats NZ (2021). 'Gender and Ethnic Pay Gaps: Stats NZ's Action Plan 2021/2022'. Available at: https://www.stats.govt.nz/corporate/gender-and-ethnic-pay-gaps-stats-nzs-action-plan-20212022/ (accessed 25 August 2022).

Stein, R. (ed.) (2004). *New Perspectives on Environmental Justice: Gender, Sexuality and Activism*. Rutgers University Press.

Steinmetz, K. (2020). 'She Coined the Term Intersectionality Over 30 Years Ago. Here's What it Means to Her Today'. *Time Magazine*. Available at: https://time.com/5786710/kimberle-crenshaw-intersectionality/ (accessed 27 August 2022).

Suchman, L. (1987). *Plans and Situated Actions: The Problem of Human-Machine Communication*. Cambridge University Press.

Suchman, L. (2007). *Human-Machine Configurations: Plans and Situated Actions*. Cambridge University Press.

Sullivan, N. and S. Murray (eds.) (2009). *Somatechnics: Queering the Technologisation of Bodies*. Routledge.

Sutherland, S. and T. Ainsworth (2021). 'Culture and Relationality: Moving Towards "Post-rational" Modes of Design'. Design Culture(s). Cumulus Conference Proceedings Roma 2021. L. Di Lucchio, L. Imbesi, A., Giambattista and V. Malakuczi (eds.). Sapienza University of Rome, Italy. 2: 4459–71.

Sweeting, B., S. Sutherland and T. Ainsworth (2021). 'Wicked Possibilities: Alternatives to Taming'. Proceedings of Relating Systems Thinking and Design (RSDX) Symposium. Available at: https://rsdsymposium.org/wicked-possibilities-alternatives-to-taming/ (accessed 25 August 2022).

Taylor, C. (1988). *Alternative World Scenarios for Strategic Planning*. Carlisle Barracks: Strategic Studies Institute.

Thackara, J. (2013). 'Republic of Salivation: Michael Burton and Michiko Nitta'. Available at: https://www.moma.org/interactives/exhibitions/2013/designand (accessed 25 February 2021).

Tham, M. (2020). 'Wicked Possibilities'. Wicked Possibilities: Designing in and with systemic complexity. University of Brighton. 15 July. Available at: https://vimeo.com/436882571 (accessed 25 August 2022).

Thompson, J. and J. Tang-Taylor (2019). 'Design. Diversity. Two Powerful Words. What Happens When They Collide?' *Idealog*. 7 May. Available at: https://idealog.co.nz/design/2019/05/design-diversity-two-powerful-words-what-happens-when-they-collide (accessed 25 August 2022).

Tlostanova, M. (2021). 'Unlearning and Relearning Design', in T. Fry and A. Nocek (eds.), *Design in Crisis: New Worlds, Philosophies and Practices*. Routledge.

Tobias, J. (2021). 'Emotional Housekeeping', in E. Lupton and J. Tobias, *Extra Bold: A Feminist Inclusive Anti-rascist Nonbinary Field Guide for Graphic Designers*. Princeton Architectural Press.

Tonkinwise, C. (2014). 'How We Intend to Future: Review of Anthony Dunne and Fiona Raby, Speculative Everything: Design, Fiction and Social Dreaming.' *Design Philosophy Papers*. 12 (2): 169–87.

Tonkinwise, C. (2014a). 'Design Away', in S. Yelavich and B. Adams (eds.), *Design as Future-Making*. Bloomsbury Academic.

Toupin, S. (2019). 'Feminist Hacking: Resistance Through Spatiality', in C. Sollfrank (ed.), *The Beautiful Warriors: Technofeminist Praxis in the 21st Century*. Minor Compositions.

Triggs, T. (2009). *Do It Yourself Girl Revolution: LadyFest, Performance and Fanzine Culture*. London College of Communication. Available at: https://ualresearchonline.arts.ac.uk/id/eprint/7875/1/TT%2Bbook.pdf (accessed 25 August 2022).

Tsing, A.L. et al. (eds.) (2020). *Feral Atlas*. Available at: https://feralatlas.org/ (accessed 28 September 2022).

Tunstall, E. (2013). 'Decolonizing Design Innovation: Design Anthropology, Critical Anthropology, and Indigenous Knowledge' in W. Gunn, T. Otto and R.C. Smith (eds.), *Design Anthropology: Theory and Practice*. Bloomsbury Academic.

UN (2021). '2 Zero Hunger'. Available at: https://unstats.un.org/sdgs/report/2021/goal-02/ (accessed 22 August 2022).

UN (2022). 'Goal 5: Achieve Gender Equality and Empower all Women and Girls'. Available at: https://sdgs.un.org/goals/goal5 (accessed 22 August 2022).

Unknown Fields. (2016). *The Breast Milk of the Volcano*. AA Publications.

UN Women (2018). 'Take Five: "If you are invisible in everyday life, your needs will not be thought of, let alone addressed, in a crisis situation"'. Available at: https://www.unwomen.org/en/news/stories/2018/7/take-five-matcha-phorn-in (accessed 22 August 2022).

UN Women (2021). 'Looking beyond traditional gender roles to a world where childcare and household chores are shared equally'. 12 January. Available at: https://eca.unwomen.org/en/news/stories/2021/01/looking-beyond-traditional-gender-roles-to-a-world (accessed 22 August 2022).

UN Women (2022). 'Progress on Sustainable Development Goals. The Gender Snapshot 2022'. Available at: https://www.unwomen.org/sites/default/files/2022-09/Progress-on-the-sustainable-development-goals-the-gender-snapshot-2022-en.pdf (accessed 22 August 2022).

UN Women (2022a). 'Explainer: How Gender Inequality and Climate Change are Interconnected'. Available at: https://www.unwomen.org/en/news-stories/explainer/2022/02/explainer-how-gender-inequality-and-climate-change-are-interconnected#:~:text=The%20climate%20crisis%20is%20not,less%20access%20to%2C%20natural%20resources (accessed 22 August 2022).

UN Women (2022b). 'UN Women Statement for the International Day Against Homophobia, Biphobia, Intersexphobia, and Transphobia'. Available at: https://www.unwomen.org/en/news-stories/statement/2022/05/un-women-statement-for-the-international-day-against-homophobia-biphobia-intersexphobia-and-transphobia#:~:text=UN%20Women%20stands%20in%20solidarity,of%20one's%20body%20and%20health (accessed 22 August 2022).

van der Velden, M. and C. Mortberg (2012). 'Between Need and Desire: Exploring Strategies for Gendering Design'. *Science, Technology, & Human Values*, November 37(6): 663–83.

Van Erden, J. (2020). 'A Davos POV About a 5th Industrial Revolution'. *RealLeaders*. Available at: https://real-leaders.com/a-5th-industrial-revolution-what-it-is-and-why-it-matters/ (accessed 20 October 2021).

Van Oost, E. (2003). 'Materialised Gender: How Shavers Configure the Users' Femininity and Masculinity', in N. Oudshoorn and T. Pinch (eds.), *How Users Matter: The Co-Construction of Users and Technology*. The MIT Press.

VNS Matrix (1991). 'A Manifesto for Cyborgs'. Available at: https://vnsmatrix.net/projects/the-cyberfeminist-manifesto-for-the-21st-century (accessed 19 September 2022).

Waggoner, L.M. (2021). 'Her Greatest Work Lay in Decorative Design: Angel De Cora Ho-Chunk Artist (1869–1919)', in B. Levit (ed.), *Baseline Shift*: *Untold Stories of Women in Graphic Design*. Princeton Architectural Press.

Wajcman, J. (1991). *Feminism Confronts Technology*. Wiley.

Wajcman, J. (2004). *Technofeminism*. Polity.

Walker, J.A. (1989). *Design History and the History of Design*. Pluto Press.

Webb, M (2013). 'Outrage: Eileen Gray's E1027 is a Scandal of French Neglect'. *Architectural Review*, 2 May. Available at: https://www.architectural-review.com/essays/outrage/outrage-eileen-grays-e-1027-is-a-scandal-of-french-neglect (accessed 22 August 2022).

West, M., R. Kraut and H.I. Chew (2019). 'I'd Blush if I Could: Closing Gender Divides in Digital Skills Through Education'. UNESCO. Available at: https://unesdoc.unesco.org/ark:/48223/pf0000367416.page=1 (accessed 22 January 2022).

Wikipedia (2022). 'Feminism'. Available at: https://en.wikipedia.org/wiki/Feminism (accessed 16 May 2022).

Wikipedia (2022a). 'Feminist Internet'. Available at: https://en.wikipedia.org/wiki/Feminist_Internet_(collective) (accessed 16 September 2022).

Wildcat, D. R. (2005). 'Indigenising the Future: Why We Must Think Spatially in the Twenty-first Century'. American Studies, 46 (3/4): 417–40.

Wilding, F. (1998). 'Where is Feminism in Cyberfeminism?' *Old Boys Network*. Available at: http://www.obn.org/reading_room/writings/html/where.html (accessed 13 July 2022).

Williams, S. (2020). *Data Action: Using Data for Public Good*. The MIT Press.

Yazzie, J. (2020). 'Why Are Diné LGBTQ+ and Two Spirit People Being Denied Access to Ceremony?' *High Country News*. 7 January. Available at: https://www.hcn.org/

issues/52.2/indigenous-affairs-why-are-dine-lgbtq-and-two-spirit-people-being-denied-access-to-ceremony(accessed 18 May 2022).

Yehaw (2020). 'Lehuauakea' *Yehaw*. Available at: https://yehawshow.com/artists/lehuauakea-fernandez (accessed 12 October 2022).

Yelavich, S. and B. Adams (eds.) (2014). *Design as Future-Making*. Bloomsbury Academic.

Young, D.R. (2019). 'Public Thinker: Jack Halberstam on Wildness, Anarchy and Growing Up Punk'. *Public Books*. Available at: https://www.publicbooks.org/public-thinker-jack-halberstam-on-wildness-anarchy-and-growing-up-punk/ (accessed 16 October 2022).

Young, J. (2021). 'Gendered Language in Design: Expanding Our Vocabulary Beyond the Binary'. *Medium*. Available at: https://josie-young.medium.com/gendered-language-in-design-1340d930e076 (accessed 28 October 2022).

FIGURES

INDEX

Entries followed by *f* indicate a page with a figure.
Entries followed by *t* indicate a page with a table.